Manheimer's Cataloging and Classification

Vol. 1   Classified Library of Congress Subject Headings, Volume 1—Classified List, *edited by James G. Williams, Martha L. Manheimer, and Jay E. Daily* (out of print; see Vol. 39, Part A)

Vol. 2   Classified Library of Congress Subject Headings, Volume 2—Alphabetic List, *edited by James G. Williams, Martha L. Manheimer, and Jay E. Daily* (out of print; see Vol. 39, Part B)

Vol. 3   Organizing Nonprint Materials, *by Jay E. Daily*

Vol. 4   Computer-Based Chemical Information, *edited by Edward McC. Arnett and Allen Kent*

Vol. 5   Style Manual: A Guide for the Preparation of Reports and Dissertations, *by Martha L. Manheimer*

Vol. 6   The Anatomy of Censorship, *by Jay E. Daily*

Vol. 7   Information Science: Search for Identity, *edited by Anthony Debons* (out of print)

Vol. 8   Resource Sharing in Libraries: Why • How • When • Next Action Steps, *edited by Allen Kent* (out of print)

Vol. 9   Reading the Russian Language: A Guide for Librarians and Other Professionals, *by Rosalind Kent*

Vol. 10   Statewide Computing Systems: Coordinating Academic Computer Planning, *edited by Charles Mosmann* (out of print)

Vol. 11   Using the Chemical Literature: A Practical Guide, *by Henry M. Woodburn*

Vol. 12   Cataloging and Classification: A Workbook, *by Martha L. Manheimer* (out of print; see Vol. 30)

Vol. 13   Multi-media Indexes, Lists, and Review Sources: A Bibliographic Guide, *by Thomas L. Hart, Mary Alice Hunt, and Blanche Woolls*

Vol. 14   Document Retrieval Systems: Factors Affecting Search Time, *by K. Leon Montgomery*

Vol. 15   Library Automation Systems, *by Stephen R. Salmon*

Vol. 16   Black Literature Resources: Analysis and Organization, *by Doris H. Clack*

Vol. 17   Copyright—Information Technology—Public Policy: Part I—Copyright—Public Policies; Part II—Public Policies—Information Technology, *by Nicholas Henry* (out of print)

Vol. 18   Crisis in Copyright, *by William Z. Nasri*

Vol. 19   Mental Health Information Systems: Design and Implementation, *by David J. Kupfer, Michael S. Levine, and John A. Nelson*

Vol. 20   Handbook of Library Regulations, *by Marcy Murphy and Claude J. Johns, Jr.* (out of print)

Vol. 21   Library Resource Sharing, *by Allen Kent and Thomas J. Galvin*

Vol. 22   Computers in Newspaper Publishing: User-Oriented Systems, *by Dineh Moghdam*

Vol. 23   The On-Line Revolution in Libraries, *edited by Allen Kent and Thomas J. Galvin*

Vol. 24   The Library as a Learning Service Center, *by Patrick R. Penland and Aleyamma Mathai*

Vol. 25   Using the Mathematical Literature: A Practical Guide, *by Barbara Kirsch Schaefer*

Vol. 26   Use of Library Materials: The University of Pittsburgh Study, *by Allen Kent et al.*

Vol. 27   The Structure and Governance of Library Networks, *edited by Allen Kent and Thomas J. Galvin*

Vol. 28   The Development of Library Collections of Sound Recordings, *by Frank W. Hoffmann*

Vol. 29   Furnishing the Library Interior, *by William S. Pierce*

Vol. 30   Cataloging and Classification: A Workbook Second Edition, Revised and Expanded, *by Martha L. Manheimer*

Vol. 31 Handbook of Computer-Aided Composition, *by Arthus H. Phillips*

Vol. 32 OCLC: Its Governance, Function, Financing, and Technology, *by Albert F. Maruskin*

Vol. 33 Scientific and Technical Information Resources, *by Krishna Subramanyam*

Vol. 34 An Author Index to Library of Congress Classification, Class P, Subclasses PN, PR, PS, PZ, General Literature, English and American Literature, Fiction in English, and Juvenile Belles Lettres, *by Alan M. Greenberg*

Vol. 35 Using the Biological Literature: A Practical Guide, *by Elisabeth B. Davis*

Vol. 36 An Introduction to Automated Literature Searching, *by Elizabeth P. Hartner*

Vol. 37 The Retrieval of Information in the Humanities and the Social Sciences: Problems as Aids to Learning, *edited by Thomas P. Slavens*

Vol. 38 The Information Professional: Survey of an Emerging Field, *by Anthony Debons, Donald W. King, Una Mansfield, and Donald L. Shirey*

Vol. 39 Classified Library of Congress Subject Headings, Second Edition: Part A—Classified List; Part B—Alphabetic List, *edited by James G. Williams, Martha L. Manheimer, and Jay E. Daily*

Vol. 40 Information Technology: Critical Choices for Library Decision-Makers, *edited by* Allen Kent and Thomas J. Galvin

Vol. 41 Structure and Subject Interaction: Toward a Sociology of Knowledge in the Social Sciences, *by Stephen Bulick*

Vol. 42 World Librarianship: A Comparative Study, *by Richard Krzys and Gaston Litton*

Vol. 43 Guide to the Successful Thesis and Dissertation: Conception to Publication: A Handbook for Students and Faculty, *by James E. Mauch and Jack W. Birch*

Vol. 44 Physical Disability: An Annotated Literature Guide, *edited by Phyllis C. Self*

Vol. 45 Effective Online Searching: A Basic Text, *by Christine L. Borgman, Dineh Moghdam, and Patti K. Corbett*

Vol. 46 Easy Access to DIALOG, ORBIT, and BRS, *by Patricia J. Klingensmith and Elizabeth E. Duncan*

Vol. 47 Subject and Information Analysis, *edited by Eleanor D. Dym*

Vol. 48 Organizing Nonprint Materials, Second Edition, *by Jay E. Daily*

Vol. 49 An Introduction to Information Science, *by Roger R. Flynn*

Vol. 50 Designing Instruction for Library Users: A Practical Guide, *by Marilla D. Svinicki and Barbara A. Schwartz*

Vol. 51 Guide to the Successful Thesis and Dissertation: Conception to Publication: A Handbook for Students and Faculty, *by James E. Mauch and Jack W. Birch*

Vol. 52 The Retrieval of Information in the Humanities and the Social Sciences: Problems as Aids to Learning. Second Edition, *compiled by Thomas P. Slavens*

Vol. 53 Manheimer's Cataloging and Classification: A Workbook, Third Edition, Revised and Expanded, *by Jerry D. Saye*

Additional Volumes in Preparation

Manheimer's Cataloging and Classification

A WORKBOOK

Third Edition
Revised and Expanded

JERRY D. SAYE

School of Information and Library Science
University of North Carolina at Chapel Hill
Chapel Hill, North Carolina

with
Desretta V. McAllister-Harper

School of Library and Information Sciences
North Carolina Central University
Durham, North Carolina

MARCEL DEKKER, INC.   New York • Basel • Hong Kong

ISBN 0-8247-8493-6

This book is printed on acid-free paper.

Marcel Dekker, Inc.
270 Madison Avenue, New York, New York 10016

Current printing (last digit):
10 9 8 7 6 5 4 3 2 1

PRINTED IN THE UNITED STATES OF AMERICA

In memory of

Martha L. Manheimer

teacher, colleague, and dear friend

Preface

I would like to express my gratitude to Martha L. Manheimer for her faith in me in asking me to undertake this revision of a text that has become a standard in the teaching of cataloging and classification in many schools. Originally, she had intended to serve as a senior advisor to this revision. Her untimely death in early 1989 left me to continue the project in her memory. Throughout this revision, my role has been to update the text and add new material needed for the instruction of catalogers in the 1990's. The concept and structure of this edition follows that of her original work. I have been assisted in this revision by Dr. Desretta V. McAllister-Harper, who revised and expanded the exercises for the Dewey Decimal Classification, developed some of the descriptive examples, and provided valuable consultation on the revision of the other parts of this book.

Changes in this edition reflect the 1988 revision of the *Anglo-American Cataloguing Rules, Second Edition* and the use of developmental order in the examples for descriptive cataloging, choice of access points, and headings. The cataloging examples have been expanded significantly to cover more fully descriptive cataloging and heading work. The Dewey Decimal Classification and the Library of Congress Classification chapters have been completely rewritten and expanded to reflect the most recent editions of these classification schemes. Additionally, the answers for these exercises now provide complete hierarchical development for the call numbers for each title. Similarly, the exercises developed to support the use of the Library of Congress subject headings have been expanded. These latter exercises are now in their own chapter rather than as a part of the treatment of the Library of Congress Classification.

Jerry D. Saye

Note to Instructors

Copies of transparency masters to support the cataloging examples illustrated in Chapters One (Descriptive Cataloging), Two (Access Points), Three (Headings for Persons), Four (Headings for Corporate Bodies), and Five (Uniform Titles) are available to instructors from the author at cost. For those instructors who wish to illustrate their presentations with these examples in MARC format, a set of transparency masters in MARC format (cataloging records without the supporting title page illustrations) is also available at cost. Please note that, in addition to making transparencies from either of these sets of masters, instructors may duplicate them for distribution to their students or for placement on reserve. To obtain these instructional materials please write or call:

Jerry D. Saye, Associate Professor
School of Information and Library Science
CB# 3360
University of North Carolina at Chapel Hill
Chapel Hill, North Carolina 27599-3360

Telephone (919) 962-8073 or 8366
Fax (919) 962-8071

Contents

Preface   v

Introduction   ix

PART I

CATALOGING

1   Rules for Description   3

2   Choice of Access Points   41

3   Headings for Persons and References   59

4   Headings for Corporate Bodies and References   75

5   Uniform Titles and References   91

PART II

SUBJECT ANALYSIS

6   Dewey Decimal Classification   101

7   Library of Congress Classification   118

8   Library of Congress Subject Headings   139

Appendices: Answers to the Exercises

A   Descriptive Cataloging Exercise   163

B   Access Points Exercise   174

C   Access Points and Forms of Headings Exercise   193

D   Dewey Decimal Classification Exercises   199

E   Library of Congress Classification Exercises   228

F   Library of Congress Subject Headings Exercises   260

Introduction

Since its first edition, this text has been designed as a workbook for a beginning course in cataloging and classification. It order to be utilized to its fullest, it should be used with the following text:

> Anglo-American Cataloguing Rules, *prepared under the direction of the Joint Steering Committee for Revision of AACR . . . [et al.]. 2nd ed., 1988 revision.* Chicago: American Library Association, 1988. [AACR2R]

In addition, the following works should be available to the student in the classroom or the laboratory:

> *Dewey Decimal Classification and Relative Index.* Edition 20. Albany, NY: Forest Press, 1989.

Library of Congress. *Classification.*

Class A	*General Works.* 4th ed. (1973)
Class B-BJ	*Philosophy. Psychology.* 3rd ed. (1979)
Class BL, BM, BP, BQ	*Religion: Religions, Hinduism, Judaism, Islam, Buddhism.* 3rd ed. (1984)
Class BR-BV	*Religion: Christianity, Bible.* 3rd ed. (1987)
Class BX	*Religion: Christian Denominations.* 3rd ed. (1985)
Class C	*Auxiliary Sciences of History.* 3rd ed. (1975)
Class D	*History: General and Old World.* 2nd ed. (1959, reprinted 1966)
Class DJK-DK	*History of Eastern Europe (General), Soviet Union, Poland.* 3rd ed. (1987)
Class DS	*History of Asia.* 3rd ed. (1987)
Class DT-DX	*History of Africa, Australia, and Ocean.* 3rd ed. (1989)
Class E-F	*History: America.* 3rd ed. (1958, reprinted 1965)
Class G	*Geography. Maps. Anthropology. Recreation.* 4th ed. (1976)
Class H-HJ	*Social Sciences: Economics.* 4th ed. (1981)
Class HM-HX	*Social Sciences: Sociology.* 4th ed. (1980)
Class J	*Political Science* 2nd ed. (1924, reprinted 1966)
Class K	*Law (General).* (1977)

Class KD	*Law of the United Kingdom and Ireland.* (1973)
Class KDZ, KG-KH	*Law of the Americas, Latin America, and the West Indies.* (1984)
Class KE	*Law of Canada.* (1976)
Class KF	*Law of the United States.* Prelim. ed. (1969)
Class KJ-KKZ	*Law of Europe.* (1989)
Class KJV-KJW	*Law of France.* (1985)
Class KK-KKC	*Law of Germany.* (1982)
Class L	*Education.* 4th ed. (1984)
Class M	*Music and Books on Music.* 3rd ed. (1978)
Class N	*Fine Arts.* 4th ed. (1970)
Class P-PZ	*Language and Literature. Tables.* (1982)
Class P-PA	*Philology, Linguistics, Classical Philology, Classical Literature.* (1928, reprinted 1968)
Class PA	*Supplement: Byzantine and Modern Greek Literature. Medieval and Modern Latin Literature.* (1942, reprinted 1968)
Class PB-PH	*Modern European Languages.* (1933, reprinted 1966)
Class PG	*Russian Literature.* (1948, reprinted 1965)
Class PJ-PK	*Oriental Philology and Literature, Indo-Iranian Philology and Literature.* 2nd ed. (1988)
Class P-PM	*Supplement: Index to Languages and Dialects.* 3rd ed. (1983)
Class PN, PR, PS, PZ	*Literature (General), English and American Literature, Fiction in English, Juvenile Belles Lettres.* 3rd ed. 1988.
PQ, Part 1	*French Literature.* (1936, reprinted 1966)
PQ, Part 2	*Italian, Spanish, and Portuguese Literatures.* (1937, reprinted 1965)
PT, Part 1	*German Literature.* (1989)
PT, Part 2	*Dutch and Scandinavian Literatures.* (1942, reprinted 1965)
Q	*Science.* 7th ed. (1989)
R	*Medicine.* 5th ed. (1987)
S	*Agriculture.* 4th ed. (1982)
T	*Technology.* 7th ed. (1971)
U	*Military Science.* 4th ed. (1974)
V	*Naval Science.* 3rd ed. (1974)
Z	*Bibliography and Library Science.* 5th ed. (1980)

Library of Congress. Subject Cataloging Division. *Library of Congress Subject Headings.* 12th ed. Washington, DC: Library of Congress, 1989.

Library of Congress. Subject Cataloging Division. *Subject Cataloging Manual: Shelflisting.* Washington, DC: Library of Congress, 1986.

Library of Congress. Subject Cataloging Division. *Subject Cataloging Manual: Subject Headings.* 3rd ed. Washington, DC: Library of Congress, 1988.

This workbook is not intended to be a stand-alone text. Rather, it was designed to provide a support medium for lectures on the cataloging process and structured exercises on cataloging, classification, and subject heading work. These exercises were designed to be self-instructional for the student. It is anticipated that instructors may wish to supplement them with graded exercises they have developed. The coverage in this workbook is general in that only situations commonly encountered are addressed. It is assumed that students interested in an in-depth coverage of cataloging and classification will have an advanced cataloging course and/or practicum later in their program.

Description of the Chapters

Chapter One covers the essential elements of International Standard Bibliographic Description (ISBD) as presented in AACR2R. Although presentation of the cataloging rules in this part is based upon the creation of catalog records for a card catalog, its principles are applicable to all types of catalogs, including online public access catalogs. Material covered in Chapter One can be reinforced by having the students catalog books from a practice collection. Students can check their own proficiency by completing the descriptive cataloging exercise at the end of this chapter.

Chapter Two covers the choice of access points and corresponds to AACR2R Chapter 21. Only commonly encountered rules are exemplified. The catalog records in this chapter and those that follow also serve as a review and continuation of the principles of descriptive cataloging. The developmental organization of this text results in the catalog records in Chapter Two indicating only the access points that would be used and not their proper form. Form of headings is covered in the succeeding chapters. At the end of Chapter Two is an exercise that calls for students to identify the access points for the records in Chapter One.

Chapters Three, Four, and Five cover forms of headings and correspond to AACR2R Chapters 22, 24, and 25. If a name in a heading appears in the Library of Congress Name Authority File and has been established under AACR2 or AACR2R, that form has been used in the examples. Name forms established by LC as "AACR2 compatible" have not been used. Appropriate references for the type of heading addressed in that chapter are given for each access point requiring a reference. Continuing the developmental order used in other chapters, the chapter dealing with personal name headings does not have corporate name headings in their proper form because those rules have not yet been addressed. Similarly, only the examples in Chapter 5 (Uniform Title) actually use uniform title headings. Within these three chapters, however, developmental order has not been adhered to, thus, in the chapter for personal name headings, dates are given with names whenever appropriate, rather than only after the rule for dates has been encountered. At the end Chapter 4 is an exercise calling for students to develop personal name and corporate name headings and their references for a group of books.

There has been no consistent attempt in this workbook to conform to all Library of Congress Rule Interpretations (LCRIs) in effect. Rather, in limited cases, particularly in descriptive cataloging, some LCRIs have been used when they provide additional guidance to the application of a particular rule. In all other cases, the catalog examples represent a catalog record as called for by AACR2R rather than AACR2R as interpreted by the Library of Congress. In no cases are LCRIs used when they contradict rules in AACR2R, unless this use is clearly indicated in the text.

Chapters Six and Seven introduce the student to the two classification systems, the Dewey Decimal Classification and the Library of Congress Classification, predominantly in use in American libraries. Each chapter consists of a brief review of the classification techniques used in the system and a series of exercises in its use. Normally, in the two steps of the classification process, a classifier first analyzes the document and its relationship to other documents in the field and in the library's collection. Secondly, the classifier translates this analysis into the paradigm of the class heading and deals with the mechanics of the classification scheme. The classification exercises in this workbook deal only with the second part of the classificatory process. The titles presented reflect, unambiguously it is hoped, the subject specification of the classification scheme. All the student is expected to do is to manipulate the scheme to create the classification notation in a way that most precisely reflects the subject content of the work. The answers to the exercises in the appendices provide hierarchical development for each of the titles so that a student can analyze how the final call number was developed.

Chapter Eight addresses the provision of subject index terms through the assignment of subject headings from the 12th edition of *Library of Congress Subject Headings* and LC's *Subject Cataloging Manual: Subject Headings*. Accompanying exercises provide a structured approach to the use of topical subdivisions, geographical subdivisions, free-floating and pattern headings. In the last exercise, subject headings are assigned to some of the titles already used in the Library of Congress Classification Exercise to allow for a comparison of the subject analysis provided by classification and alphabetical subject indexing.

Manheimer's
Cataloging
and
Classification

Part I

CATALOGING

CHAPTER ONE

Rules for Description

Topic Outline

Rules

1.0   General Rules

1.1   Title and Statement of Responsibility Area

1.2   Edition Area

1.4   Publication, Distribution, Etc., Area

1.5   Physical Description Area

1.6   Series Area

1.7   Notes Area

1.8   Standard Number and Terms of Availability Area

Readings: *Anglo-American Cataloguing Rules.* 2nd ed., 1988 revision.
              Chicago: American Library Association, 1988. (AACR2R)
                  General Introduction, p. 1-4; Introduction, p. 7-9;
                  Chapter 1, General Rules for Description, p. 11-59;
                  Chapter 2, Books, Pamphlets, and Printed Sheets, p. 60-85.

                  Refer also to:
                  Appendix A, Capitalization, p. 563-599;
                  Appendix B, Abbreviations, p. 600-610;
                  Appendix C, Numerals, p. 611-614;
                  Appendix D, Glossary, p. 615-624.

Resources: Saye, Jerry D. and Vellucci, Sherry L. *Notes in the Catalog
              Record: Based on AACR2 and LC Rule Interpretations.* Chicago:
              American Library Association, 1989.
              or
              Salinger, Florence A. and Zagon, Eileen. *Notes for Catalogers: A
              Sourcebook for Use with AACR 2.* White Plains, N.Y.:
              Knowledge Industry Publications, 1985.

Rule Citations. To the right of each catalog record in this workbook is the AACR2R rule the example is intended to illustrate. Catalog records illustrating general rules for description have the relevant rule numbers from Chapter 1 to their right. For examples illustrating situations covered by rules in both the general chapter for description (Chapter 1) and in the chapter for books (Chapter 2), reference is made only to the rules in Chapter 1, if the rule in Chapter 2 only refers to the general rule.

Levels of Description. In 1978, the publication of AACR2 provided catalogers with a cataloging code which allowed for the description of documents using different levels of detail. Prior to this, national cataloging codes had provided a standard of description which, in general, met the more demanding description needs of academic and research libraries. AACR2R Rule 1.0D provides for three levels of detail. For each level, the elements stated are the minimum requirements for that level, provided that they are appropriate to the document being described. Additional descriptive elements can be added at a library's option. It should be noted that variation in the information recorded in a description can affect the provision of access points for the document. The three examples that follow illustrate the differences in description for the same document at each of the levels of description.

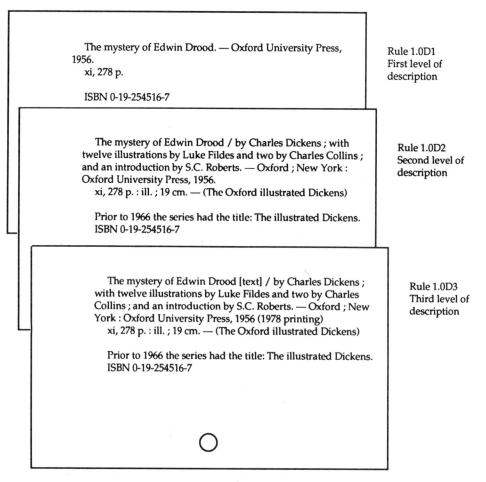

The mystery of Edwin Drood. — Oxford University Press, 1956.
    xi, 278 p.

ISBN 0-19-254516-7

Rule 1.0D1
First level of description

The mystery of Edwin Drood / by Charles Dickens ; with twelve illustrations by Luke Fildes and two by Charles Collins ; and an introduction by S.C. Roberts. — Oxford ; New York : Oxford University Press, 1956.
    xi, 278 p. : ill. ; 19 cm. — (The Oxford illustrated Dickens)

Prior to 1966 the series had the title: The illustrated Dickens.
ISBN 0-19-254516-7

Rule 1.0D2
Second level of description

The mystery of Edwin Drood [text] / by Charles Dickens ; with twelve illustrations by Luke Fildes and two by Charles Collins ; and an introduction by S.C. Roberts. — Oxford ; New York : Oxford University Press, 1956 (1978 printing)
    xi, 278 p. : ill. ; 19 cm. — (The Oxford illustrated Dickens)

Prior to 1966 the series had the title: The illustrated Dickens.
ISBN 0-19-254516-7

Rule 1.0D3
Third level of description

Areas of Description. In AACR2R, the elements of the description are divided into eight areas, each identified by a number. This area numbering has a direct relationship in the numbering of the rules in the chapters for description. The example that follows illustrates the elements in each area for a second level description.

Title proper : other title information / statement of responsibility ; subsequent statement of responsibility. —	*Area 1*
Edition statement / statement of responsibility relating to the	*Area 2*
edition. — Place : publisher, date (Place : printer)	*Area 4*
pagination, no. of p. of plates : illustrative matter ;	*Area 5*
dimensions + accompanying material. — (Series ; number)	*Area 6*
Notes.	*Area 7*
ISBN	*Area 8*

N.B. The style of indentions and alignment used in the catalog examples that follow is that used by the Library of Congress on its printed cards. The level of description used in this text is the second level. The examples in this chapter illustrate only descriptive cataloging elements. The selection of access points, their proper formatting, and the assignment of call numbers and subject headings are treated in the chapters that follow.

1

Robertson, R.B.

    Of whales and men / by R.B. Robertson. — 1st ed. — New York : Knopf, 1954.
    xii, 299 p. : ill. ; 22 cm.

    "Portions of this book appeared originally in the New Yorker in different form"—T.p. verso.
    "A Borzoi book"—T.p. verso.

I. Title

Rule 2.0B1
Standard title page

2

Meier, August

    From plantation to ghetto / by August Meier and Elliott Rudwick. — Rev. ed. — New York : Hill and Wang, 1970.
    x, 340 p. : maps ; 21 cm. — (American century series)

    Includes bibliographical references (p. 299-326) and index.
    ISBN 0-8090-4791-8. — ISBN 0-8090-0096-2 (pbk.)

I. Rudwick, Elliott. II. Title. III Series

Rule 2.0B1
Facing title pages

3

Munn, Ralph.

    Carnegie Library of Pittsburgh : a brief history and description / by Ralph Munn. — [Pittsburgh] : The Library, [1968]
    [10] p. ; 23 cm.

    Cover title.
    "May 1, 1968."

I Title

Rule 2.0B1
Title page substitute

4

Rinehart, Mary Roberts

    Isn't that just like a man! / by Mary Roberts Rinehart. Oh, well, you know how women are! / by Irvin S. Cobb. — New York : G.H. Doran, c1920.
    2 v. in 1 ; 20 cm.

I. Cobb, Irvin S.. Oh well, you know how women are! II Title

Rule 1.0H1a
Two title pages treated as a single source

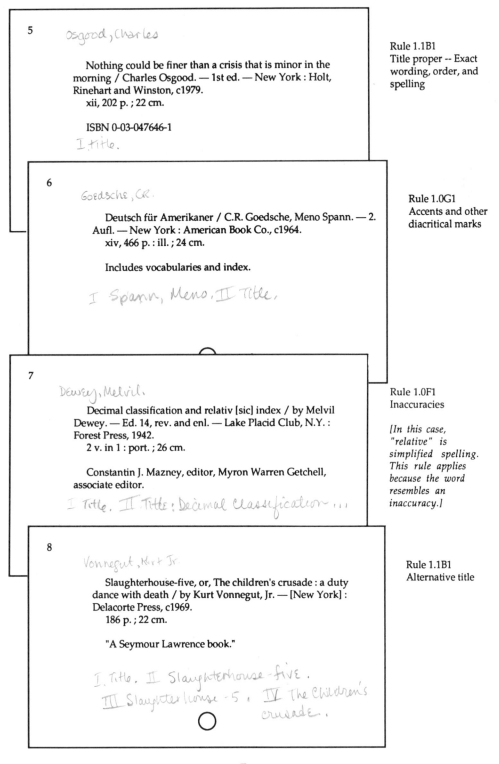

5

Osgood, Charles

Nothing could be finer than a crisis that is minor in the morning / Charles Osgood. — 1st ed. — New York : Holt, Rinehart and Winston, c1979.
  xii, 202 p. ; 22 cm.

  ISBN 0-03-047646-1

I. title.

Rule 1.1B1
Title proper -- Exact wording, order, and spelling

6

Goedsche, C.R.

Deutsch für Amerikaner / C.R. Goedsche, Meno Spann. — 2. Aufl. — New York : American Book Co., c1964.
  xiv, 466 p. : ill. ; 24 cm.

  Includes vocabularies and index.

I Spann, Meno. II Title.

Rule 1.0G1
Accents and other diacritical marks

7

Dewey, Melvil.

Decimal classification and relativ [sic] index / by Melvil Dewey. — Ed. 14, rev. and enl. — Lake Placid Club, N.Y. : Forest Press, 1942.
  2 v. in 1 : port. ; 26 cm.

  Constantin J. Mazney, editor, Myron Warren Getchell, associate editor.

I Title. II Title: Decimal Classification ...

Rule 1.0F1
Inaccuracies

[In this case, "relative" is simplified spelling. This rule applies because the word resembles an inaccuracy.]

8

Vonnegut, Kurt Jr.

Slaughterhouse-five, or, The children's crusade : a duty dance with death / by Kurt Vonnegut, Jr. — [New York] : Delacorte Press, c1969.
  186 p. ; 22 cm.

  "A Seymour Lawrence book."

I. Title. II Slaughterhouse-five.
III Slaughterhouse - 5. IV The Children's crusade.

Rule 1.1B1
Alternative title

Title proper, cont'd.

9 *Baugh, Albert C.*

> Chaucer's major poetry / Albert C. Baugh, editor. —
> Englewood Cliffs, N.J. : Prentice-Hall, c1963.
>   xlvii, 616 p. ; 26 cm.
>
> Includes bibliographical references (p. xliii-xlv).

Rule 1.1B2
Title proper
includes a statement
of responsibility

10 *McKerrow, Ronald Brunlees*

> Ronald Brunlees McKerrow : a selection of his essays /
> compiled by John Phillip Immroth. — Metuchen, N.J. :
> Scarecrow Press, 1974.
>   viii, 240 p. ; 23 cm. — (The Great bibliographers series ; no. 1)
>
> Includes bibliographical references.
>   ISBN 0-8108-0690-8   *I Imroth, John Phillip II series*

Rule 1.1B3
Title proper consists
solely of the name
of the person
responsible for the
item

11 *McBain, Ed.*

> Three from the 87th / Ed McBain. — Garden City, N.Y. : N.
> Doubleday, [197-]
>   470 p. : ill. ; 22 cm.
>
> "Book club edition"—Jacket.
> Contents: Hail, hail, the gang's all here — Jigsaw — Fuzz.
>   *I Title. II Hail, hail… III Jigsaw, IV Fuzz.*

Rule 1.1B10
Collective title and
the titles of the
individual works
appear on the chief
source of
information

1.1D   Parallel titles

12 *Title*

> Simon and Schuster's international dictionary,
> English/Spanish, Spanish/English = Diccionario internacional
> Simon and Schuster, Inglés/Espanol, Espanol/Inglés / Tana de
> Gámez, editor in chief. — New York : Simon and Schuster ;
> [Englewood Cliffs, N.J.?] : Distributed by Prentice-Hall Trade,
> c1973.
>   xviii, 1605 p. ; 29 cm.
>   *I. = Title*
>   ISBN 0-671-21507-8. — ISBN 0-671-21267-2 (thumb-indexed)

Rule 1.1D2
Parallel title --
Second level
description

13

Title

> Murallas de San Juan = Forts of San Juan. — 1st ed. — San
> Juan, P.R. : Escudo de Oro Caribe [distributor], 1984.
>   [34] p. : col. ill. ; 25 cm.
>
> In English, French, German, Spanish.
> Cover title.
> ISBN 84-378-1041-8
>   *I Forts of San Juan.*

Rule 1.1B5
Word appears once,
but is intended to be
read more than once

14

Lane, Harlan

The wild boy of Burundi : a study of an outcast child / Harlan Lane & Richard Pillard. — 1st ed. — New York : Random House, c1978.
xiv, 188 p., [8] p. of plates : ill., map ; 24 cm.

Foreword by B.F. Skinner.
Includes index.
ISBN 0-394-41252-4

I. Pillard, Richard . II . Title .

Rule 1.1E1
Other title information -- Subtitle

15

Robbins, Chandler S.

Birds of North America : a guide to field identification / by Chandler S. Robbins, Bertel Bruun, and Herbert S. Zim ; illustrated by Arthur Singer. — New York : Golden Press, c1966.
340 p. : col. ill., col. maps ; 19 cm. — (Golden field guide series)

Includes bibliographical references (p. 326-327) and index.
ISBN 0-307-13656-6. — ISBN 0-307-47002-4 (invalid)

I. Bruun, Bertel. II. Zim, Herbert S. III. Title.

Rule 1.1E5
Other title information transcribed after the title proper

16

Lavallee, David.

Gray lady down : a novel : original title, Event 1000 / by David Lavallee. — Warner Books ed. — New York : Warner Books, [1972], c1971.
269 p. : ill. ; 18 cm.

ISBN 0-446-89429-X

I. Title.

Rule 1.1D3
Other title information -- Original title in the same language as the title proper

---

17

Sellar, Walter Carruthers

1066 and all that : a memorable history of England . . . / by Walter Carruthers Sellar and Robert Julian Yeatman ; illustrated by John Reynolds. — New York : Dutton, c1931.
xii, 116 p. : ill. ; 20 cm.

I. Yeatman, Robert Julian. II. Title.

Rule 1.1E3
Lengthy other title information abridged

18

Keillor, Garrison

    Lake Wobegon days / Garrison Keillor. — New York, N.Y. : Viking, 1985.
      x, 337 p. : ill. ; 24 cm.

    "Portions of this book appeared originally in The Atlantic monthly"—T.p. verso.
      ISBN 0-670-80514-9

Rule 1.1F1
Statement of responsibility

19

Title

    Pictorial treasury of U.S. stamps / [edited and published by Collectors Institute ; Elena Marzulla, editor]. — Omaha, Neb. : The Institute, c1974.
      viii, 223 p. : col. ill. ; 29 cm. — (Collectors Institute reference library)

    Includes bibliographical references (p. 218-219) and index.

I. Marzulla, Elena.
II. Collectors Institute.
III. Series.

Rule 1.1F1
Statement of responsibility from other than the chief source of information

20

Mencken, H.L.

    The American scene : a reader / H.L. Mencken ; selected and edited, and with an introduction and commentary by Huntington Cairns. — 1st Vintage Books ed. — New York : Vintage Books, 1982, c1965.
      xxvii, 542 p. ; 21 cm.

    Reprint. Originally published: New York : Knopf, 1965.
    Includes bibliographical references (p. 541-542).
      ISBN 0-394-75214-7

I. Cairns, Huntington. II. Title.

Rule 1.1F3
Statement of responsibility preceding the title proper transcribed in its required position

21

Woolley, Sir Leonard

    Digging up the past / Sir Leonard Woolley. — 2nd ed. — Baltimore, Md. : Penguin, 1960, c1954.
      141 p., 32 p. of plates : ill. ; 18 cm. — (A Pelican book)

    "Based on a series of six broadcast talks broadcast by the BBC"—T.p. verso.
    Includes index.

I. Title.

Rule 1.1F7
Inclusion of a British term of honor

Statements of responsibility, cont'd.

22

Layton, Edwin T.

"And I was there" : Pearl Harbor and Midway-- breaking the secrets / by Edwin T. Layton with Roger Pineau and John Costello. — New York : W. Morrow, c1985.
596 p., [24] p. of plates : ill. ; 25 cm.

Includes bibliographical references (p. 570-581) and index.
ISBN 0-688-04883-8

I. Pineau, Roger. II. Costello, John. III. Title.

Rule 1.1F7
Omission of titles
and qualifications

23

Parsons, Lucy.

Famous speeches of the eight Chicago anarchists / [compiled by] Lucy Parsons. — New York : Arno Press & the New York Times, 1969.
121 p. : ports. ; 24 cm. — (Mass violence in America)

Spine title: Speeches of the eight Chicago anarchists.
Reprint with new editorial note. Originally published: [2nd ed.] Chicago : L.E. Parsons, 1910.
Contains speeches by August Spies, Michael Schwab, Oscar Neebe, Adolph Fischer, Louis Lingg, George Engel, Samuel Fielden and Albert R. Parsons.

I. Title.

Rule 1.1F8
Addition of a
short phrase

24

Title.

Outdoor education / Julian W. Smith . . . [et al.]. — Englewood Cliffs, N.J. : Prentice-Hall, 1963.
ix, 322 p. : ill. ; 24 cm.

Includes bibliographies and index.

I. Smith, Julian W.

Rule 1.1F5
More than three
persons or
corporate bodies
performing the
same function

25

Leverence, John.

Irving Wallace : a writer's profile / by John Leverence ; with an introduction by Jerome Weidman ; an interview by Sam L. Grogg, Jr. ; and an afterword by Ray B. Browne. — Bowling Green, Ohio : Popular Press, 1974.
454 p. : ill. ; 24 cm. — (Profiles in popular culture ; no. 1)

Includes index.
ISBN 0-87972-063-8

I. Title. II. Series.

Rule 1.1F6
More than one
statement of
responsibility

26

From Anne to Victoria.

    From Anne to Victoria / essays by various hands ; edited by
Bonamy Dobrée. — New York : Scribner's, 1937.
    x, 630 p. ; 22 cm.

    Includes index.

I. Dobrée, Bonamy

Rule 1.1F14
Statement of
responsibility
even if no person
or body is named
specifically

27

Sewell, Samuel

    The diary of Samuel Sewall / edited and abridged with an
introduction by Harvey Wish. — Capricorn Books ed. — New
York : Capricorn Books, 1967.
    189 p. ; 20 cm.

    Includes bibliographical references.

I. Wish, Harvey. II. Title.

Rule 1.1F13
Person associated
with responsibility
for the item is
named in the title

28

Cobb, Lyman

    Cobb's spelling book : being a just standard for pronouncing
the English language . . . designed to teach the orthography and
orthoepy of J. Walker / by Lyman Cobb. — Rev. ed. —
Baltimore : Joseph Jewett, [1825]
    168 p. ; 17 cm.

I. Walker, J.
II. Title.
III. Title: Spelling Book.

Rule 1.1F13
Person associated
with responsibility
for the item is
named in the title
and in a separate
statement of
responsibility

○

1.1G   Items without a collective title

29

Anderson, Robert.

    Solitaire ; & Double solitaire / by Robert Anderson. — New
York : Random House, c1972.
    83 p. ; 22 cm.

    Two plays.

I Title: Solitaire. II Title: Double Solitaire.

Rule 1.1G2
Work lacking a
collective title
cataloged as a unit

Rule 1.1G3
Transcription of
individual titles

○

1.2   EDITION AREA
1.2B   Edition statement

30

Binns, Norman E.

    An introduction to historical bibliography / by Norman E.
Binns. — 2nd ed., rev. and enl. — London : Association of
Assistant Librarians, 1962.
    387 p. : ill. ; 23 cm.

    Includes bibliographical references and index.

I. Title.

○

Rule 1.2B1
Edition statement

Rule C.8A
Ordinal numbers

Rule B.9
Abbreviations

1.2C   Statements of responsibility relating to the edition

31

Harvey-Gibson, R.J.

    Two thousand years of science : the wonders of nature and
their discoverers / by R.J. Harvey-Gibson. — 2nd ed. / revised
and enlarged by A.W. Titherley. — London : A. & C. Black,
1931.
    x, 508 p., [1] leaf of plates : ill. ; 22 cm.

    Includes index.

I. Titherly, A.W. II Title.

○

Rule 1.2C1
Statement of
responsibility that
does not relate to all
editions of the work

1.2D   Statement relating to a named revision of an edition

32

Title

    Spas, hot tubs & home saunas / by the editors of Sunset
Books and Sunset magazine ; [research & text, Susan Watson,
Paul Spring]. — 2nd ed., 2nd printing, updated. — Menlo Park,
Calif. : Lane Pub. Co., 1987, c1986.
    80 p. : col. ill. ; 27 cm.

    At head of title: Sunset.
    Includes index.
    ISBN 0-376-01247-1

I Watson, Susan. II Spring, Paul III Sunset Books.

○

Rule 1.2D1
Named revision of
an edition

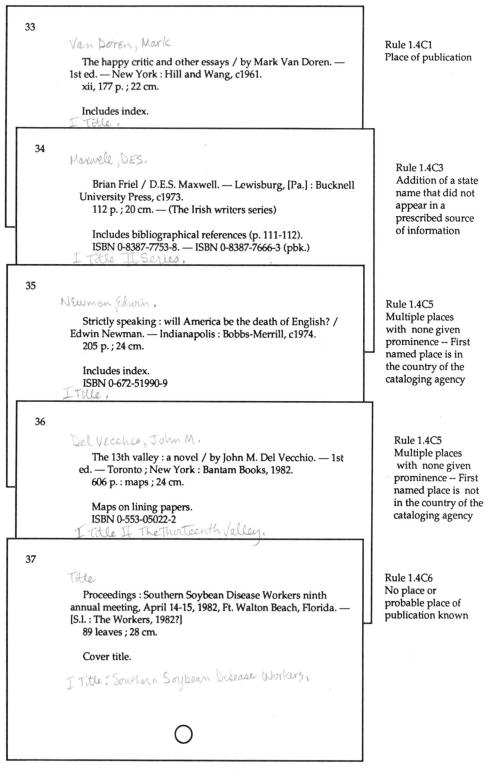

33

Van Doren, Mark

    The happy critic and other essays / by Mark Van Doren. —
1st ed. — New York : Hill and Wang, c1961.
    xii, 177 p. ; 22 cm.

    Includes index.

I Title.

Rule 1.4C1
Place of publication

34

Maxwell, DES.

    Brian Friel / D.E.S. Maxwell. — Lewisburg, [Pa.] : Bucknell
University Press, c1973.
    112 p. ; 20 cm. — (The Irish writers series)

    Includes bibliographical references (p. 111-112).
    ISBN 0-8387-7753-8. — ISBN 0-8387-7666-3 (pbk.)

I Title II Series.

Rule 1.4C3
Addition of a state
name that did not
appear in a
prescribed source
of information

35

Newman, Edwin.

    Strictly speaking : will America be the death of English? /
Edwin Newman. — Indianapolis : Bobbs-Merrill, c1974.
    205 p. ; 24 cm.

    Includes index.
    ISBN 0-672-51990-9

I Title.

Rule 1.4C5
Multiple places
with none given
prominence -- First
named place is in
the country of the
cataloging agency

36

Del Vecchio, John M.

    The 13th valley : a novel / by John M. Del Vecchio. — 1st
ed. — Toronto ; New York : Bantam Books, 1982.
    606 p. : maps ; 24 cm.

    Maps on lining papers.
    ISBN 0-553-05022-2

I Title II The Thirteenth Valley.

Rule 1.4C5
Multiple places
with none given
prominence -- First
named place is not
in the country of the
cataloging agency

37

Title

    Proceedings : Southern Soybean Disease Workers ninth
annual meeting, April 14-15, 1982, Ft. Walton Beach, Florida. —
[S.l. : The Workers, 1982?]
    89 leaves ; 28 cm.

    Cover title.

I Title : Southern Soybean Disease Workers.

Rule 1.4C6
No place or
probable place of
publication known

38

Beschloss, Michael R.

Kennedy and Roosevelt : the uneasy alliance / Michael R. Beschloss ; foreword by James MacGregor Burns. — 1st ed. — New York : Norton, c1980.
318 p. : ill. ; 24 cm.

Includes bibliographical references (p. [281]-285) and index.
ISBN 0-393-01335-9

I Title.

Rule 1.4D1
Name of the publisher

Rule 1.4D2
Name of the publisher in the shortest form in which it can be understood and identified internationally

39

Horticultural Society

Printed books, 1481-1900, in the Horticultural Society of New York / a listing by Elizabeth Cornelia Hall. — New York : The Society, 1970.
xiii, 279 p. ; 24 cm.

I. Hall, Cornelia.

Rule 1.4D4
Publisher's name appears in a recognizable form in Area 1 -- In Area 4 it is recorded in the shortest form possible

40

Gid, Richard

Secrecy and power : the life of J. Edgar Hoover / Richard Gid Powers. — New York : Free Press, c1987.
x, 624 p., [16] p. of plates : ill. ; 23 cm.

Includes bibliographical references (p. 591-605) and index.
ISBN 0-02-925061-7 (pbk.). — ISBN 0-02-925060-9

I Title.

Rule 1.4D5
Work with two publishers described in terms of the first

41

Title

Raising laboratory animals : a handbook for biological and behavioral research / James Silvan. — 1st ed. — Garden City, N.Y. : Published for the American Museum of Natural History [by] the Natural History Press, 1966.
viii, 225 p., [16] p. of plates : ill. ; 22 cm.

Includes bibliographical references (p. [209]-215) and index.

I American Museum of Natural History. II Title.

Rule 1.4D5a
Work with two publishers described in terms of both -- The first and subsequently named entity are linked in a single statement

---

42

Hudson, W.H.

    Rare, vanishing & lost British birds / compiled from notes by
W.H. Hudson by Linda Gardiner ; with 25 coloured plates by
H. Gronvold. — London : Dent ; New York : Dutton, 1923.
    xix, 120 p., [25] leaves of plates : col. ill. ; 23 cm.

    Enl. ed. of the author's Lost British birds. London, 1894.
    Includes bibliographical references (p. 115) and index.

I Gardiner, Linda   II Gronvold, H.   III Title

Rule 1.4D5d
Work with two
publishers
described in terms
of both -- The first
named publisher is
not in the country
of the cataloging
agency and a
subsequently
named publisher is

43

Cardona Bonet, Walter A.

    Shipwrecks in Puerto Rico's history / by Walter A. Cardona
Bonet. — 1st ed. — San Juan, P.R. : [s.n.], c1989 (Puerto Rico :
Model Offset Printing)
    v. : ill. (some col.) ; 23 cm.

    Includes bibliographical references.
    Contents: v. 1. 1502-1650

I Title.

Rule 1.4D7
Name of the
publisher is
unknown

Rule 1.4G1
Place and name of
the manufacturer

44

Weinstein, Allen.

    Perjury : the Hiss-Chambers case / by Allen Weinstein. —
1st ed. — New York : Knopf : Distributed by Random House,
1978.
    xxi, 674 p., [16] p. of plates : ill. ; 25 cm.

    "A Borzoi book"—T.p. verso.
    Includes bibliographical references (p. [645]-656) and index.
    ISBN 0-394-49176-9

I. Title.

Rule 1.4D3a
Phrase indicating
the function of the
distributor

45

Kater, David A.

    The printed word : professional word processing with
Microsoft Word on the Apple Macintosh / David A. Kater,
Richard L. Kater. — Bellevue, Wash. : Microsoft Press ; New
York : Harper and Row [distributor], c1985.
    xiv, 293 p. : ill. ; 24 cm.

    Includes index.
    ISBN 0-914845-53-5

I Kater, Richard L.   II Title

Rule 1.4D6
Optionally,
Place and name of
the distributor

Rule 1.4E1
Optional addition
Addition of the
term "distributor"

46

Poyer, Joe

    Tunnel war / Joe Poyer. — 1st ed. — New York : Atheneum, 1979.
    x, 339 p. : ill. ; 24 cm.

    ISBN 0-689-11009-X

I Tunnel War.

Rule 1.4F1
Date of publication

47

Lanes, Selma G.

    Down the rabbit hole : adventures & misadventures in the realm of children's literature / Selma G. Lanes. — 1st Atheneum pbk. ed. — New York : Atheneum, 1976, c1971.
    xiii, 241 p. : ill. ; 23 cm.

    "College edition"—Cover.
    Includes bibliographical references (p. 212-233) and index.
    ISBN 0-689-70533-6

I Title.

Rule 1.4F5
Optional addition
Date of publication and the latest copyright date differ

48

Steinberg, S.H.

    Five hundred years of printing / by S.H. Steinberg ; with a foreword by Beatrice Warde. — 2nd ed., fully rev., Reprinted with revisions. — Harmondsworth, Middlesex, England ; Baltimore, Md. : Penguin, 1966, c1961.
    394 p. : ill. ; 18 cm. — (A Pelican book)

    Includes bibliographical references (p. 367-369) and index.

I Title : Five Hundred Years of Printing.
II Title : 500 Years of Printing.

Rule 1.4F3
Date of a named revision of an edition previously specified in Area 2

49

Orczy, Baroness.

    Petticoat rule / by Baroness Orczy. — New York : Hodder & Stoughton, c1910.
    380 p. ; 20 cm.

I Petticoat Rule.

Rule 1.4F6
Copyright date

Date of publication, distribution, etc., cont'd.

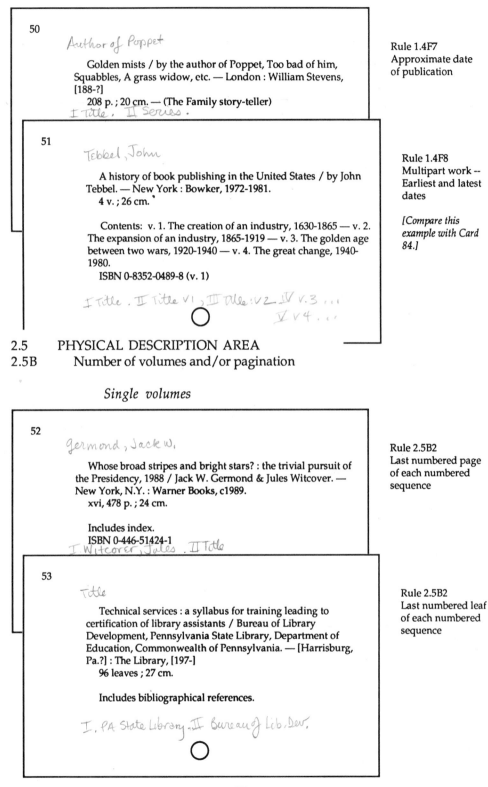

50

Author of Poppet

    Golden mists / by the author of Poppet, Too bad of him, Squabbles, A grass widow, etc. — London : William Stevens, [188-?]
    208 p. ; 20 cm. — (The Family story-teller)

I Title. II Series.

Rule 1.4F7
Approximate date
of publication

51

Tebbel, John

    A history of book publishing in the United States / by John Tebbel. — New York : Bowker, 1972-1981.
    4 v. ; 26 cm.

    Contents: v. 1. The creation of an industry, 1630-1865 — v. 2. The expansion of an industry, 1865-1919 — v. 3. The golden age between two wars, 1920-1940 — v. 4. The great change, 1940-1980.
    ISBN 0-8352-0489-8 (v. 1)

I Title. II Title V1, III Title : V2 IV v.3 ... V v4 ...

Rule 1.4F8
Multipart work --
Earliest and latest
dates

[Compare this example with Card 84.]

2.5   PHYSICAL DESCRIPTION AREA
2.5B   Number of volumes and/or pagination

Single volumes

52

Germond, Jack W.

    Whose broad stripes and bright stars? : the trivial pursuit of the Presidency, 1988 / Jack W. Germond & Jules Witcover. — New York, N.Y. : Warner Books, c1989.
    xvi, 478 p. ; 24 cm.

    Includes index.
    ISBN 0-446-51424-1

I Witcover, Jules. II Title

Rule 2.5B2
Last numbered page
of each numbered
sequence

53

Title

    Technical services : a syllabus for training leading to certification of library assistants / Bureau of Library Development, Pennsylvania State Library, Department of Education, Commonwealth of Pennsylvania. — [Harrisburg, Pa.?] : The Library, [197-]
    96 leaves ; 27 cm.

    Includes bibliographical references.

I. PA State Library. II Bureau of Lib. Dev.

Rule 2.5B2
Last numbered leaf
of each numbered
sequence

Date of publication, distribution, etc., cont'd.

54

Eliot, George.

Daniel Deronda / George Eliot ; edited with an introduction by Graham Handley. — Oxford ; New York : Oxford University Press, 1988.
xxii, [3], 727 p. : facsim. ; 19 cm. — (The World's classics) (Oxford paperbacks)

Includes bibliographical references (p. [xxv]).
ISBN 0-19-281787-6 (pbk.)

I. Daniel Deronda. II Handley, Graham. III Title.

Rule 2.5B3
Unnumbered sequence includes pages referred to in a note

55

Moore, Margaret.

Certainly, Carrie, cut the cake : poems A-Z / by Margaret and John Travers Moore ; illustrated by Laurie Anderson. — Indianapolis : Bobbs-Merrill, c1971.
[30] p. : ill. ; 19 cm.

Summary: Each letter of the alphabet is accompanied by a poem using words beginning with that letter.

I. Moore, John Travers. II Anderson, Laurie. III title.

Rule 2.5B7
Work unnumbered, but the number of pages is readily ascertainable

---

56

Trudeau, Gary.

The Doonesbury chronicles / G.B. Trudeau ; with an introduction by Garry Wills. — New York : Holt, Rinehart and Winston, [1975?]
ca. 200 p. : ill. (some col.) ; 29 cm.

ISBN 0-03-014906-1

I Title.

Rule 2.5B7
Work unnumbered, and the number of pages is not readily ascertainable – Estimate of the number of pages

---

57

Viertel, Arthur T.

Trees, shrubs and vines : a pictorial guide to the ornamental woody plants of the northern United States exclusive of conifers / Arthur T. Viertel. — Syracuse, N.Y. : Syracuse University Press, c1970.
1 v. (unpaged) : ill., map ; 26 cm.

Includes bibliographical references and index.
ISBN 0-8156-0068-2

II. title.

Rule 2.5B7
Work unnumbered, and the number of pages is not readily ascertainable

[Library of Congress practice for a non-children's book.]

58

Coulter, Bailey M. Jr. (handwritten)

Compressible flow manual : a handbook for the design of compressible flow piping systems and a complete source of gas properties / Bailey M. Coulter, Jr. — Melbourne, FL : Fluid Research and Pub., c1984.

1 v. (various pagings) : ill. ; 28 cm.

Place of publication from label on t.p. verso.

I Title. (handwritten)

Rule 2.5B8c
Complicated or irregular paging

59

Title (handwritten)

Library of Congress rule interpretations. — 2nd ed. — Washington, D.C. : Cataloging Distribution Service, Library of Congress, 1989-

1 v. (loose-leaf) ; 30 cm.

Formulated by Office for Descriptive Cataloging Policy, Library of Congress.
Editor: Robert M. Hiatt.
Updated with quarterly supplements. Base text April 1989.
Includes index.
ISBN 0-8444-0639-2 (loose-leaf)

I L.C. Office for " (handwritten)

Rule 2.5B9
Loose-leaf publication designed to receive additions

60

Johanson, Donald C. (handwritten)

Lucy : the beginnings of humankind / Donald C. Johanson and Maitland A. Edey. — Warner Books ed. — New York, N.Y. : Warner Books, [1982], c1981.

409 p., [8] p. of plates : ill. (some col.) ; 21 cm.

Includes bibliographical references (p. 385-409) and index.
ISBN 0-446-37036-3 (U.S.A.). — ISBN 0-446-37342-7 (Canada)

I Edey, Maitland A. (handwritten)
II Title (handwritten)

[The plates are located between pages 96 and 97.]

Rule 2.5B10
Unnumbered pages of plates

61

Oliphant, Mrs. (handwritten)

The makers of Florence : Dante, Giotto, Savonarola, and their city / by Mrs. Oliphant ; with portrait of Savonarola by C.H. Jeens and illustrations from drawings by Professor Delamotte. — New ed. — London : Macmillan, 1881.

xx, 422 p., [8] leaves of plates : ill. ; 19 cm.

Includes index.

I Title (handwritten)

how do you know (handwritten)
because of this? (handwritten)

Rule 2.5B10
Unnumbered leaves of plates

Date of publication, distribution, etc., cont'd.

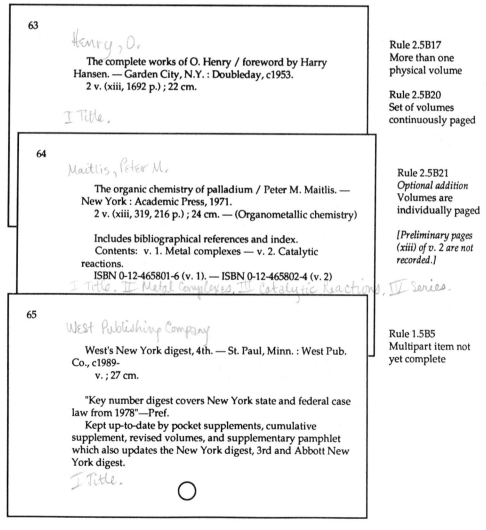

62

Alcock, Leslie

Was this Camelot? : excavations at Cadbury Castle, 1966-1970 / Leslie Alcock. — New York : Stein and Day, 1972. 224 p. : ill. (some col.) ; 26 cm. — (New aspects of archaeology)

Report of research conducted by the Camelot Research Committee.
Includes bibliographical references and index.
ISBN 0-8128-1505-X

I Title.

[The plates are located between pages 32-49, 56-61, 84-101, etc.]

Rule 2.5B10
Unnumbered leaves of plates

[In this instance, the rule does not apply because the plates do not meet the definitional requirement for plates, i.e., they "do not form part of . . . the main sequence of pages or leaves."]

Publications in more than one volume

63

Henry, O.

The complete works of O. Henry / foreword by Harry Hansen. — Garden City, N.Y. : Doubleday, c1953.
2 v. (xiii, 1692 p.) ; 22 cm.

I Title.

Rule 2.5B17
More than one physical volume

Rule 2.5B20
Set of volumes continuously paged

64

Maitlis, Peter M.

The organic chemistry of palladium / Peter M. Maitlis. — New York : Academic Press, 1971.
2 v. (xiii, 319, 216 p.) ; 24 cm. — (Organometallic chemistry)

Includes bibliographical references and index.
Contents: v. 1. Metal complexes — v. 2. Catalytic reactions.
ISBN 0-12-465801-6 (v. 1). — ISBN 0-12-465802-4 (v. 2)

I Title. II Metal Complexes. III Catalytic Reactions. IV Series.

Rule 2.5B21
Optional addition
Volumes are individually paged

[Preliminary pages (xiii) of v. 2 are not recorded.]

65

West Publishing Company

West's New York digest, 4th. — St. Paul, Minn. : West Pub. Co., c1989-
v. ; 27 cm.

"Key number digest covers New York state and federal case law from 1978"—Pref.
Kept up-to-date by pocket supplements, cumulative supplement, revised volumes, and supplementary pamphlet which also updates the New York digest, 3rd and Abbott New York digest.

I Title.

Rule 1.5B5
Multipart item not yet complete

Date of publication, distribution, etc., cont'd.

66

Youngman, Henny.

    The best of Henny Youngman : three volumes in one / drawings by Sheila Greenwald and Fred Hausman. — New York : Gramercy Pub. Co., [1978]
    3 v. in 1 : ill. ; 21 cm.

    Contents: How do you like me so far? — 400 traveling salesmen's jokes — Henny Youngman's bar bets, bar jokes, bar tricks.
    ISBN 0-517-25714-9

I Title. II How do you like me so far? III 400 Traveling salesmen Jokes; IV Four Hundred ... V Henny Youngman's ... VI Bar Bets, ...

Rule 2.5B19
Number of bibliographic volumes differs from the number of physical volumes

---

[Special formats]

67

Sayers, Dorothy L.

    Strong poison / by Dorothy L. Sayers. — Large type ed. — New York, N.Y. : Franklin Watts, [196-?], c1930.
    252 p. (large print) ; 29 cm.

    "A Lord Peter Wimsey novel"—Jacket.
    "A Keith Jennison book."

I Title.

Rule 2.5B24
Large print intended for the visually impaired

2.5C   Illustrative matter

68

Anderson, John.

    Burning down the house : MOVE and the tragedy of Philadelphia / John Anderson and Hilary Hevenor. — 1st ed. — New York : Norton, c1987.
    xv, 409 p. : ill. ; 25 cm.

    Includes index.
    ISBN 0-393-02460-1

I Hevenor, Hilary. II Title.

Rule 2.5C1
Illustrated work

69

Bowman, Francis Favill.

    Why Wisconsin / by Francis Favill Bowman. — Madison, Wis. : F. F. Bowman, 1948.
    210 p., vi : map ; 24 cm.

    Map on lining papers.
    Includes bibliographical references and index.

I Title.

Rule 2.5C2
Specific type of illustration

Date of publication, distribution, etc., cont'd.

70

Lorant, Stefan.

    Pittsburgh : the story of an American city / Stefan Lorant,
with contributions by Henry Steele Comanger . . . [et al.]. —
Rev., enl. and updated Bicentennial ed. — Lenox, Mass. :
Authors Edition, c1975.
    608 p. : ill. (some col.), facsims., maps, plans, ports. ; 32 cm.

    Includes bibliographical references (p. 595-600) and index.
I Title.

Rule 2.5C2
General and specific
types of illustrations

71

Goodman, Joan Elizabeth.

    The secret life of Walter Kitty / story and pictures by Joan
Elizabeth Goodman. — New York : Golden Book, c1986.
    [24] p. : col. ill. ; 21 cm. — (A Big little golden book)

    Summary: When unlawful badgers take over a city park, a
young cat dons a mask and cape and becomes the super hero,
Wonder Cat.
    ISBN 0-307-10260-2. — ISBN 0-307-68260-9 (lib. bdg.)
I Title. II Series.

Rule 2.5C3
Colored
illustrations

72

Boardman, John.

    Greek art / John Boardman. — Rev. ed. — New York :
Praeger, c1973.
    252 p. : ill. (some col.) ; 21 cm. — (Praeger world of art series)

    "Books that matter"—T.p. verso.
    Includes bibliographical references (p. 238-241) and index.
I Title. II Series.

Rule 2.5C4
Some illustrations in
color

73

Theroux, Paul,

    Riding the Iron Rooster : by train through China / Paul
Theroux. — New York : Putnam's, c1988.
    480 p. : map ; 25 cm.

    Map on lining papers.
    ISBN 0-399-13309-7
I Title.

Rule 2.5C5
All of the
illustrations appear
on the lining papers

74

Ward, Lynd.

    Gods' man : a novel in woodcuts / by Lynd Ward. — New
York : St. Martin's Press, [1978?], c1929.
    [117] p. : all ill. ; 21 cm.

    ISBN 0-312-33100-2 (cloth). — ISBN 0-312-33101-0 (pbk.)

I Title.

Rule 2.5C6
Work consists
wholly of
illustrations

2.5D Dimensions

75

Parker, Rowland.

Men of Dunwich : the story of a vanished town / Rowland Parker. — New York : Holt, Rinehart and Winston, 1979, c1978. 272 p. : ill., maps ; 22 cm.

Map on lining papers.
Includes bibliographical references (p. 267) and index.
ISBN 0--03-046801-9

1 Title,   *[The book measures 21.6 cm.]*

Rule 2.5D1
Height of the item in centimeters, rounded to the next whole centimeter

76

Reader's Digest Association,

Reader's Digest complete do-it-yourself manual. — Pleasantville, N.Y. : Reader's Digest Association, c1973. 600 p. : ill. (some col.) ; 23 x 28 cm.

Includes index.
ISBN 0-89577-010-5

I. Title. II Complete Do-it-Yourself Manual

Rule 2.5D2
Width of the item is greater than the height

1.5E Accompanying material

77

Place, Irene.

Records management : controlling business information / Irene Place, David J. Hyslop. — Reston, Va. : Reston Pub. Co., c1982.
    xi, 371 p. : ill. ; 24 cm. + 1 instructor's manual (84 p. : ill. ; 23 cm.)

Includes bibliographical references (p. 348-353) and index.
ISBN 0-8359-6606-2 — ISBN 0-8359-6607-0 (instructor's manual)

I Hyslop, David J. II Title.

Rule 1.5Ed
Accompanying material -- Number and name of physical units

Optional addition
Physical description of accompanying material

[Description made according to Rule 2.5).]

78

Allen, Sue.

Victorian bookbindings : a pictorial survey / Sue Allen. — Rev. ed. — Chicago : University of Chicago Press, c1976.
    v, 53 p. ; 21 cm. + 3 microfiches (col. ill.). — (A University of Chicago Press text/fiche)

Reduction ratio varies.
Microfiches in pocket.
"List of books illustrated:" p. 39-53.
ISBN 0-226-68787-2

I Title . II Series.

Rule 1.5Ed
Accompanying material -- Number and name of physical units

Optional addition
Physical description of accompanying material

[Description made according to Rule 11.5).]

Please explain: Format related

Accompanying material, cont'd.

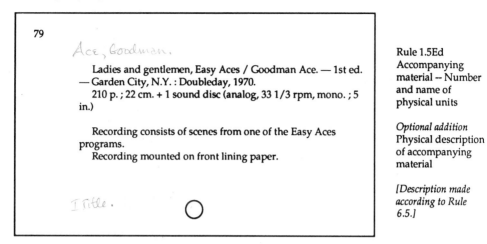

79

Ace, Goodman.

    Ladies and gentlemen, Easy Aces / Goodman Ace. — 1st ed. — Garden City, N.Y. : Doubleday, 1970.
    210 p. ; 22 cm. + 1 sound disc (analog, 33 1/3 rpm, mono. ; 5 in.)

    Recording consists of scenes from one of the Easy Aces programs.
    Recording mounted on front lining paper.

I Title.   ◯

Rule 1.5Ed
Accompanying material -- Number and name of physical units

Optional addition
Physical description of accompanying material

[Description made according to Rule 6.5.]

1.6   SERIES AREA
1.6B   Title proper of series

80

Doors + Windows.

    Doors and windows / by the editors of Time-Life Books. — Chicago, Ill. : Time-Life ; Morristown, N.J. : School and library distribution by Silver Burdett, 1980, c1978.
    128 p. : col. ill. ; 26 cm. — (Home repair and improvement)

    "Second printing. Revised 1980"—T.p. verso.
    Includes index.
    ISBN 0-8094-2408-8. — ISBN 0-8094-2407-X (lib. bdg.)

I Time Life Books. ◯
II Series.

Rule 1.6B1
Title proper of series

1.6E   Statements of responsibility relating to series

81

National Association of Accountants.

    Accounting for costs of capacity. — New York, N.Y. : National Association of Accountants, c1963.
    64 p. : ill. ; 23 cm. — (Research report / National Association of Accountants ; no. 39)

    Cover title.
    "May 1, 1963"—P. 2 of cover.
    Includes bibliographical references.
I Title.
II Series: National Association of Accountants Research Report # 39
    ◯

Rule 1.6E1
Statement of responsibility relating to the series

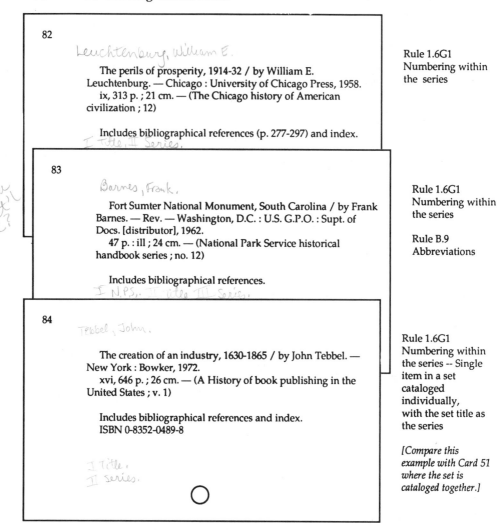

82

Leuchtenburg, William E.

    The perils of prosperity, 1914-32 / by William E.
Leuchtenburg. — Chicago : University of Chicago Press, 1958.
    ix, 313 p. ; 21 cm. — (The Chicago history of American
civilization ; 12)

    Includes bibliographical references (p. 277-297) and index.

I Title. II Series.

Rule 1.6G1
Numbering within
the series

83

Barnes, Frank.

    Fort Sumter National Monument, South Carolina / by Frank
Barnes. — Rev. — Washington, D.C. : U.S. G.P.O. : Supt. of
Docs. [distributor], 1962.
    47 p. : ill ; 24 cm. — (National Park Service historical
handbook series ; no. 12)

    Includes bibliographical references.

I N.P.S. II Title III Series.

Rule 1.6G1
Numbering within
the series

Rule B.9
Abbreviations

How do you
figure Nat'l
Park Svc?

84

Tebbel, John.

    The creation of an industry, 1630-1865 / by John Tebbel. —
New York : Bowker, 1972.
    xvi, 646 p. ; 26 cm. — (A History of book publishing in the
United States ; v. 1)

    Includes bibliographical references and index.
    ISBN 0-8352-0489-8

I Title.
II series.

Rule 1.6G1
Numbering within
the series -- Single
item in a set
cataloged
individually,
with the set title as
the series

*[Compare this
example with Card 51
where the set is
cataloged together.]*

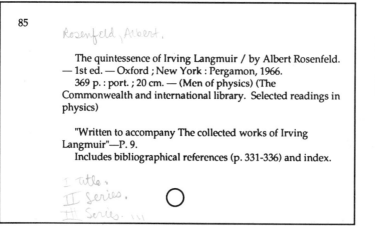

85

Rosenfeld, Albert.

    The quintessence of Irving Langmuir / by Albert Rosenfeld.
— 1st ed. — Oxford ; New York : Pergamon, 1966.
    369 p. : port. ; 20 cm. — (Men of physics) (The
Commonwealth and international library. Selected readings in
physics)

    "Written to accompany The collected works of Irving
Langmuir"—P. 9.
    Includes bibliographical references (p. 331-336) and index.

I Title.
II Series.
III Series. ...

Rule 1.6J1
Multiple series

Rule 1.6H1
Subseries

1.7 NOTE AREA
1.7A Form of notes

86

Christie, Agatha.

What Mrs. McGillicuddy saw! / by Agatha Christie. — New York : Dodd, Mead, c1957.
192 p. ; 22 cm. — (Red badge detective)

"This book serialized under the title Eye witness to murder"—T.p. verso.

I Title.

Rule 1.7A3
Quotation

[Source is other than the chief source of information.]

1.7B Notes

87

Adams, Henry.

The education of Henry Adams / edited with an introduction and notes by Ernest Samuels, Jane N. Samuels, assistant editor. — Boston : Houghton Mifflin, [1973], c1918.
xxx, 705 p. ; 20 cm. — (Riverside editions)

Autobiographical.
Includes bibliographical references (p. 537-538) and index.
ISBN 0-395-16620-9 (pbk.). — ISBN 0-035-16810-4 (hardbound)

I Samuels, Ernest. II Samuels, Jane N. III Title.

Rule 2.7B1
Nature of the work note

88

Eco, Umberto.

The name of the rose / Umberto Eco ; translated from the Italian by William Weaver. — San Diego : Harcourt Brace Jovanovich, c1983.
502 p. ; 25 cm.

Translation of: Il nome della rosa.
"A Helen and Kurt Wolff book."
ISBN 0-15-144647-4

I Title.

Rule 2.7B2
Translation note

89

Defense Intelligence Agency

Defense Intelligence Agency organization, mission and key personnel. — [Washington, D.C. : The Agency, 1987]
vi, 73 p. ; 22 x 28 cm.

Cover title.
"Prepared by the Directorate for Human Resources"—Pref.
"November 1987."
"DRS-2600-926-87."

I Title.

Rule 2.7B3
Source of title proper note

[See also Rule 1.1B1.]

Why isn't this under title?

90

Burstein, Milton B.

What you should know about selling and salesmanship / by Milton B. Burstein. — Dobbs Ferry, N.Y. : Oceana Publications, 1969.
x, 85 p. ; 20 cm. — (Business almanac series ; no. 18)

Cover title: Selling and salesmanship.
"Oceana book number 297-18"—T.p. verso.

I Title. II Title. III Selling + Salesmanship. IV Series.

Rule 2.7B4
Variations in title note

91

Ewen, David.

Great men of American popular song / David Ewen. — Rev. and enl. ed. — Englewood Cliffs, N.J. : Prentice-Hall, c1972.
x, 404 p. ; 25 cm.

Subtitle: The history of the American popular song told through the lives, careers, achievements, and personalities of its foremost composers and lyricists—from William Billings of the Revolutionary War through Bob Dylan, Johnny Cash, Burt Bacharach.

I Title.

Rule 2.7B5
Other title information note

[See also Rule 1.1E3.]

92

See answer . . .

Classification. Class KJ-KKZ, law of Europe / Subject Cataloging Division, Processing Services, Library of Congress. — Washington : The Library, 1988.
xxxi p., 599 leaves ; 28 cm.

Cover title: Law of Europe.
"Prepared in the Subject Cataloging Division by Jolande E. Goldberg"—P. iii.
ISBN 0-8444-0643-0

Rule 2.7B6
Statement of responsibility note

[See also Rule 1.1F2.]

93

Defoe, Daniel.

A journal of the plague year : being observations or memorials of the most remarkable occurrences . . . during the last great visitation in 1665 / written by a citizen who continued all the while in London. — London : W. Clowes ; Totowa, N.J. : distributed in the USA by Rowman & Littlefield, 1974.
302 p. : facsim. ; 24 cm. — (The Shakespeare Head edition of the novels & selected writings of Daniel Defoe)

Reprint. Originally published: Oxford : B. Blackwell, 1928.
Facsim. on lining papers.
ISBN 0-87471-500-8

I. Title.
II Series.

Rule 2.7B7
Edition and history note

Notes, cont'd.

94

Tse-Tung, Mao.

Quotations from Chairman Mao Tse-Tung. — 1st ed. —
Peking : Foreign Languages Press ; San Francisco : U.S.
distributors, China Books & Periodicals, 1966.
311 p. : port. ; 14 cm.

Distributor statement stamped on t.p.

I Title.

Rule 2.7B9
Publication,
distribution, etc.
note

95

Title.

Report to Topmakers III / J.R. Eley . . . [et al.]. — Belmont,
Vic., Australia : CSIRO Division of Textile Industry, [1985]
6 leaves : ill. ; 30 cm. — (Report ; no. G52)

"July, 1985."
Includes bibliographical references (leaf 6).
ISBN 0-643-03940-6

I Eley, J.R.

Rule 2.7B9
Publication,
distribution, etc.,
note -- Transmittal
date

96

Galloway, John.

Origins of modern art, 1905-1914 / by John Galloway. —
New York : McGraw-Hill, c1965.
47 p. : ill. ; 25 cm. + 24 slides (col.). — (Color slide program of
the world's art)

Slides mounted in pocket.

I Title.

Rule 2.7B11
Accompanying
material note

97

Konig, Hans.

Death of a schoolboy / Hans Koning. — 1st ed. — New
York : Harcourt Brace Jovanovich, c1974.
187 p. ; 21 cm.

"A Helen and Kurt Wolff book."
ISBN 0-15-124155-4

I Title.

Rule 2.7B12
Series note --
Phrase naming an
in-house editor or
another official of
the firm

Notes, cont'd.

98

Shepherd, Jean.

    A fistful of fig newtons / by Jean Shepherd ; illustrated by the author. — Doubleday Dolphin ed. — Garden City, N.Y. : Doubleday, 1983, c1981.
    xii, 265 p. : ill. ; 21 cm.

    "A Doubleday Dolphin book."
    ISBN 0-385-18843-9

I. Title.

○

Rule 2.7B12
Series note --
Publisher's
characterization of
the work

99

Viorst, Judith.

    Alexander and the terrible, horrible, no good, very bad day / Judith Viorst ; illustrated by Ray Cruz. — 2nd Aladdin Books ed. — New York : Aladdin Books, 1987, c1972.
    [32] p. : ill. ; 18 x 23 cm.

    Summary: One day when everything goes wrong for him, Alexander is consoled by the thought that other people have bad days too.
    ISBN 0-689-71173-5

I. Cruz, Ray. II. Title.

○

Rule 2.7B17
Summary note

100

Mortimer, John.

    Rumpole and the age of miracles / John Mortimer. — New York : Penguin, 1989, c1988.
    225 p. ; 18 cm.

    Contents: Rumpole and the bubble reputation — Rumpole and the barrow boy — Rumpole and the age of miracles — Rumpole and the tap end — Rumpole and the chambers party — Rumpole and Portia — Rumpole and the quality of life.
    ISBN 0-14-013116-7

I. Title.

○

Rule 2.7B18
Contents note --
Works by one
author

101

Title.

Shakespeare : lectures on five plays / by A. Fred Sochatoff . . .
[et al.]. — Pittsburgh : Carnegie Institute of Technology, 1958.
83 p. ; 23 cm. — (Carnegie series in English ; no. 4)

Contents: Much ado about nothing / A. Fred Sochatoff —
Measure for measure / Robert C. Slack — Antony and
Cleopatra / Austin Wright — Cymbeline / Neal Woodruff, Jr.
— The tempest / John A. Hart.

I Sochatoff, A. Fred. I. Series.

essays

Rule 2.7B18
Contents note --
Works by different
authors

102

Wiener, Joel H.

A descriptive finding list of unstamped British periodicals,
1830-1836 / by Joel H. Wiener. — London : Bibliographical
Society, 1970.
xiii, 74 p. ; 26 cm.

Includes bibliographical references (p. 72-74) and index.

I Title.

Rule 2.7B18
Contents note --
Bibliography and
index note

*[This is the format
currently used by the
Library of Congress.]*

103

Galanides, Antonio M.

Useful information for newly commissioned officers. — 1985
ed. / prepared by Antonio M. Galanides. — [Pensacola, Fla.?] :
Naval Education and Training Program Development Center,
[1985]
viii, 168 p. : ill., forms ; 13 x 19 cm.

"NAVEDTRA 10802-AG."
Stock ordering no.: 0502-LP-054-0200.

*I Naval Educ. . . . .
II. Title.*

Rule 2.7B19
Numbers note

In addition to the note examples under Area 7, notes have been added, when appropriate, to the preceding examples. In the list below, following the number and heading for the note, are references to card examples in this chapter that provide additional examples of notes. Some very commonly used notes, e.g., bibliographical reference notes and index notes, have not been included in this index.

Rule
2.7B1   Nature, scope or artistic form
         29, 65
2.7B2   Language of the item and/or translation or adaptation
         13   (Other languages)
2.7B3   Source of the title proper
         3, 13, 37, 81
2.7B4   Variations in title
         92   (Cover title)
         23   (Spine title)
2.7B6   Statements of responsibility
         7, 14, 59, 62, 92
         32   ("At head of title")
2.7B7   Edition and history
         21   ("Based on")
         1, 18, 42, 85, 86   (Bibliographic history)
         11, 47, 106   (Edition information)
         20, 23   (Reprint)
         80   (Revision statement)
         81   (Transmittal date)
2.7B9   Publication, distribution, etc.
         3
         58   (Publisher information on label)
         89   (Transmittal date)
         59, 65   (Updates)
2.7B10   Physical description
         36, 69, 73, 75, 93   (Illustrations on lining papers)
2.7B11   Accompanying material
         78   (Details)
         78, 79   (Location)
         79   (Nature)
2.7B12   Series
         1, 9, 44, 67, 84, 88   (Publisher's characterization)
         67, 72   (Series-like statement)
         94   (Series no.)
2.7B17   Summary
         55, 71
2.7B18   Contents
         11, 43, 51, 64, 66   (Formal contents)
         23, 78   (Informal contents)
2.7B19   Numbers
         89, 90

104

Grizzard, Lewis.

    Elvis is dead and I don't feel so good myself / Lewis
Grizzard. — Warner Books ed. — New York, N.Y. : Warner
Books, [1986], c1984.
    269 p. ; 18 cm.

    ISBN 0-446-34099-5
    [ISBN taken from the back cover.]

I Title.

Rule 1.8B1
International
Standard Book
Number

105

Rich, Daniel Catton

    Edgar-Hilaire-Germain Degas / text by Daniel Catton Rich.
— New York : Henry N. Abrams, [1966?]
    124 p. : ill. (some col.) ; 33 cm. — (The Library of great
painters)

    ISBN 0-8109-0067-X

I Degas, Edgar-Hilaire-Germain.
II title.

Rule 1.8B1
International
Standard Book
Number

*[Library of Congress
policy is to convert a
Standard Book
Number (SBN) to an
ISBN.]*

106

Wall, Joseph Frazier.

    Andrew Carnegie / Joseph Frazier Wall. — [2nd ed.]. —
Pittsburgh, Pa. : University of Pittsburgh Press, c1989.
    xiii, 1137 p., [16] p. of plates : ill. ; 25 cm.

    2nd ed. contains "no additions, no deletions and no
corrections" from the 1st ed.
    Originally published: New York : Oxford University Press,
1970.
    Includes bibliographical references and index.
    ISBN 0-8229-5904-6 (pbk.). — ISBN 0-8229-3828-6

I Title.   ◯   *[The work in hand is the pbk. ed.]*

Rule 1.8B2
Multiple ISBNs

Optionally
Other ISBNs

*[Library of Congress
policy is to record
first the ISBN for the
item being described.]*

DESCRIPTIVE CATALOGING EXERCISE

Using the information from the title pages, title page versos, and the
descriptive paragraph that follows them, descriptively catalog each of the
following books. Answers to this exercise appear in Appendix A.

Title page

HOUSE DESIGN
FOR
MODERN LIVING

ROBERT GROGAN

With Illustrations by
Patty Brown

Third Edition

ALBATROSS PRESS, INC.
New York Chicago

1979

Title page verso

© 1963, 1969, 1977
by Albatross Press, Inc.

1st Printing   1977
2nd Printing   1979

ISBN 0-9876-4321-0

The book is 22 cm. high and 17 cm. wide. The last numbered preliminary page is xii. The first numbered page of text is 1 and the last numbered page is 306. The book is illustrated with black & white reproductions of photographs and line drawings. There are 12 unnumbered pages of colored plates.

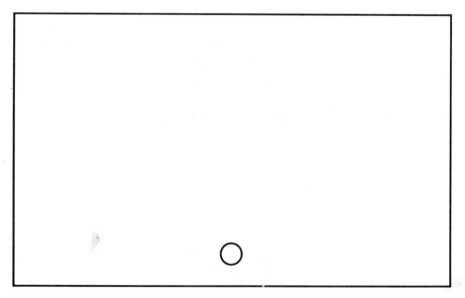

Title page

**ENVIRONMENTAL EFFECTS
OF THE USE OF ASBESTOS**

Horace Lemper, M.D.
Justine McCabe, Ph.D.

Introduction by
J. Wells Sinclair

Photographs by
Ann Reed & Ella Julianno

THE OSGOOD PUBLISHING COMPANY
LONDON   STOCKHOLM   NEW YORK

1972

Title page verso

©
Under
International Agreement

Second Revised Edition
1969

Reprinted 1972

SBN 683-49361-2

Printed in Stockholm

The last numbered preliminary page is vi. The first page of text is numbered 7 and the last numbered page of text is 398. The book is 22.3 cm. high. The book has several tables and is illustrated with line drawings and black and white photographs. There is a bibliography that begins on unnumbered page 361 and continues through numbered page 388. There is an index beginning on page 389 and continuing to page 398.

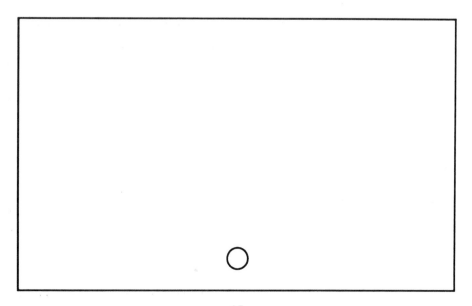

Title page

THE PROBLEMS OF EARTH

READINGS IN ECOLOGY

by

Adam Smith
Helen R. Roberts
John A. Kirschwin
A. N. Untermeyer

ECOLOGY ASSOCIATION PRESS
Bloomington, Indiana

1976

Title page verso

© 1968

First Published 1969
Second Printing 1973
Third Printing 1976

Number IX

*Series on the
Environmental Sciences*

Series Editor:
Oscar W. Friedlander

ISBN 0-2345-9870-1
ISBN 0-2345-9871-2
(paperback)

The book is 24 cm. high. The last numbered page of text is 296, although the text continues for 5 more pages. There is a bibliography at the end of each separately written section, on pages 73, 141, 212, and 296. The only illustrations are maps of the Eastern and Western Hemispheres on the end papers. This is the hardcover edition.

**AMERICAN BOOK
ILLUSTRATORS**
A BIBLIOGRAPHY

by KAREN GALE

AMERICAN BINDERS
A BIBLIOGRAPHY

by HUGO TREES

GAMBIT PRESS

Pittsburgh, Pennsylvania

© 1987

*BOOKS
FOR
COLLECTORS*

ISBN 0-5678-9012-3

The book is 27.6 cm. high. The pagination goes from 1-116 and 1-125. The book is not illustrated, but at the back of the book are pockets containing 120 2x2 inch colored slides showing the work of illustrators and binders. There is an index to the slides at the end of the book. The title on the book's spine reads "American Book Illustrators and Binders."

Department of the Navy
Office of the Judge Advocate General

**THE
OFFICIAL GUIDE
TO
POST-SERVICE
EMPLOYMENT OPPORTUNITIES**

May 1989

JAG P-19913

Page following the Table of Contents

A revision of
*The Reference Guide to
Post-Service Employment
Opportunities for Naval
Personnel.*

Compiled by
Nelson F. Halleck.

The book is 21.2 cm. high. There is no title page or title page verso. There are 7 unnumbered preliminary pages. The last numbered page is 96. The book is not illustrated, but does have bibliographic footnotes and an index. The binding is paperback. No place of publication is known, but one can assume it was published in the United States.

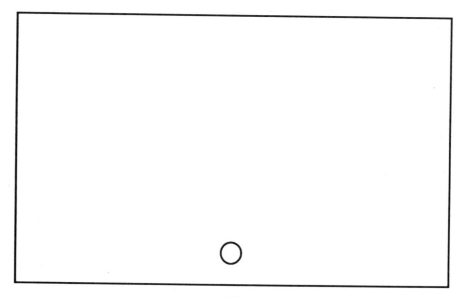

Title page

The Feminist Struggle
Volume Seven

THE RIGHT OF WOMEN

Our Struggle for the Vote

by

Alice Faberman

A Susan Ebert / Karen Norris book

Philadelphia
THE FEMINIST PRESS
1990

Title page verso

FIRST EDITION

Photo-offset reproduction of the work originally published in Philadelphia by J. P. Lippincott in 1911 from the copy in the Van Pelt Library of the University of Pennsylvania.

Limited to 500 copies.
Copy 173

ISBN 0-361-45927-5

The book is 23 cm. high. The pagination sequences end with xiii and 389. There are no illustrations other than a frontispiece portrait of the author that precedes the numbered preliminary pages (consider this a leaf). On the series title page, the series title reads: The Feminist Struggle Series, volume seven.

Title page

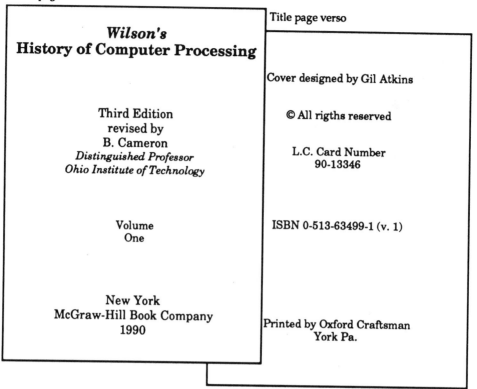

Wilson's
History of Computer Processing

Third Edition
revised by
B. Cameron
Distinguished Professor
Ohio Institute of Technology

Volume
One

New York
McGraw-Hill Book Company
1990

Title page verso

Cover designed by Gil Atkins

L.C. Card Number
90-13346

ISBN 0-513-63499-1 (v. 1)

Printed by Oxford Craftsman
York Pa.

The book is 27 cm tall. The preface indicates that this is the first of a planned three volume work. To date, this is the only volume that has been published. It has preliminary pagination ending with page xi and a main sequence ending with page 457. The work has black and white photographs occurring between pages 262 and 263. The work has bibliographical references at the end of most chapters and an index at the end of the book.

CHAPTER TWO

Choice of Access Points

Topic Outline

Rules

21.1   General Rule

21.4   Works for Which a Single Person or Corporate Body is Responsible

21.5   Works of Unknown or Uncertain Authorship or by Unnamed Groups

21.6   Works of Shared Responsibility

21.7   Collections of Works Produced under Editorial Direction

WORKS THAT ARE MODIFICATIONS OF OTHER WORKS

Modifications of Texts

21.10   Adaptations of Texts

21.11   Illustrated Texts

21.12   Revisions of Texts

21.14   Translations

21.15   Texts Published with Biographical/Critical Material

MIXED RESPONSIBILITY IN NEW WORKS

21.24   Collaboration between Artist and Writer

21.25   Reports of Interviews or Exchanges

RELATED WORKS

21.28   Related Works

21.30   Specific Rules

Readings: *Anglo-American Cataloguing Rules.* 2nd ed., 1988 revision
               Part II, Headings, Uniform Titles, and References:
                  Introduction, p. 306-307;
                     Chapter 21: Choice of Access Points, p. 307-338.

CARD FORMAT

Format for a main entry unit card

```
Call        Main entry.
number          Title proper : other title information / statement of
            responsibility ; subsequent statements of responsibility. —
            Edition statement / statement of responsibility relating to the
            edition. — Place : publisher, date (Place : printer)
                no. of pages, no. of plates : illustration statement ; size +
            accompanying material. — (Series ; number)

                Notes.
                ISBN

                1. Subject heading.  I. Added entry.
                            O
```

Format for a title main entry unit card

```
Call        Title proper : other title information / statement of responsibility ;
number          subsequent statements of responsibility. — Edition statement /
            statement of responsibility relating to the edition. — Place :
            publisher, date (Place : printer)
                no. of pages, no. of plates : illustration statement ; size +
            accompanying material. — (Series ; number)

                Notes.
                ISBN

                1. Subject heading.  I. Added entry.
                            O
```

This book generates five entries for a dictionary catalog

Z6824
.S4
1967

Sealock, Richard B., 1907-
    Bibliography of place-name literature : United States and
Canada / by Richard B. Sealock and Pauline A. Seely. — 2nd
ed. — Chicago : American Library Association, 1967.
    x, 352 p. ; 24 cm.

    Includes indexes.

    1. Names, Geographical--United States--Bibliography. 2.
Names, Geographical--Canada--Bibliography. I. Seely, Pauline
A. (Pauline Augusta), 1905-   II. Title.

        O

Seely, Pauline A. (Pauline Augusta), 1905-
Z6824   Sealock, Richard B., 1907-
.S4
1967

Z6824   Sealock, Richard B., 1907-
.S4
1967

NAMES, GEOGRAPHICAL--UNITED STATES--
        BIBLIOGRAPHY.
Z6824   Sealock, Richard B., 1907-
.S4   Bibliography of place-name literature : United States and
1967   Canada / by Richard B. Sealock and Pauline A. Seely. -- 2nd

NAMES, GEOGRAPHICAL--CANADA--BIBLIOGRAPHY.
Z6824   Sealock, Richard B., 1907-
.S4
1967

Bibliography of place-name literature.
Z6824   Sealock, Richard B., 1907-
.S4   Bibliography of place-name literature : United States and
1967   Canada / by Richard B. Sealock and Pauline A. Seely. — 2nd
    ed. — Chicago : American Library Association, 1967.
    x, 352 p. ; 24 cm.

    Includes indexes.

    1. Names, Geographical--United States--Bibliography. 2.
Names, Geographical--Canada--Bibliography. I. Seely, Pauline
A. (Pauline Augusta), 1905-   II. Title.

        O

Cards are arranged in the same order as the books appear on the shelves.

Z7165
.U5W9
1969

Wynkoop, Sally.
    Directories of government agencies / compiled by Sally
Wynkoop and David W. Parish. — Rochester, N.Y. : Libraries
Unlimited, 1969.
    242 p. ; 23 cm.

Z7165
.U5W88
1969

Wynar, Lubomyr R., 1932-
    American political parties : a selective guide to parties and
movements of the 20th century / compiled by Lubomyr R.
Wynar. — Littleton, Colo. : Libraries Unlimited, 1969.
    427 p. ; 24 cm.

Z7164
.T8M4
1966

Metcalf, Kenneth N., 1923-1965.
    Transportation information sources : an annotated guide to
publications, agencies, and other data sources concerning air,
rail, water, road, and pipeline transportation / Kenneth N.
Metcalf ; foreword by Charles C. Cain, III. — Detroit : Gale
Research Co., 1966, c1965.
    307 p. ; 23 cm. — (Management information guide ; 8)

Z7164
.E2M45
1971

Melnyk, Peter.
    Economics : a bibliographic guide to reference books and
information resources / Peter Melnyk. — Littleton, Colo. :
Libraries Unlimited, 1971.
    263 p. ; 24 cm.

    1. Economics—Bibliography. I. Title.

Z6824
.S4
1967

Sealock, Richard B., 1907-
    Bibliography of place-name literature : United States and
Canada / by Richard B. Sealock and Pauline A. Seely. — 2nd
ed. — Chicago : American Library Association, 1967.
    x, 352 p. ; 24 cm.

    Includes indexes.

    1. Names, Geographical--United States--Bibliography. 2.
Names, Geographical--Canada--Bibliography. I. Seely, Pauline
A. (Pauline Augusta), 1905-   II. Title.

N.B. In the examples that follow, the headings, main and added, merely indicate the appropriate headings to use. As is done in Chapter 21 of AACR2R, the headings are not in their proper form. The forms of personal, and corporate headings are addressed in Chapters 3 and 4 of this workbook. In some of the examples, the notes and tracings have been moved up on the catalog record from where they normally would appear on a printed catalog card, i.e., near the bottom of the card, in order to conserve space.

21.1   GENERAL RULE
21.1A   Works of personal authorship

21.4   WORKS FOR WHICH A SINGLE PERSON OR CORPORATE BODY
        IS RESPONSIBLE
21.4A   Works of single personal authorship

107

Flanner, Janet.
    London was yesterday, 1934-1939 / Janet Flanner ; edited by
Irving Drutman. — New York : Viking, 1975.
    160 p. : ill. ; 25 cm.

    "A Studio book."
    "The text in this volume originally appeared in The New
Yorker"—T.p. verso.
    Includes index.
    ISBN 0-670-43753-0

    I. Drutman, Irving. II. Title.

Rule 21.1A2
Personal authorship

Rule 21.4A1
Work of single
personal authorship

108

Bakewell, K. G. B.
    Management principles and practice : a guide to information
sources / K.G.B. Bakewell. — Detroit, Mich. : Gale Research
Co., c1977.
    xix, 519 p. ; 23 cm. — (Management information guide ; 32)

    Includes indexes.
    ISBN 0-8103-0832-0

    I. Title. II. Series.

Rule 21.1A2
Personal authorship

Rule 21.4A1
Work of single
personal authorship
-- Compiler of a
bibliography

109

Breathed, Berke.
    Penguin dreams and stranger things / Berke Breathed. —
Boston : Little, Brown, c1985.
    120 p. : ill. (some col.) ; 23 x 26 cm.

    Selections from the author's Bloom County comic strip.
    "A Bloom County book."
    ISBN 0-316-10725-5

    I. Title. II. Title: Bloom County.

Rule 21.1A2
Personal authorship

Rule 21.4A1
Work of single
personal authorship
-- Writer of a comic
strip

Works of single personal authorship, cont'd.

110

Dunne, Finley Peter.
    Mr. Dooley in the hearts of his countrymen. — Boston :
Small, Maynard, 1899.
    xi, 285 p. ; 18 cm.

    Preface signed: F.P.D. [i.e., Finley Peter Dunne].
"Third edition (10,000 copies) October, 1899"—T.p. verso.

    I. Title. II. Title: Mister Dooley in the hearts of his
countrymen.

◯

Rule 21.1A2
Personal authorship

Rule 21.4A1
Work of single
personal authorship
-- Person is not
named in the work

21.1   GENERAL RULE
21.1B   Entry under corporate body

21.4   WORKS FOR WHICH A SINGLE PERSON OR CORPORATE BODY
       IS RESPONSIBLE
21.4B   Works emanating from a single corporate body

111

Inglewood Public Library.
    Library of Congress classification adapted for children's
books / [produced by John W. Perkins, Paul N. Clingen, Paul C.
Jones]. — Inglewood, Calif. : Inglewood Public Library, c1971.
    162 p. ; 28 cm.

    Cover title.

    I. Perkins, John W. II. Clingen, Paul N. III. Jones, Paul C. IV.
Title.

Rule 21.1B2a
Corporate
authorship --
Administrative
work

Rule 21.4B1
Work emanating
from a single
corporate body

112

Folio Society.
    Folio 21 : a bibliography of the Folio Society, 1947-1967 /
with an appraisal by Sir Francis Meynell. — London : Folio
Press, 1968.
    208 p. : ill. (some col.), facsims. ; 29 cm.

    Includes indexes.

    I. Meynell, Sir Francis. II. Title. III. Title: Folio twenty-one.

◯

Rule 21.1B2a
Corporate
authorship --
Administrative
work

Rule 21.4B1
Work emanating
from a single
corporate body

Works emanating from a single corporate body, cont'd.

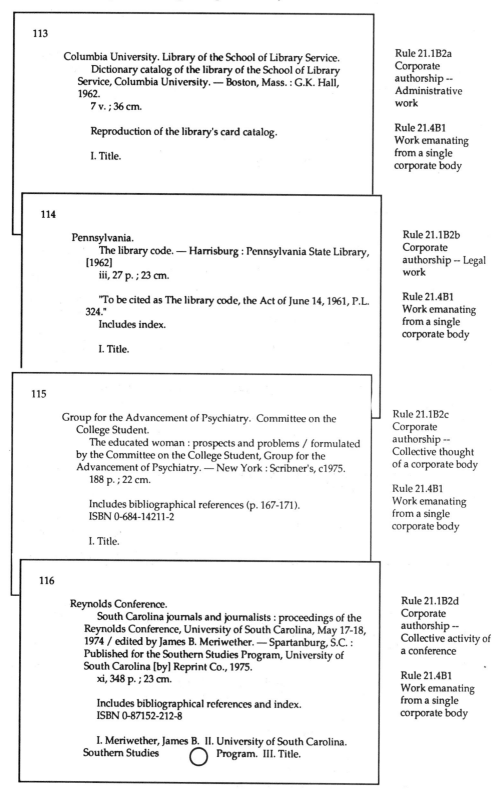

113

Columbia University. Library of the School of Library Service.
    Dictionary catalog of the library of the School of Library
    Service, Columbia University. — Boston, Mass. : G.K. Hall,
    1962.
        7 v. ; 36 cm.

    Reproduction of the library's card catalog.

        I. Title.

Rule 21.1B2a
Corporate
authorship --
Administrative
work

Rule 21.4B1
Work emanating
from a single
corporate body

114

Pennsylvania.
    The library code. — Harrisburg : Pennsylvania State Library,
    [1962]
        iii, 27 p. ; 23 cm.

        "To be cited as The library code, the Act of June 14, 1961, P.L.
    324."
        Includes index.

        I. Title.

Rule 21.1B2b
Corporate
authorship -- Legal
work

Rule 21.4B1
Work emanating
from a single
corporate body

115

Group for the Advancement of Psychiatry. Committee on the
    College Student.
        The educated woman : prospects and problems / formulated
    by the Committee on the College Student, Group for the
    Advancement of Psychiatry. — New York : Scribner's, c1975.
        188 p. ; 22 cm.

        Includes bibliographical references (p. 167-171).
        ISBN 0-684-14211-2

        I. Title.

Rule 21.1B2c
Corporate
authorship --
Collective thought
of a corporate body

Rule 21.4B1
Work emanating
from a single
corporate body

116

Reynolds Conference.
    South Carolina journals and journalists : proceedings of the
    Reynolds Conference, University of South Carolina, May 17-18,
    1974 / edited by James B. Meriwether. — Spartanburg, S.C. :
    Published for the Southern Studies Program, University of
    South Carolina [by] Reprint Co., 1975.
        xi, 348 p. ; 23 cm.

        Includes bibliographical references and index.
        ISBN 0-87152-212-8

        I. Meriwether, James B. II. University of South Carolina.
    Southern Studies   Program. III. Title.

Rule 21.1B2d
Corporate
authorship --
Collective activity of
a conference

Rule 21.4B1
Work emanating
from a single
corporate body

Works emanating from a single corporate body, cont'd.

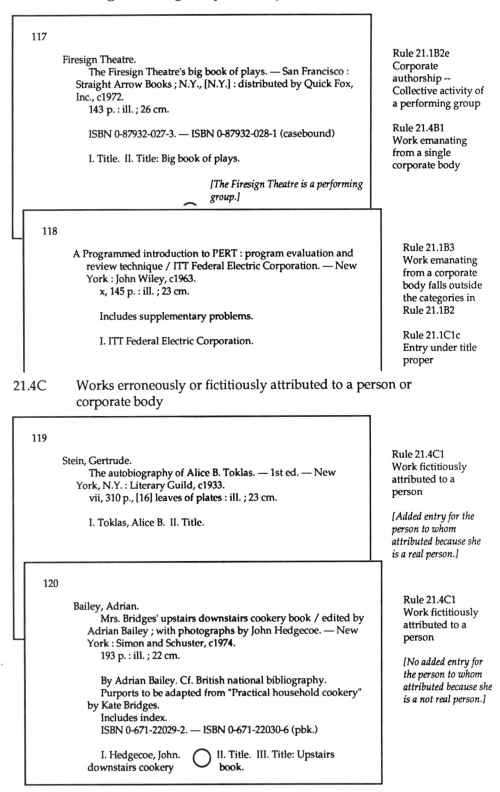

117

Firesign Theatre.
    The Firesign Theatre's big book of plays. — San Francisco :
Straight Arrow Books ; N.Y., [N.Y.] : distributed by Quick Fox,
Inc., c1972.
    143 p. : ill. ; 26 cm.

    ISBN 0-87932-027-3. — ISBN 0-87932-028-1 (casebound)

    I. Title. II. Title: Big book of plays.

                  [The Firesign Theatre is a performing
                     group.]

Rule 21.1B2e
Corporate
authorship --
Collective activity of
a performing group

Rule 21.4B1
Work emanating
from a single
corporate body

118

A Programmed introduction to PERT : program evaluation and
    review technique / ITT Federal Electric Corporation. — New
York : John Wiley, c1963.
    x, 145 p. : ill. ; 23 cm.

    Includes supplementary problems.

    I. ITT Federal Electric Corporation.

Rule 21.1B3
Work emanating
from a corporate
body falls outside
the categories in
Rule 21.1B2

Rule 21.1C1c
Entry under title
proper

21.4C   Works erroneously or fictitiously attributed to a person or
          corporate body

119

Stein, Gertrude.
    The autobiography of Alice B. Toklas. — 1st ed. — New
York, N.Y. : Literary Guild, c1933.
    vii, 310 p., [16] leaves of plates : ill. ; 23 cm.

    I. Toklas, Alice B. II. Title.

Rule 21.4C1
Work fictitiously
attributed to a
person

*[Added entry for the
person to whom
attributed because she
is a real person.]*

120

Bailey, Adrian.
    Mrs. Bridges' upstairs downstairs cookery book / edited by
Adrian Bailey ; with photographs by John Hedgecoe. — New
York : Simon and Schuster, c1974.
    193 p. : ill. ; 22 cm.

    By Adrian Bailey. Cf. British national bibliography.
    Purports to be adapted from "Practical household cookery"
by Kate Bridges.
    Includes index.
    ISBN 0-671-22029-2. — ISBN 0-671-22030-6 (pbk.)

    I. Hedgecoe, John.   II. Title. III. Title: Upstairs
downstairs cookery   book.

Rule 21.4C1
Work fictitiously
attributed to a
person

*[No added entry for
the person to whom
attributed because she
is a not real person.]*

21.4D Works by heads of state, other high government officials, popes, and other high ecclesiastical officials

121

United States. President (Truman)
The economic reports of the President as transmitted to the Congress, January 1949, January 1947, July 1947, January 1948, July 1948, together with the Joint Congressional Committee reports of 1947 & 1948 / introduction by the Council of Economic Advisers. — New York : Harcourt, Brace, [1949?]
1 v. (various pagings) : ill. ; 23 cm.
Includes the Annual economic review, January 1949, and the economic situation at midyear 1948, reports to the President by the Council of Economic Advisers.
Includes index.
I. Truman, Harry S. II. United States. Congress. Joint Economic Committee. ◯ III. Council of Economic Advisers.
IV. Title.

Rule 21.4D1
Official communications of a head of state

[Added entry for the person holding the office.]

122

Wilson, Woodrow.
President Wilson's state papers and addresses / introduction by Albert Shaw. — New York : G.H. Doran, c1918.
xiv, 484 p. ; 22 cm.

Includes index.

I. Shaw, Albert. II. United States. President (Wilson) III. Title.

◯

Rule 21.4D3
Collection of official communications of a head of state and other works

[Added entry for the office of the head of state.]

123

Kennedy, John F.
Profiles in courage / John F. Kennedy. — Memorial ed. — New York : Harper & Row, [1964?]
287 p., [9] p. of plates : ill. ; 22 cm.

Foreword by Robert F. Kennedy.
Includes bibliographical references (p. 269-281) and index.

I. Title.

◯

Rule 21.4D2
Other works by a head of state

21.5 WORKS OF UNKNOWN OR UNCERTAIN AUTHORSHIP OR BY UNNAMED GROUPS

124

The Copyright dilemma : proceedings of a conference held at
Indiana University, April 14-15, 1977 / edited by Herbert S.
White. — Chicago : American Library Association, 1978.
xiii, 199 p. ; 23 cm.

Sponsored by the Indiana University Graduate Library
School.
ISBN 0-8389-0262-6

I. White, Herbert S. II. Indiana University. Graduate Library
School.

Rule 21.5A
Work emanates
from a body that
lacks a name

125

Nobody.
The notion-counter : a farrago of foibles : being notes about
nothing / by Nobody ; illustrated by Somebody. — Boston :
Atlantic Monthly Press, c1922.
108 p. : ill. ; 16 cm.

I. Title.

Rule 21.5C
Personal author
unknown, but chief
source of information
has a characterizing
word

126

Author of Widder Bagshaw.
Namby pamby, or, A hotch potch of poetic tit-bits / by the
author of Widder Bagshaw and her nevvy Samul's
Whissentoidr trip fro' Chowbent to New Brighton, etc., etc., etc.
— Liverpool : William Gilling, [18--]
vii, 256 p. ; 19 cm.

I. Title. II. Title: Namby pamby. III. Title: A hotch potch of
poetic tit-bits.

Rule 21.5C
Personal author
unknown, but chief
source of information
has a characterizing
phrase

21.6 WORKS OF SHARED RESPONSIBILITY
21.6B Principal responsibility indicated

127

Menninger, Karl.
The vital balance : the life process in mental health and
illness / Karl Menninger with Martin Mayman and Paul
Pruyser. — New York : Viking, 1963.
531 p. ; 25 cm.

Includes bibliographical references (p. 491-509) and index.

I. Mayman, Martin. II. Pruyser, Paul. III. Title.

Rule 21.6B1
Work of shared
responsibility with
principal
responsibility
attributed to an
individual

21.6C   Principal responsibility not indicated

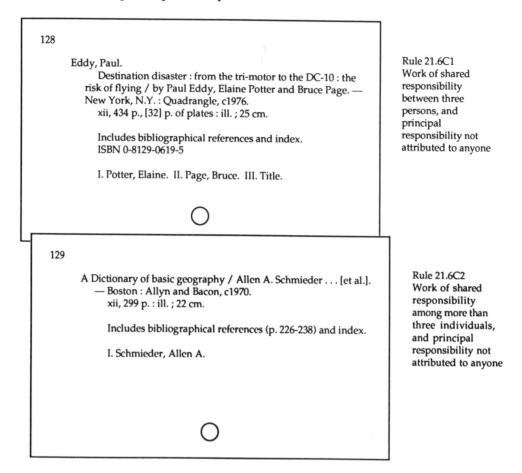

128

Eddy, Paul.
    Destination disaster : from the tri-motor to the DC-10 : the
risk of flying / by Paul Eddy, Elaine Potter and Bruce Page. —
New York, N.Y. : Quadrangle, c1976.
    xii, 434 p., [32] p. of plates : ill. ; 25 cm.

    Includes bibliographical references and index.
    ISBN 0-8129-0619-5

    I. Potter, Elaine. II. Page, Bruce. III. Title.

Rule 21.6C1
Work of shared
responsibility
between three
persons, and
principal
responsibility not
attributed to anyone

129

A Dictionary of basic geography / Allen A. Schmieder . . . [et al.].
    — Boston : Allyn and Bacon, c1970.
    xii, 299 p. : ill. ; 22 cm.

    Includes bibliographical references (p. 226-238) and index.

    I. Schmieder, Allen A.

Rule 21.6C2
Work of shared
responsibility
among more than
three individuals,
and principal
responsibility not
attributed to anyone

21.6D   Shared pseudonyms

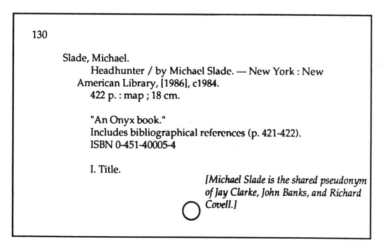

130

Slade, Michael.
    Headhunter / by Michael Slade. — New York : New
American Library, [1986], c1984.
    422 p. : map ; 18 cm.

    "An Onyx book."
    Includes bibliographical references (p. 421-422).
    ISBN 0-451-40005-4

    I. Title.

*[Michael Slade is the shared pseudonym
of Jay Clarke, John Banks, and Richard
Covell.]*

Rule 21.6D1
Shared pseudonym

21.7 COLLECTIONS OF WORKS PRODUCED UNDER EDITORIAL DIRECTION

21.7B With collective title

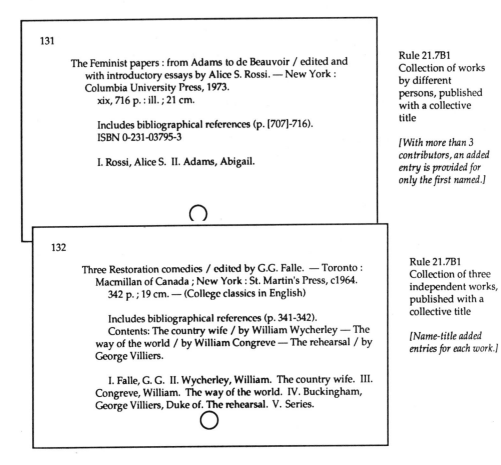

131

The Feminist papers : from Adams to de Beauvoir / edited and with introductory essays by Alice S. Rossi. — New York : Columbia University Press, 1973.
xix, 716 p. : ill. ; 21 cm.

Includes bibliographical references (p. [707]-716).
ISBN 0-231-03795-3

I. Rossi, Alice S. II. Adams, Abigail.

Rule 21.7B1
Collection of works by different persons, published with a collective title

[With more than 3 contributors, an added entry is provided for only the first named.]

132

Three Restoration comedies / edited by G.G. Falle. — Toronto : Macmillan of Canada ; New York : St. Martin's Press, c1964.
342 p. ; 19 cm. — (College classics in English)

Includes bibliographical references (p. 341-342).
Contents: The country wife / by William Wycherley — The way of the world / by William Congreve — The rehearsal / by George Villiers.

I. Falle, G. G. II. Wycherley, William. The country wife. III. Congreve, William. The way of the world. IV. Buckingham, George Villiers, Duke of. The rehearsal. V. Series.

Rule 21.7B1
Collection of three independent works, published with a collective title

[Name-title added entries for each work.]

21.7C Without collective title

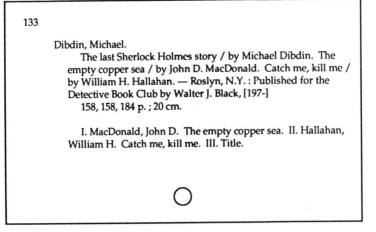

133

Dibdin, Michael.
The last Sherlock Holmes story / by Michael Dibdin. The empty copper sea / by John D. MacDonald. Catch me, kill me / by William H. Hallahan. — Roslyn, N.Y. : Published for the Detective Book Club by Walter J. Black, [197-]
158, 158, 184 p. ; 20 cm.

I. MacDonald, John D. The empty copper sea. II. Hallahan, William H. Catch me, kill me. III. Title.

Rule 21.7C1
Collection of works by different persons, published without a collective title

[Name-title added entries for the 2nd and 3rd works.]

21.10   ADAPTATIONS OF TEXTS

134

Grossbach, Robert.
   The cheap detective / a novelization by Robert Grossbach ;
based on the original screenplay by Neil Simon. — Warner
Books ed. — New York, N.Y. : Warner Books, c1978.
   221 p. ; 18 cm.

   ISBN 0-446-89557-1

   I. Simon, Neil. The cheap detective. II. Title.

Rule 21.10A
Adaptation of a text

21.11   ILLUSTRATED TEXTS

135

Loos, Anita.
   "Gentlemen prefer blondes" : the illuminating diary of a
professional lady / by Anita Loos ; intimately illustrated by
Ralph Barton. — New York : Boni & Liveright, 1925.
   217 p. : ill. ; 20 cm.

   I. Barton, Ralph. II. Title.

Rule 21.11A1
Text for which an
artist has provided
illustrations

136

Doré, Gustave.
   A Doré treasury : a collection of the best engravings of
Gustave Doré / edited and with an introduction by James
Stevens. — [New York] : Bounty Books, c1970.
   ix, 246 p. : chiefly ill. ; 31 cm.

   I. Stevens, James. II. Title.

Rule 21.11B1
Illustrations by an
artist published
separately

21.12   REVISIONS OF TEXTS
21.12A   Original author considered responsible

137

Esdaile, Arundell.
　　Esdaile's manual of bibliography. — 4th rev. ed. / revised
edition by Roy Stokes. — London : Allen & Unwin ; New York :
Barnes & Noble, 1967.
　　x, 336 p., [8] p. of plates : ill. ; 22 cm.

　　Includes bibliographical references and index.
　　ISBN 06-492032-1 (U.S.). — ISBN 04-010001-4 (British)

　　I. Stokes, Roy. II. Title. III. Title: Manual of bibliography.

Rule 21.12A1
Work that has been
revised and, (1) the
original author is
named in the title,
and (2) no one is
named in the Area 1
statement of
responsibility

21.12B   Original author no longer considered responsible

138

Abrams, M. H.
　　A glossary of literary terms / by M.H. Abrams ; based on the
original version by Dan S. Norton and Peters Rushton. — New
York : Rinehart, c1957.
　　105 p. ; 23 cm. — (The Rinehart English pamphlet series)

　　I. Norton, Dan S. A glossary of literary terms. II. Title. III.
Series.

Rule 21.12B1
Person responsible
for the original
work is no longer
considered
responsible for it

*[Name-title added
entry for the original
author.]*

21.14   TRANSLATIONS

139

Milne, A. A.
　　Winnie ille Pu / A.A. Milnei ; liber celeberrimus omnibus
fere pueris puellisque notus nunc primum de angelico sermone
in Latinum conversus auctore Alexandro Lenardo. — Novi
Eboraci [New York] : Sumptibus Duttonis, 1960.
　　121 p. : ill., map ; 20 cm.

　　Map on lining papers.

　　I. Leonard, Alexander. II. Title.

Rule 21.14A
Translation

140

Mahler, Alma.
    Gustav Mahler : memories and letters / by Alma Mahler. —
Enl. ed. / revised and edited and with an introduction by
Donald Mitchell ; translated by Basil Creighton. — New York :
Viking, 1969.
    xl, 369 p., [16] p. of plates : ill., facsims., ports. ; 25 cm.

    Translated from Gustav Mahler : erinnerunger und briefe.
Includes bibliographical references (p. [343]-353) and index.

    I. Mahler, Gustav. II. Mitchell, Donald. III. Title.

Rule 21.15A
Work by a writer,
with biographical or
critical material by
another person and
the work is
presented as a
biographical or
critical work

141

Beethoven, Ludwig van.
    Beethoven's letters : a critical edition / with explanatory
notes by Alf C. Kalischer ; translated with preface by J.S.
Shedlock. — Freeport, N.Y. : Books for Libraries Press, 1969.
    2 v. : ill., facsims., music, ports. ; 23 cm. — (Select
bibliographies reprint series)

    Reprint. Originally published: 1909.
ISBN 0-8369-5110-7

    I. Kalischer, Alf C. II. Title. III. Series.

Rule 21.15B
Biographical or
critical work in
which the
biographer or critic
is presented as an
editor, compiler, etc.

MIXED RESPONSIBILITY IN NEW WORKS

21.24   COLLABORATION BETWEEN ARTIST AND WRITER

142

Lewis, Taylor.
    Washington's Mount Vernon / photographs by Taylor
Lewis, Jr. ; text by Joanne Young. — 1st ed. — New York : Holt,
Rinehart and Winston, c1973.
    [63] p. : col. ill. ; 19 x 27 cm.

    Illustrations on lining papers.
ISBN 0-03-003961-4

    I. Young, Joanne. II. Title.

Rule 21.24A
Collaborative work
between artist and
writer

143

Erikson, Erik H.
    In search of common ground : conversations with Erik H.
Erikson and Huey P. Newton / introduced by Kai T. Erikson.
— 1st ed. — New York : Norton, c1973.
    143 p. ; 22 cm.

    ISBN 0-393-05483-7

    I. Newton, Huey P. II. Title.

Rule 21.25A
Report essentially
confined to the
words of the
persons
interviewed

144

Bragg, Melvyn.
    Speak for England : an oral history of England, 1900-1975,
based on interviews with the inhabitants of Wigton,
Cumberland / Melvyn Bragg. — 1st American ed. — New York
: Knopf : Distributed by Random House, 1977, c1976.
    498 p., [32] p. of plates : ill., maps ; 25 cm.

    "A Borzoi book"—T.p. verso.
    ISBN 0-394-40855-1

    I. Title.

Rule 21.25B
Report to a
considerable extent
in the words of the
reporter

RELATED WORKS

21.28   RELATED WORKS

145

Bristol, Roger P.
    Supplement to Charles Evans' American bibliography / by
Roger P. Bristol. — Charlottesville : Published for the
Bibliographical Society of America and the Bibliographical
Society of the University of Virginia [by the] University Press of
Virginia, 1970.
    xix, 636 p. ; 29 cm.
    A chronological list, 1646-1800, of items "not-in-Evans."
    Includes bibliographical references (p. [xiii]-xvi).
    ISBN 0-8139-0287-8
    I. Evans, Charles. American bibliography. II. Biblio-
graphical Society of America. III. Bibliographical Society
of the University of   Virginia. IV. Title.

Rule 21.28B1
Related works

21.30   SPECIFIC RULES
21.30J   Titles

146

Horne, Bernard S.
   The compleat angler, 1653-1967 : a new bibliography / by
Bernard S. Horne. — [Pittsburgh, Pa.] : Pittsburgh Bibliophiles :
Distributed by the University of Pittsburgh Press, 1970.
   xx, 350 p. : ill., facsims., col. port. ; 26 cm.

   "Edition of 500 copies"—Colophon.
   Includes index.
   Copy no. 155.
   ISBN 0-8229-4036-1

   I. Title. II. Title: The complete angler, 1653-1967.

Rule 21.30J1
Title added entries

147

McCluskey, John.
   Mr. America's last season blues : a novel / by John
McCluskey, Jr. — Baton Rouge : Louisiana State University
Press, 1983.
   243 p. ; 24 cm.

   ISBN 0-8071-1120-1

   I. Title. II. Title: Mister America's last season blues.

Rule 21.30J1
Title added entries

148

Ellis, L. Ethan.
   40 million schoolbooks can't be wrong : myths in American
history / by L. Ethan Ellis. — New York : Macmillan, c1975.
   x, 100 p. : ill. ; 24 cm.

   Includes bibliographical references (p. 95) and index.
   ISBN 0-02-733450-3

Rule 21.30J1
Title added entries

149

Hogarth, Paul.
   Paul Hogarth's walking tours of old Philadelphia : through
Independence Square, Society Hill, Southwark, and Washington
Square. — Barre, Mass. : Barre Pub. ; New York : Distributed by
Crown, c1976.
   xiii, 154 p. : ill. (some col.) ; 22 cm.

   Includes bibliographical references (p. 149) and index.
   ISBN 0-517-52385-X (pbk.). — ISBN 0-517-52384-1

   I. Title. II. Title: Walking tours of old Philadelphia.

Rule 21.30J1
Title added entries

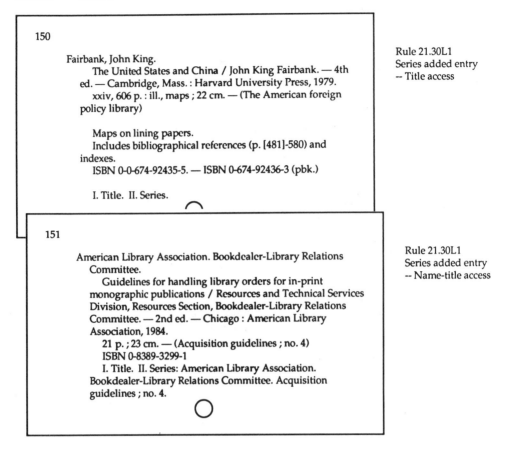

150

Fairbank, John King.
    The United States and China / John King Fairbank. — 4th
ed. — Cambridge, Mass. : Harvard University Press, 1979.
    xxiv, 606 p. : ill., maps ; 22 cm. — (The American foreign
policy library)

    Maps on lining papers.
    Includes bibliographical references (p. [481]-580) and
indexes.
    ISBN 0-0-674-92435-5. — ISBN 0-674-92436-3 (pbk.)

    I. Title. II. Series.

Rule 21.30L1
Series added entry
-- Title access

151

American Library Association. Bookdealer-Library Relations
Committee.
    Guidelines for handling library orders for in-print
monographic publications / Resources and Technical Services
Division, Resources Section, Bookdealer-Library Relations
Committee. — 2nd ed. — Chicago : American Library
Association, 1984.
    21 p. ; 23 cm. — (Acquisition guidelines ; no. 4)
    ISBN 0-8389-3299-1
    I. Title. II. Series: American Library Association.
Bookdealer-Library Relations Committee. Acquisition
guidelines ; no. 4.

Rule 21.30L1
Series added entry
-- Name-title access

CHOICE OF ACCESS POINTS EXERCISE

For each of the card examples in Chapter 1 (Rules for Description), indicate
on the card the main and added entries that should be made for each record. It
would be useful to consult the title pages and title page verso on the
transparencies when developing the answers. They will help in determining
whether a person or body is prominently named, etc. Answers to this exercise
appear in Appendix B.

CHAPTER THREE

Headings for Persons and References

Topic Outline

Rules

CHOICE OF NAME

22.1   General Rule

22.2   Choice among Different Names

22.3   Choice among Different Forms of the Same Name

ENTRY ELEMENT

22.5   Entry under Surname

22.6   Entry under Title of Nobility

22.8   Entry under Given Name, etc.

22.10   Entry under Initials, Letters, or Numerals

22.11   Entry under Phrase

ADDITIONS TO NAMES

General

22.12   Titles of Nobility and Terms of Honour

22.14   Spirits

22.15   Additions to Names entered under Surname

22.16   Additions to Names entered under Given Name, etc.

Additions to Distinguish Identical Names

22.17   Dates

22.18   Fuller Forms

22.19   Distinguishing Terms

Readings: *Anglo-American Cataloguing Rules.* 2nd ed., 1988 revision
Chapter 22, Headings for Persons, p. 379-418;
Chapter 26, References, p. 539-549.

NAME AUTHORITY AND REFERENCE CARD FORMAT

The style used on a name authority record and on a reference card for the public catalog is a local option. Similarly, the amount of information one records may also vary from library to library. Despite these differences, the function of these records remains constant.

Entries in a name authority file record the established form of a name used in the catalog, whether as a main or added entry. They also record references from unauthorized or unused forms of the name ("x" or "see" references) and references from other authorized names for the person or corporate body used in the public catalog ("xx" or "see also" references).

The reference cards in a public catalog provide instructions or links for catalog users to the correct name or names to consult in the catalog. These references reflect decisions recorded in the name authority file.

The following name authority file and public catalog reference cards indicate that the library has used the pseudonym S.S. Van Dine in the catalog and has not used the author's real name, Willard Huntington Wright, as an access point.

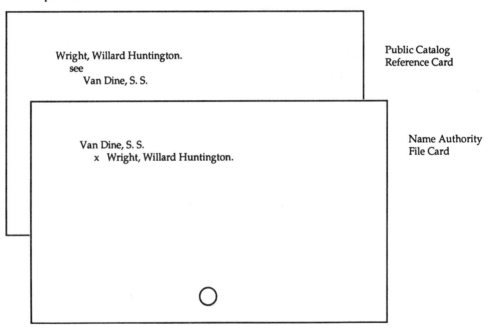

The name authority records and public catalog reference cards that follow are based upon a library's collection that includes works by this person under the names Robert Ludlum, Jonathan Ryder, and Michael Shepherd. Here, the "see also" references refer a catalog user from one name that has been used to the other two names that have also been used in the catalog.

Shepherd, Michael, 1927-
　　see also
　　　　Ludlum, Robert, 1927-
　　　　Ryder, Jonathan, 1927-

Ryder, Jonathan, 1927-
　　see also
　　　　Ludlum, Robert, 1927-
　　　　Shepherd, Michael, 1927-

Ludlum, Robert, 1927-
　　see also
　　　　Ryder, Jonathan, 1927-
　　　　Shepherd, Michael, 1927-

Public Catalog
Reference Cards

Shepherd, Michael, 1927-
　　xx Ludlum, Robert, 1927-
　　xx Ryder, Jonathan, 1927-

Ryder, Jonathan, 1927-
　　xx Ludlum, Robert, 1927-
　　xx Shepherd, Michael, 1927-

Ludlum, Robert, 1927-
　　xx Ryder, Jonathan, 1927-
　　xx Shepherd, Michael, 1927-

Name Authority
File Cards

61

There are times when more information in a "see also" reference allows a patron to make a more informed decision about which name to consult. One of these situations occurs when a heading for a corporate body varies over time. The examples that follow illustrate such a situation. The use of "see also" references in this case assumes that the library has documents under both names. If this were not the case, an explanatory "see" reference would have been made from the name not used.

LTV Corporation.
    In 1972 Ling-Temco-Vought changed its name to LTV
    Corporation. For entries in the catalog for this firm before that
    date see also
        Ling-Temco-Vought.

Ling-Temco-Vought.
    In 1972 Ling-Temco-Vought changed its name to LTV
    Corporation. For entries in the catalog for this firm after that
    date see also
        LTV Corporation.

L.T.V. Corporation.
    see
        LTV Corporation.

Public Catalog
Reference Cards

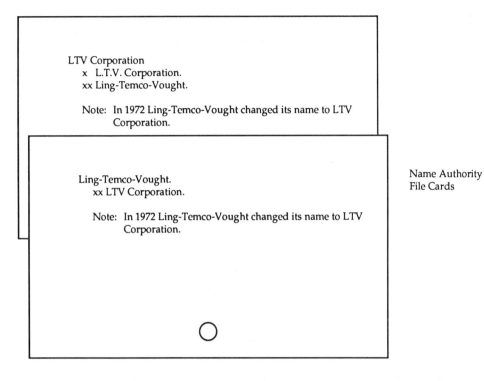

Name Authority
File Cards

N.B. In the examples that follow, an indication is given at the bottom of the card of name references that would be required for personal name access points for that work. This is not the proper location for this information, normally it would be recorded on a name authority record. The references provided are not exhaustive, but rather, are those references likely to have been used in a typical catalog. No references for corporate names are provided in this chapter. References for corporate names are addressed in Chapter 4 of this workbook.

CHOICE OF NAME

22.1   GENERAL RULE

152

    Carter, Jimmy, 1924-
        The blood of Abraham / Jimmy Carter. — Boston :
    Houghton Mifflin, 1985.
        xx, 257 p., [6] p. of plates : maps ; 24 cm.

        Includes index.
        ISBN 0-395-37722-6

        I. Title.

                            x   *Carter, James Earl, 1924-*

Rule 22.1A/22.1B
Name by which a
person is commonly
known

153

Neuharth, Allen H.
Confessions of an S.O.B. / Al Neuharth. — 1st ed. — New York : Doubleday, 1989.
372 p. ; 24 cm.

Includes index.
ISBN 0-385-24942-X

I. Title.

x   Neuharth, Al.

[Name commonly used in his works is Allen H. Neuharth]

Rule 22.1A/22.1B
Name by which a person is commonly known

22.1D   Diacritical marks and hyphens

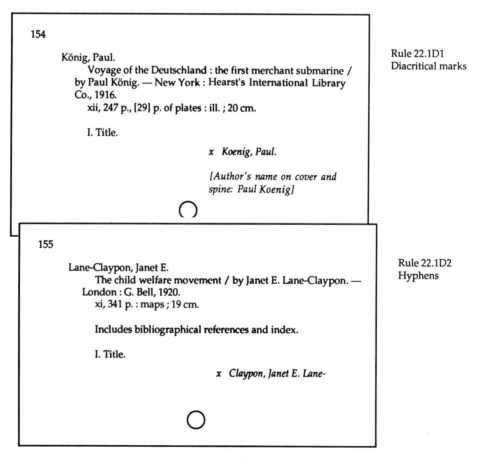

154

König, Paul.
Voyage of the Deutschland : the first merchant submarine / by Paul König. — New York : Hearst's International Library Co., 1916.
xii, 247 p., [29] p. of plates : ill. ; 20 cm.

I. Title.

x   Koenig, Paul.

[Author's name on cover and spine: Paul Koenig]

Rule 22.1D1
Diacritical marks

155

Lane-Claypon, Janet E.
The child welfare movement / by Janet E. Lane-Claypon. — London : G. Bell, 1920.
xi, 341 p. : maps ; 19 cm.

Includes bibliographical references and index.

I. Title.

x   Claypon, Janet E. Lane-

Rule 22.1D2
Hyphens

22.2   CHOICE AMONG DIFFERENT NAMES
22.2B   Pseudonyms

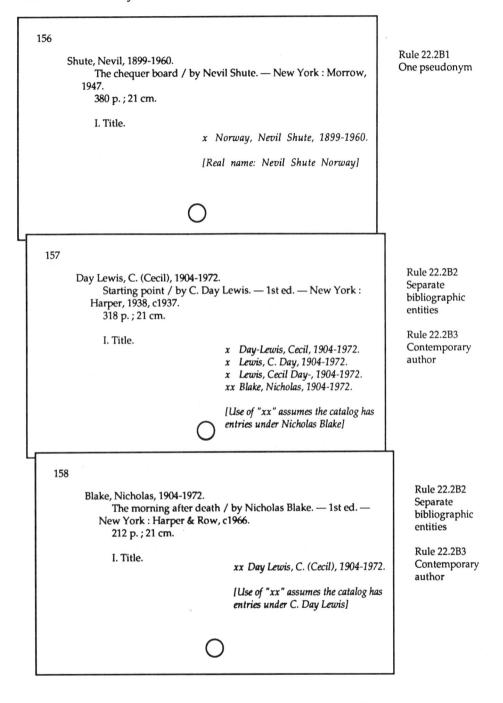

156

Shute, Nevil, 1899-1960.
    The chequer board / by Nevil Shute. — New York : Morrow,
1947.
    380 p. ; 21 cm.

    I. Title.

                                x   Norway, Nevil Shute, 1899-1960.

                            [Real name: Nevil Shute Norway]

Rule 22.2B1
One pseudonym

157

Day Lewis, C. (Cecil), 1904-1972.
    Starting point / by C. Day Lewis. — 1st ed. — New York :
Harper, 1938, c1937.
    318 p. ; 21 cm.

    I. Title.

                        x   Day-Lewis, Cecil, 1904-1972.
                        x   Lewis, C. Day, 1904-1972.
                        x   Lewis, Cecil Day-, 1904-1972.
                        xx Blake, Nicholas, 1904-1972.

                        [Use of "xx" assumes the catalog has
                        entries under Nicholas Blake]

Rule 22.2B2
Separate
bibliographic
entities

Rule 22.2B3
Contemporary
author

158

Blake, Nicholas, 1904-1972.
    The morning after death / by Nicholas Blake. — 1st ed. —
New York : Harper & Row, c1966.
    212 p. ; 21 cm.

    I. Title.

                        xx Day Lewis, C. (Cecil), 1904-1972.

                        [Use of "xx" assumes the catalog has
                        entries under C. Day Lewis]

Rule 22.2B2
Separate
bibliographic
entities

Rule 22.2B3
Contemporary
author

22.3 CHOICE AMONG DIFFERENT FORMS OF THE SAME NAME
22.3A Fullness

159

Shaw, Bernard, 1856-1950.
    Everybody's political what's what? / by Bernard Shaw. —
London : Constable, 1944.
    viii, 380 p., [1] leaf of plates : port. ; 21 cm.

    Includes index.

    I. Title.

                 *x Shaw, G. B. (George Bernard),
                    1856-1950.*
                 x Shaw, George Bernard, 1856-1950.

            ○   *[Full name: George Bernard Shaw]*

Rule 22.3A1
Variation in fullness
of name -- Use of
the form commonly
found

ENTRY ELEMENT

22.5 ENTRY UNDER SURNAME
22.5C Compound surnames

160

Lloyd George, David, 1863-1945.
    Coal and power : the report of an enquiry presided over by
the Right Hon. D. Lloyd George, O.M., M.P. — London :
Hodder and Stoughton, [1924]
    xiv, 139 p., [16] p. of plates : ill. ; 18 cm.

    I. Title.

                 x George, David Lloyd, 1863-1945.
                 *x Lloyd George of Dwyfor, David
                    Lloyd George, Earl, 1863-1945.*

Rule 22.5C2
Compound
surname —
Preferred form
known

161

Panter-Downes, Mollie, 1906-
    London war notes, 1939-1945 / Mollie Panter-Downes ;
edited by William Shawn. — New York : Farrar, Strauss and
Giroux, c1971.
    378 p., [1] leaf of plates : ill. ; 25 cm.

    "All of the material in this book appeared originally in the
New Yorker"—T.p. verso.
    ISBN 0-374-1-9022-4

    I. Shawn, William. II. Title.

         ○   *x Downes, Mollie Panter-, 1906-*

Rule 22.5C3
Compound
(hyphenated)
surname

Compound surnames, cont'd.

162

Rinehart, Mary Roberts, 1876-1958.
    The swimming pool / Mary Roberts Rinehart. — New York : Rinehart, c1952.
    312 p. ; 22 cm.

    I. Title.

Rule 22.5C5
Compound surname -- Married woman whose surname consists of her surname before marriage and her husband's surname

163

Post, Melville Davisson, 1871-1930.
    The complete Uncle Abner / Melville Davisson Post ; with introduction and annotated bibliography by Allen J. Hubin ; illustrations by Darrel Millsap. — Del Mar, CA : Publication of University Extension, University of California, San Diego in cooperation with Publisher's Inc., c1977.
    xvi, 423 p. : ill. ; 21 cm. — (The Mystery library ; 4)

    Includes bibliographical references (p. 399-410).
    ISBN 0-89163-028-7

    I. Title. II. Series.

○ *[No reference is required — the name is not treated as a compound surname in reference sources]*

Rule 22.5C6
Nature of surname uncertain

164

Schlesinger, Arthur M. (Arthur Meier), 1917-
    A thousand days : John F. Kennedy in the White House / Arthur M. Schlesinger, Jr. — Boston : Houghton Mifflin, 1965.
    xiv, 1087 p. ; 22 cm.

    Includes bibliographical references and index.

    I. Title.

Rule 22.5C8
Omission of a word indicating relationship following the surname

22.5D   Surnames with separately written prefixes

165

De La Roche, Mazo, 1885-1961.
    The building of Jalna / by Mazo De La Roche. — Whiteoak ed. — Boston : Little, Brown, 1944.
    366 p. ; 19 cm.

    "An Atlantic Monthly Press book."

    I. Title.

x La Roche, Mazo de, 1885-1961.
x Roche, Mazo de la, 1885-1961.

○

Rule 22.5D1
Articles and prepositions -- English

Compound surnames, cont'd.

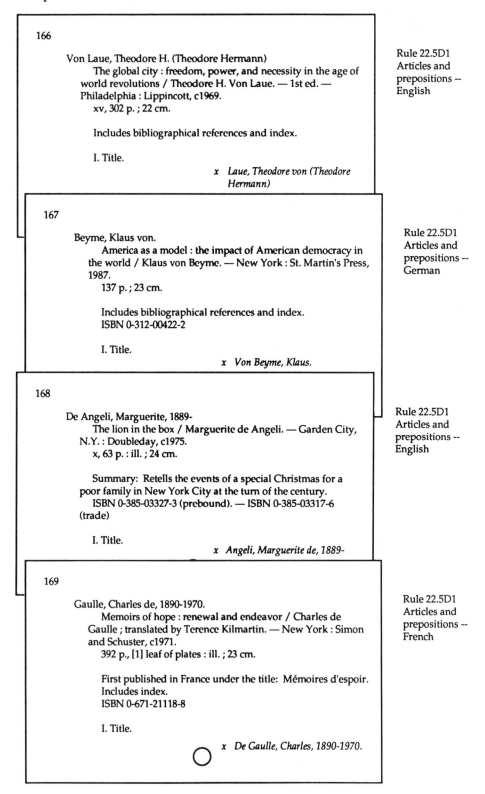

166

Von Laue, Theodore H. (Theodore Hermann)
    The global city : freedom, power, and necessity in the age of world revolutions / Theodore H. Von Laue. — 1st ed. — Philadelphia : Lippincott, c1969.
    xv, 302 p. ; 22 cm.

    Includes bibliographical references and index.

    I. Title.

                        x Laue, Theodore von (Theodore Hermann)

Rule 22.5D1
Articles and prepositions --
English

167

Beyme, Klaus von.
    America as a model : the impact of American democracy in the world / Klaus von Beyme. — New York : St. Martin's Press, 1987.
    137 p. ; 23 cm.

    Includes bibliographical references and index.
    ISBN 0-312-00422-2

    I. Title.

                    x Von Beyme, Klaus.

Rule 22.5D1
Articles and prepositions --
German

168

De Angeli, Marguerite, 1889-
    The lion in the box / Marguerite de Angeli. — Garden City, N.Y. : Doubleday, c1975.
    x, 63 p. : ill. ; 24 cm.

    Summary: Retells the events of a special Christmas for a poor family in New York City at the turn of the century.
    ISBN 0-385-03327-3 (prebound). — ISBN 0-385-03317-6 (trade)

    I. Title.

                  x Angeli, Marguerite de, 1889-

Rule 22.5D1
Articles and prepositions --
English

169

Gaulle, Charles de, 1890-1970.
    Memoirs of hope : renewal and endeavor / Charles de Gaulle ; translated by Terence Kilmartin. — New York : Simon and Schuster, c1971.
    392 p., [1] leaf of plates : ill. ; 23 cm.

    First published in France under the title: Mémoires d'espoir.
    Includes index.
    ISBN 0-671-21118-8

    I. Title.

                  x De Gaulle, Charles, 1890-1970.

Rule 22.5D1
Articles and prepositions --
French

Compound surnames, cont'd.

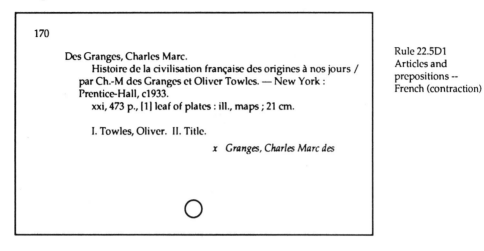

170

Des Granges, Charles Marc.
    Histoire de la civilisation française des origines à nos jours /
par Ch.-M des Granges et Oliver Towles. — New York :
Prentice-Hall, c1933.
    xxi, 473 p., [1] leaf of plates : ill., maps ; 21 cm.

I. Towles, Oliver. II. Title.

    x Granges, Charles Marc des

Rule 22.5D1
Articles and
prepositions --
French (contraction)

22.6   ENTRY UNDER TITLE OF NOBILITY
22.6A   General rule

171

Lytton, Edward Bulwar Lytton, Baron, 1803-1873.
    The coming race / by Lord Lytton ; footnotes and additional
material by Emerson M. Clymer. — Knebworth ed. —
Quakerstown, Pa. : Philosophical Pub. Co., 1973.
    vi, 186, 27 p. ; 23 cm.

Edited and revised by Manuela Auerbach.

I. Clymer, Emerson M. II. Auerbach, Manuela. III. Title.

    x Bulwar, Edward Lytton,
      1803-1873.
    x Bulwar-Lytton, Edward George,
      1803-1873.

Rule 22.6A1
Title of nobility

22.6B   Special rules

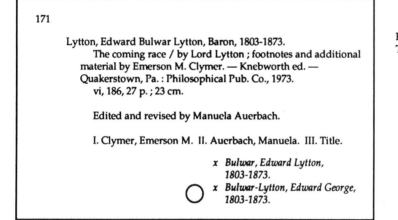

172

Webb, Sidney, 1859-1947.
    The decay of capitalist civilization / by Sidney and Beatrice
Webb. — New York : Harcourt, Brace, c1923.
    xvii, 242 p. ; 20 cm.

Includes bibliographical references and index.

I. Webb, Beatrice, 1858-1943. II. Title.

x Passfield, Sidney James Webb,   *x Potter, Beatrice, 1858-1943.*
  Baron, 1859-1947.   *x Passfield, Beatrice Potter Webb,*
                                 Baroness, 1858-1943.

[Renounced the title: Baron Passfield]   *[Renounced the title: Baroness Passfield]*

Rule 22.6B3
Disclaimer of a title

Rule 22.2C
Change of name --
Latest name

22.8 ENTRY UNDER GIVEN NAME, ETC.
22.8A General rule

173

Leonardo da Vinci, 1452-1519.
    Leonardo da Vinci's note-books / arranged and rendered
into English with introductions by Edward McCurdy. — New
York : Empire State Book Co., 1923.
    xiv, 289 p., [14] leaves of plates : ill. ; 22 cm.

    I. McCurdy, Edward, b. 1871. II. Title.

                    x Da Vinci, Leonardo, 1452-1519.
                    x Vinci, Leonardo da, 1452-1519.

Rule 22.8A1
Name does not
include a surname

22.10 ENTRY UNDER INITIALS, LETTERS, OR NUMERALS

174

M.
    The sensuous man : the first how-to book for the man who
wants to be a great lover / by M. — New York, N.Y. : Lyle
Stuart, c1971.
    253 p. ; 21 cm.

    I. Title.

Rule 22.10A
Name consists of an
initial

22.11 ENTRY UNDER PHRASE

175

Captain X, 1922-
    Unfriendly skies : revelations of a deregulated airline pilot /
Captain X and Reynolds Dodson. — New York : Berkley Books,
1989.
    xiv, 236 p. ; 18 cm.

    ISBN 0-425-12182-8

    I. Dodson, Reynolds. II. Title.

Rule 22.11A
Name is a phrase or
appellation

176

Author of the Cloud of unknowing.
    The pursuit of wisdom and other works / by the author of
the Cloud of unknowing ; translated, edited, and annotated by
James A. Walsh ; preface by George A. Maloney. — New York :
Paulist Press, c1988.
    ix, 325 p. ; 23 cm. — (Classics of western spirituality)

    Writings of a 14th century mystic.
    Includes bibliographical references (p. 314-319) and index.
    ISBN 0-8091-2972-8 (pbk.). — ISBN 0-8091-0404-0

    I. Walsh, James, 1920-   II. Title. III. Series.
                    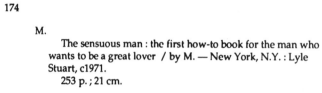 x Cloud of unknowing, Author of

Rule 22.11D
Phrase naming
another work

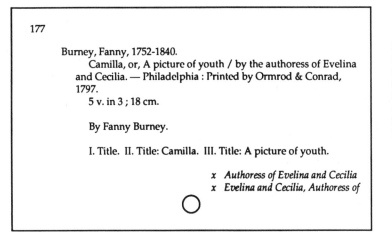

177

Burney, Fanny, 1752-1840.
    Camilla, or, A picture of youth / by the authoress of Evelina
and Cecilia. — Philadelphia : Printed by Ormrod & Conrad,
1797.
        5 v. in 3 ; 18 cm.

    By Fanny Burney.

    I. Title. II. Title: Camilla. III. Title: A picture of youth.

                                    x   *Authoress of Evelina and Cecilia*
                                    x   *Evelina and Cecilia, Authoress of*

Rule 22.11D
Person commonly
identified by her
real name was
identified on a chief
source of
information by the
titles of other works

ADDITIONS TO NAMES

General

22.12   TITLES OF NOBILITY AND TERMS OF HONOUR
22.12B   British terms of honour

178

Montagu, Lady Mary Wortley, 1689-1762.
    Essays and poems ; and, Simplicity : a comedy / Lady Mary
Wortley Montagu ; edited by Robert Halsband and Isobel
Grundy. — Oxford : Clarendon Press, 1977.
        viii, 412 p., [7] p. of plates : ill. ; 23 cm.

    Includes bibliographical references and indexes.
    ISBN 0-19-812444-9

    I. Halsband, Robert, 1914-   II. Grundy, Isobel. III. Title.
    IV. Title: Essays and poems. V. Title: Simplicity.

Rule 22.12B1
British term of
honor

*[The Library of
Congress would
change the location of
the title "Lady" to:
Montagu, Mary
Wortley, Lady,
1689-1762.]*

179

Fraser, Antonia, 1932-
    Mary, Queen of Scots / by Antonia Fraser. — 1st American
ed. — New York : Delacorte Press, c1969.
        xv, 613 p., [24] p. of plates : ill., geneal. tables ; 25 cm.

    Includes bibliographical references (p. [585]-594) and index.

    I. Title.
                                    [Born: Lady Antonia Pakenham Fraser]

Rule 22.12B1
British term of
honor does not
commonly appear
with the name in
the person's works

22.14   SPIRITS

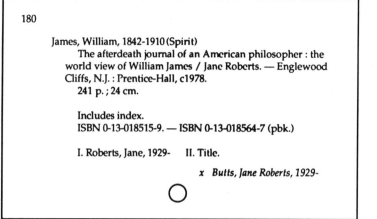

180

James, William, 1842-1910 (Spirit)
    The afterdeath journal of an American philosopher : the
world view of William James / Jane Roberts. — Englewood
Cliffs, N.J. : Prentice-Hall, c1978.
    241 p. ; 24 cm.

    Includes index.
    ISBN 0-13-018515-9. — ISBN 0-13-018564-7 (pbk.)

    I. Roberts, Jane, 1929-   II. Title.

                    x Butts, Jane Roberts, 1929-

Rule 22.14A
Spirit
communication

[See also Rule 21.26.]

22.15   ADDITIONS TO NAMES ENTERED UNDER SURNAME

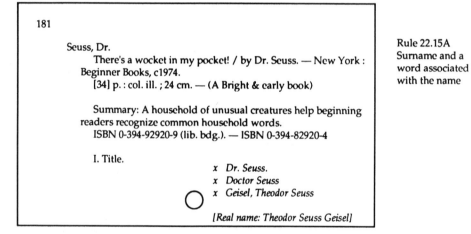

181

Seuss, Dr.
    There's a wocket in my pocket! / by Dr. Seuss. — New York :
Beginner Books, c1974.
    [34] p. : col. ill. ; 24 cm. — (A Bright & early book)

    Summary: A household of unusual creatures help beginning
readers recognize common household words.
    ISBN 0-394-92920-9 (lib. bdg.). — ISBN 0-394-82920-4

    I. Title.

                    x Dr. Seuss.
                    x Doctor Seuss
                    x Geisel, Theodor Seuss

                    [Real name: Theodor Seuss Geisel]

Rule 22.15A
Surname and a
word associated
with the name

22.15B   Terms of address of married women

182

Chesterton, Mrs. Cecil, 1888-
    Young China and new Japan / by Mrs. Cecil Chesterton. —
Philadelphia : Lippincott, [1933?]
    310 p., [31] p. of plates : ill., map ; 22 cm.

    I. Title.

                    *x Chesterton, Ada Elizabeth Jones,
                        1888-*

Rule 22.15B1
Term of address of a
married woman

*[The Library of
Congress would
change the location of
the term "Mrs." to:
Chesterton, Cecil,
Mrs., 1888-   ]*

72

22.16   ADDITIONS TO NAMES ENTERED UNDER GIVEN NAME, ETC.
22.16A   Royalty

183

George III. King of Great Britain, 1738-1820.
    The correspondence of King George the Third with Lord
North, 1768 to 1783 / edited with an introduction and notes by
W. Bodham Donne. — New York : Da Capo Press, 1971.
    2 v. (lcii, 307, 452) ; 24 cm. — (The Era of the American
Revolution)
    "A Da Capo Press reprint edition"—T.p. verso.
    Reprint. Originally published: London : J. Murray, 1867.
    Running title: George the Third's Letters to Lord North.
    Includes bibliographical references.
    ISBN 0-306-70155-3
    I. North, Frederick, 1732-1792. II. Donne, William Bodham,
1807-1882. III. Title.   ◯   IV. Title: George the Third's
Letters to Lord North.   V. Series.
                    x Donne, W. Bodham. 1807-1882.

Rule 22.16A1
Person with royal
status within a state

Additions to Distinguish Identical Names

22.17   DATES

Hill, James Edward

Hill, James Edward, 1931-

Hill, James Edward, 1942-

Forbes, James, 1629?-1712

Forbes, James, d. 1810.

Forbes, James, ca. 1750-1811

Smith, William, fl. 1755

Smith, William, fl. 1762-1778

Smith, William, fl. ca. 1800

Johnson, Cecil, 1900-

Johnson, Cecil, 1900 Jan. 19-

Johnson, Cecil, 1900 Mar. 2-

```
┌─────────────────────────────────────────────────────────────┐
│ 184                                                          │
│                                                              │
│     Mack, William P., 1915-                                  │
│          South to Java : a novel / by William P. Mack and    │
│     William P. Mack, Jr. — Baltimore, Md. : Nautical &       │
│     Aviation Pub. Co. of America, c1987.                     │
│          460 p. ; 24 cm.                                     │
│                                                              │
│          ISBN 0-933852-70-3                                  │
│                                                              │
│          I. Mack, William P., 1943-    II. Title.            │
│                                                              │
└─────────────────────────────────────────────────────────────┘
```

Rule 22.17A
Addition of dates

22.18   FULLER FORMS

```
┌─────────────────────────────────────────────────────────────┐
│ 185                                                          │
│                                                              │
│     Lewis, C. S. (Clive Staples), 1898-1963.                 │
│          That hideous strength : a modern fairy-tale for     │
│     grown-ups / by C.S. Lewis. — New York : Macmillan, 1946. │
│          viii, 459 p. ; 21 cm.                               │
│                                                              │
│          I. Title.                                           │
│                          x  Lewis, Clive Staples, 1898-1963. │
│     ┌─────────────────────────────────────────────────────┐ │
│     │ 186                                                 │ │
│     │                                                     │ │
│     │   Buckley, William F. (William Frank), 1925-        │ │
│     │        Marco Polo, if you can / William F. Buckley, │ │
│     │   Jr. — 1st ed. — Garden City, N.Y. : Doubleday,    │ │
│     │   1982.                                             │ │
│     │        233 p. ; 21 cm.                              │ │
│     │                                                     │ │
│     │        ISBN 0-385-15232-9                           │ │
│     │                                                     │ │
│     │        I. Title.                                    │ │
│     │                                                     │ │
│     │                     ◯                               │ │
│     └─────────────────────────────────────────────────────┘ │
└─────────────────────────────────────────────────────────────┘
```

Rule 22.18A
Addition of a fuller
form of a person's
name

Rule 22.18A
Addition of a fuller
form of a person's
name

22.19   DISTINGUISHING TERMS
22.19B   Names in which the entry element is a surname

Smith, William, M.A.

Smith, William, D.D.

Smith, William, Gent.

Smith, William, managing director

Smith, William, soldier

Smith, William, Vice-Admiral

CHAPTER FOUR

Headings for Corporate Bodies and References

Topic Outline

Rules

24.1   General Rule

24.2   Variant Names. General Rules

24.3   Variant Names. Special Rules

ADDITIONS, OMISSIONS, AND MODIFICATIONS

24.4   Additions

24.5   Omissions

24.7   Conferences, Congresses, Meetings, etc.

24.10   Local Churches, etc.

SUBORDINATE AND RELATED BODIES

24.12   General Rule

24.13   Subordinate and Related Bodies Entered Subordinately

24.14   Direct or Indirect Subheading

Special Rules

24.15   Joint Committees, Commissions, etc.

GOVERNMENT BODIES AND OFFICIALS

24.17   General Rule

24.18   Government Agencies Entered Subordinately

24.19   Direct or Indirect Subheading

Special Rules

24.20   Government Officials

24.21   Legislative Bodies

24.24   Armed Forces

Readings: *Anglo-American Cataloguing Rules.* 2nd ed., 1988 revision.
Chapter 24, Corporate Bodies, p. 439-479;
Chapter 26, References, p. 549-557.

N.B. In the examples that follow, an indication is given at the bottom of the card of name references that would be required for corporate access points for that work. The references provided are not exhaustive, but rather, are those references likely to have been used in a typical catalog. In order to conserve space, only references for corporate bodies are provided.

24.1   GENERAL RULE

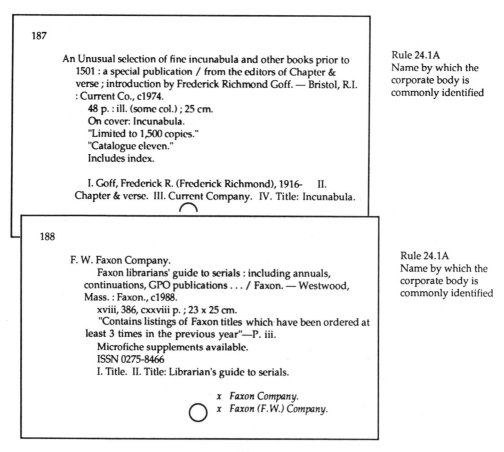

187

> An Unusual selection of fine incunabula and other books prior to 1501 : a special publication / from the editors of Chapter & verse ; introduction by Frederick Richmond Goff. — Bristol, R.I. : Current Co., c1974.
> 48 p. : ill. (some col.) ; 25 cm.
> On cover: Incunabula.
> "Limited to 1,500 copies."
> "Catalogue eleven."
> Includes index.
>
> I. Goff, Frederick R. (Frederick Richmond), 1916-   II. Chapter & verse. III. Current Company. IV. Title: Incunabula.

Rule 24.1A
Name by which the corporate body is commonly identified

188

> F. W. Faxon Company.
> Faxon librarians' guide to serials : including annuals, continuations, GPO publications . . . / Faxon. — Westwood, Mass. : Faxon., c1988.
> xviii, 386, cxxviii p. ; 23 x 25 cm.
> "Contains listings of Faxon titles which have been ordered at least 3 times in the previous year"—P. iii.
> Microfiche supplements available.
> ISSN 0275-8466
> I. Title. II. Title: Librarian's guide to serials.
>
>   x   *Faxon Company.*
>   x   *Faxon (F.W.) Company.*

Rule 24.1A
Name by which the corporate body is commonly identified

24.1C   Changes of name

Rule 24.1C1
Change of corporate
body name

*[The United States
Steel Corporation was
renamed U.S.X.
Corporation in 1986.]*

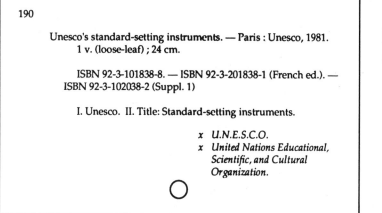

189

United States Steel Corporation.
   United States Steel Corporation T.N.E.C. papers : comprising
the pamphlets and charts submitted by United States Steel
Corporation to the Temporary National Economic Committee.
— [New York?] : The Corp., 1940.
   3 v. : ill. (some col.), maps ; 29 cm.
      Contents: v. 1. Economic and related studies — v. 2. Chart
studies — v. 3. The basing point method.
      I. United States. Temporary National Economic Committee.
II. Title. III. Title: T.N.E.C. papers. IV. Title: Temporary
National Economic Committee papers.

x U.S.X. Corporation.
x U.S. Steel (Firm)
x US Steel (Firm)

*x Temporary National Economic
   Committee.*
x T.N.E.C.
x TNEC.

24.2   VARIANT NAMES. GENERAL RULES

Rule 24.2D
Variant names--
Brief form

190

Unesco's standard-setting instruments. — Paris : Unesco, 1981.
   1 v. (loose-leaf) ; 24 cm.

   ISBN 92-3-101838-8. — ISBN 92-3-201838-1 (French ed.). —
ISBN 92-3-102038-2 (Suppl. 1)

   I. Unesco. II. Title: Standard-setting instruments.

x U.N.E.S.C.O.
*x United Nations Educational,
   Scientific, and Cultural
   Organization.*

24.3   VARIANT NAMES. SPECIAL RULES
24.3B   Language. International bodies

Rule 24.3B1
International body

*[The name appears in
English in some of the
organization's
publications.]*

191

Principles of the Universal Decimal Classification (UDC) and rules
for its revision and publication = Principes de la Classification
Décimale Universelle (CDU) et règles pour sa révision et sa
publication. — 5th ed. — The Hague : Federation Internationale
de Documentation, 1981.
   35 p. ; 30 cm. — (FID publication ; 598)
   English, French, and German.
   "Supersedes the 'Universal Decimal Classification (UDC)
revision and publication procedure', FID 429"—Pref.
   ISBN 92-66-00598-3
      I. International Federation for Documentation. II. Title:
Principes de la Classification Décimale Universelle (CDU) et
règles pour sa révision et sa publication.

x F.I.D.
x FID.

*x Fédération internationale de
   documentation*

24.4 ADDITIONS

24.4B Names not conveying the idea of a corporate body

192

    Keith Hogg (Firm)
        Bibliographica : a catalogue of books offered for sale by
    Keith Hogg. — Tenterden, Kent, England : K. Hogg, [197-]
    43 p. ; 21 cm. — (Catalogue ; no. 100)

    Cover title.

    I. Title.

                 x *Hogg, Keith (Firm)*

Rule 24.4B1
Addition of a
designation to
indicate the body is
a corporate body

193

    Monty Python (Comedy troupe)
        Monty Python's the meaning of life / written and performed
    by Graham Chapman . . . [et al.]. — [London] : Methuen, [1983]
    [128] p. : col. ill. ; 28 cm. — (A Methuen paperback)

    From the motion picture of the same title.
    ISBN 0-413-53380-8

    I. Chapman, Graham, 1941?-   II. The meaning of life
    (Motion picture) III. Title. IV. Title: The meaning of life.

Rule 24.4B1
Addition of a
designation to
indicate the body is
a corporate body

24.4C Two or more bodies with the same or similar names

194

    National Gallery of Art (U.S.)
        Early Netherlandish painting / John Oliver Hand, Martha
    Wolff. — Washington : National Gallery of Art, c1986.
        xv, 271 p. : ill. (some col.) ; 29 cm. — (The Collections of the
    National Gallery of Art : systematic catalogue)
        Includes bibliographical references and index.
        ISBN 0-894-68093-5 (pbk.). — ISBN 0-521-34016-0
        I. Hand, John Oliver, 1941-   II. Wolff, Martha. III. Title. IV.
    Series: National Gallery of Art (U.S.). Collections of the
    National Gallery of Art.

x *Smithsonian Institution. National*   x *Collections of the National Gallery*
   Gallery of Art.   *of Art.*
x *United States. National Gallery of*
   Art.

Rule 24.4C2
Addition of a
country

Two or more bodies with the same or similar names, cont'd.

195

Becker, Carl M.
    The village : a history of Germantown, Ohio, 1804-1976 /
Carl M. Becker . — Germantown, Ohio : Historical Society of
Germantown ; [Athens] : Ohio University Press [distributor],
c1981.
    xvi, 214 p. : ill. ; 24 cm.

    Includes bibliographical references (p. [203]-207) and index.
    ISBN 0-8214-0550-0

    I. Historical Society of Germantown (Ohio) II. Title.

    ◯ x *Germantown Historical Society
             (Ohio)*

Rule 24.4C2
Addition of a state

196

Sets, series & ensembles in African art / George Nelson Preston ;
    introduction, Susan Vogel ; catalogue, Polly Nooter. — New
    York : Center for African Art, c1985.
    96 p. : ill. (some col.) ; 31 cm.

    "Published in conjunction with the exhibition, Sets, series &
    ensembles organized by the Center for African Art, July 17,
    1985-October 27, 1985"—T.p. verso.
    Includes bibliographical references (p. 94-95) and index.
    ISBN 0-8109-1637-1

    I. Preston, George Nelson. II. Center for African Art (New
York, N.Y.) III. Title: ◯ Sets, series and ensembles in
African art.

Rule 24.4C3
Addition of a local
place name

Rule 24.4C4
Body is located
outside the British
Isles

197

Introductions to Shakespeare : being the introductions to the
    individual plays in the Folio Society edition, 1950-76 / with a
    foreword by Charles Ede. — London : The Society, 1977.
    245 p., [12] leaves of plates : col. ill. ; 23 cm.

    I. Folio Society (London, England)

Rule 24.4C3
Addition of a local
place name

Rule 24.4C5
Body located in the
British Isles

    ◯

24.5   OMISSIONS
24.5A   Initial articles

198

Mangum, Garth L.
    Coming of age in the ghetto : a dilemma of youth
unemployment : a report to the Ford Foundation / Garth
Mangum and Stephen F. Seninger. — Baltimore : Johns Hopkins
University Press, c1978.
    vii, 114 p. : ill. ; 21 cm. — (Policy studies in employment and
welfare ; no. 33)

    Includes bibliographical references and index.
    ISBN 0-8018-2125-8

    I. Seninger, Stephen F. II. Ford Foundation. III. Title. IV.
Series.   ◯

Rule 24.5A1
Omission of an
initial article

24.5C   Terms indicating incorporation and certain other terms

199

Pantone two color selector. — Moonachie, N.J. : Pantone, c1985.
    1 v. (various pagings) : col. ill. ; 23 cm.

    I. Pantone, Inc.

Rule 24.5C1
Term indicating
incorporation

◯

24.7   CONFERENCES, CONGRESSES, MEETINGS, ETC.

200

Conference on Satellite Meteorology and Oceanography (3rd : 1988
    : Anaheim, Calif.)
    Third conference on satellite meteorology and
oceanography, Feb. 1-5, 1988, Anaheim, Calif. / sponsored by
American Meteorological Society. — Boston, Mass. : The
Society, c1987.
    xv, 432, [64] p. : ill., maps ; 28 cm.
    "Preprints"—P. 1 of cover.
    Includes bibliographical references and index.
    "D (VT) 500 1/88"—P. 4 of cover.
    I. American Meteorological Society. II. Title. III. Title: 3rd
conference on satellite meteorology and oceanography.
            ◯   x A.M.S.
                x AMS

Rule 24.7A1
Omission of a
conference number
from its name

Rule 24.7B2
Addition of number

Rule 24.7B3
Addition of date

Rule 24.7B4
Addition of location

24.10   LOCAL CHURCHES, ETC.

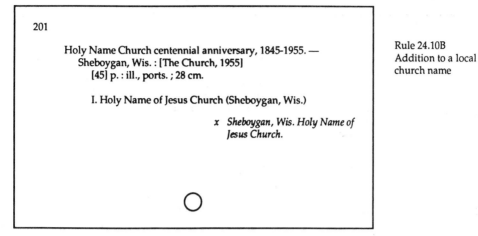

201

Holy Name Church centennial anniversary, 1845-1955. —
Sheboygan, Wis. : [The Church, 1955]
[45] p. : ill., ports. ; 28 cm.

I. Holy Name of Jesus Church (Sheboygan, Wis.)

x   *Sheboygan, Wis. Holy Name of*
Jesus Church.

Rule 24.10B
Addition to a local
church name

SUBORDINATE AND RELATED BODIES

24.12   GENERAL RULE

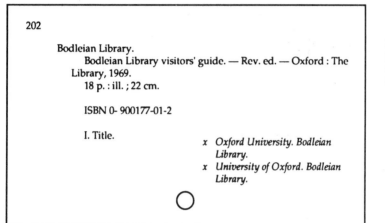

202

Bodleian Library.
Bodleian Library visitors' guide. — Rev. ed. — Oxford : The
Library, 1969.
18 p. : ill. ; 22 cm.

ISBN 0- 900177-01-2

I. Title.

x   *Oxford University. Bodleian*
Library.
x   *University of Oxford. Bodleian*
Library.

Rule 24.12A
Non-government
subordinate body
under its own name

24.13   SUBORDINATE AND RELATED BODIES ENTERED
SUBORDINATELY

203

B. H. Blackwell Ltd. Antiquarian Department.
A centenary catalogue of antiquarian and rare modern
books. — Oxford, England : Blackwell's Antiquarian Dept.,
[1979?]
vii, 135 p., [1] leaf of plates : ill., facsims. ; 25 cm. —
(Blackwell's catalogue ; A-1)

On cover: Blackwell's centenary antiquarian catalogue.
Includes bibliographical references.

I. Title. II. Title: Blackwell's centenary antiquarian catalogue.

x   *Blackwell (B. H.) Ltd.*

Rule 24.13A
Type 1
Term in the name
implies the body is
part of another

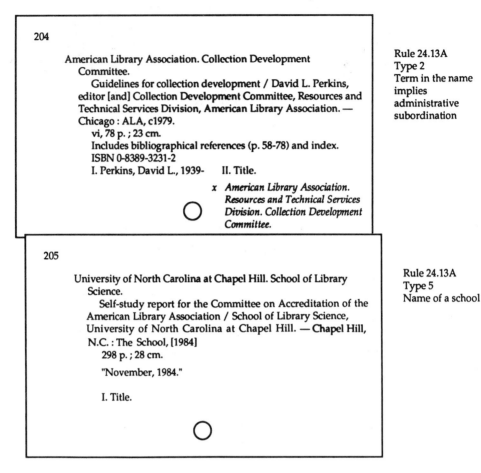

204

American Library Association. Collection Development
   Committee.
     Guidelines for collection development / David L. Perkins,
editor [and] Collection Development Committee, Resources and
Technical Services Division, American Library Association. —
Chicago : ALA, c1979.
     vi, 78 p. ; 23 cm.
     Includes bibliographical references (p. 58-78) and index.
     ISBN 0-8389-3231-2
     I. Perkins, David L., 1939-   II. Title.

     x American Library Association.
       Resources and Technical Services
       Division. Collection Development
       Committee.

Rule 24.13A
Type 2
Term in the name
implies
administrative
subordination

205

University of North Carolina at Chapel Hill. School of Library
   Science.
     Self-study report for the Committee on Accreditation of the
American Library Association / School of Library Science,
University of North Carolina at Chapel Hill. — Chapel Hill,
N.C. : The School, [1984]
     298 p. ; 28 cm.

     "November, 1984."

     I. Title.

Rule 24.13A
Type 5
Name of a school

24.14   DIRECT OR INDIRECT SUBHEADING

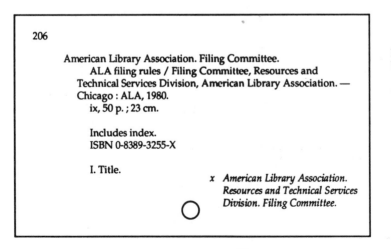

206

American Library Association. Filing Committee.
     ALA filing rules / Filing Committee, Resources and
Technical Services Division, American Library Association. —
Chicago : ALA, 1980.
     ix, 50 p. ; 23 cm.

     Includes index.
     ISBN 0-8389-3255-X

     I. Title.

     x American Library Association.
       Resources and Technical Services
       Division. Filing Committee.

Rule 24.14A
Direct subheading

24.15   JOINT COMMITTEES, COMMISSIONS, ETC.

207

Joint Committee of the American Society for Metals and the Special
Libraries Association.
  ASM/SLA metallurgical literature classification / prepared
by a Joint Committee of the American Society for Metals and
the Special Libraries Association. — Cleveland : A.S.M., c1950.
  49 p. : ill. ; 28 cm. + 1 punch card
  Punch card inserted in text.
  I. American Society for Metals. II. Special Libraries
Association. III. Title. IV. Title: Metallurgical literature
classification.

x   *American Society of Metals*   x   *S.L.A.*
x   *A.S.M.*   x   *SLA.*
x   *ASM.*

Rule 24.15A
Joint committee

GOVERNMENT BODIES AND OFFICIALS

24.17   GENERAL RULE

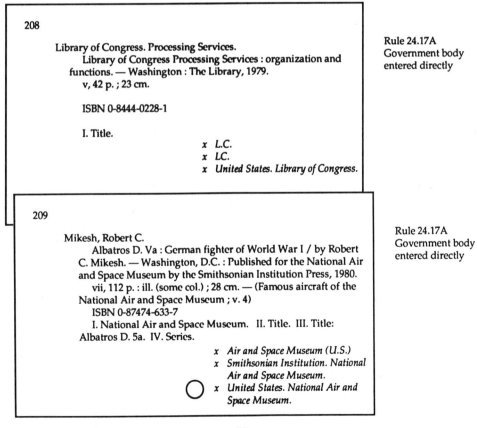

208

Library of Congress. Processing Services.
  Library of Congress Processing Services : organization and
functions. — Washington : The Library, 1979.
  v, 42 p. ; 23 cm.

  ISBN 0-8444-0228-1

  I. Title.

          x   *L.C.*
          x   *LC.*
          x   *United States. Library of Congress.*

Rule 24.17A
Government body
entered directly

209

Mikesh, Robert C.
  Albatros D. Va : German fighter of World War I / by Robert
C. Mikesh. — Washington, D.C. : Published for the National Air
and Space Museum by the Smithsonian Institution Press, 1980.
  vii, 112 p. : ill. (some col.) ; 28 cm. — (Famous aircraft of the
National Air and Space Museum ; v. 4)
  ISBN 0-87474-633-7
  I. National Air and Space Museum. II. Title. III. Title:
Albatros D. 5a. IV. Series.

          x   *Air and Space Museum (U.S.)*
          x   *Smithsonian Institution. National*
              Air and Space Museum.
          x   *United States. National Air and*
              Space Museum.

Rule 24.17A
Government body
entered directly

210

Wise home buying / U.S. Department of Housing and Urban
Development. — Washington, D.C. : The Dept., [1974]
36 p. : ill. ; 21 cm.

Cover title.
"August, 1974"—P. [4] of cover.
"HUD-267-F(4)"—P. [4] of cover.

I. United States. Department of Housing and Urban
Development.

    x H.U.D.
    x HUD.
    x United States. Housing and Urban
    *   Development, Department of.*

Rule 24.18A
Type 1
Term in the agency
name implies the
body is part of
another

211

United States. Commission on Civil Rights.
    Comparable worth : an analysis and recommendation : a
report of the United States Commission on Civil Rights. —
Washington, D.C. : The Commission, [1985]
v, 81 p. ; 26 cm.

"June, 1985."
Includes bibliographical references.

I. Title.

    x Civil Rights Commission (U.S.)
    x Commission on Civil Rights (U.S.)
    x United States. Civil Rights
    *   Commission.*

Rule 24.18A
Type 2
Term in the agency
name implies
administrative
subordination

212

Great Britain. Ministry of Housing and Local Government.
    Northampton, Bedford and North Bucks study : an
assessment of inter-related growth / Ministry of Housing and
Local Government. — London : H.M.S.O., 1965.
x, 86 p. : ill., maps ; 30 cm.

I. Title.

    x Great Britain. Ministry of Local
    *   Government.*

Rule 24.18A
Type 5
Ministry

213

> United States. Bureau of Alcohol, Tobacco, and Firearms.
>   Explosives usage policy / Department of the Treasury,
> Bureau of Alcohol, Tobacco and Firearms. — [Washington,
> D.C.] : The Bureau, [1985]
>   1 v. (loose-leaf) ; 28 cm. — (Order ; ATF 0 3320.4)
>
>   Cover title.
>   "10/18/85."
>
>   I. Title. II. Series: United States. Bureau of Alcohol, Tobacco,
>   and Firearms. Order ; ATF 0 3320.4.
>
> *x   United States. Treasury*   *x   Order (United States. Bureau of*
> *Department. Bureau of Alcohol,*   ◯   *Alcohol, Tobacco and Firearms)*
> *Tobacco, and Firearms.*

Rule 24.19A
Direct subheading

Special Rules

24.20   GOVERNMENT OFFICIALS
24.20B   Heads of state, etc.

214

> England and Wales. Sovereign (1603-1625 : James I)
>   Royal proclamations of King James I, 1603-1625 / edited by
> James F. Larkin and Paul L. Hughes. — Oxford : Clarendon
> Press, 1973.
>   xxxiv, 679 p. ; 24 cm. — (Stuart royal proclamations ; v. 1)
>
>   Includes bibliographical references and index.
>
>   I. James I, King of England, 1566-1625. II. Larkin, James F.
>   (James Francis), 1912-   III. Hughes, Paul L. IV. Title. V.
>   Series: England and Wales. Sovereign. Stuart royal
>   proclamations ; v. 1.
>
> *x   Great Britain. Sovereign*   *x   Stuart royal proclamations.*
> *(1603-1625 : James I)*   ◯

Rule 24.20B1
Head of State --
Sovereign

Rule 24.18A
Type 9
Head of state

215

> United States. President (1963-1969 : Johnson)
>   No retreat from tomorrow : President Lyndon B. Johnson's
> 1967 messages to the 90th Congress. — [S.l. : s.n., 1968?]
>   241 p. : ill. (some col.) ; 29 cm.
>
>   I. Johnson, Lyndon B. (Lyndon Baines), 1908-1973. II. United
>   States. 90th Congress : 1st session, 1967. III. Title.
>
>   ◯

Rule 24.20B1
Head of State --
President

Rule 24.18A
Type 9
Head of state

216

United States. Congress. Senate. Committee on Foreign Relations.
    The Vietnam hearings / with an introduction by J. William
Fulbright. — 1st Vintage Books ed. — New York : Vintage
Books, 1966.
    xiv, 294 p. ; 19 cm.
    Complete statements and excerpts from the testimony of
Dean Rusk, James M. Gavin, George F. Kennan, and Maxwell D.
Taylor given during hearings by the Senate Foreign Relations
Committee held Jan. 26-Feb. 18, 1966.
    First published under the title: Supplemental foreign
assistance, fiscal year 1966, Vietnam.
    I. Title.

    x *United States. Congress.*
       Committee on Foreign Relations.
    x *United States. Congress. Senate.*
       Foreign Relations Committee.

Rule 24.21B
Committee of a
legislature

217

United States. Congress. House. Committee on Agriculture.
    Subcommittee on Livestock and Grains.
    Sale of wheat to Russia : hearings before the Subcommittee
on Livestock and Grains of the Committee on Agriculture,
House of Representatives, Ninety-second Congress, second
session, September 14, 18, and 19, 1972. — Washington : U.S.
G.P.O. : for sale by the Supt. of Docs., 1972.
    iv, 293 p. : ill. ; 24 cm.
    "Serial no. 92-KK."
    I. Title.

    x *United States. Congress. House.*
       Subcommittee on Livestock and
       Grains.

Rule 24.21C
Legislative
subcommittee of the
U.S. Congress

218

Memorial addresses and other tributes in the Congress of the
    United States on the life and contributions of William Benton /
    Ninety-third Congress, first session ; [compiled under the
    direction of the Joint Committee on Printing]. — Washington :
    U. S. G.P.O., 1973.
    vi, 110 p. : port. ; 24 cm.
    Cover title: William Benton, late senator from Connecticut,
memorial addresses and tributes to the Congress of the United
States.
    I. United States. 93rd Congress, 1st session, 1973. II. United
States. Congress. Joint Committee on Printing. III. Title:
William Benton, late senator from Connecticut.

Rule 24.21D
Successive
legislature
numbered
consecutively

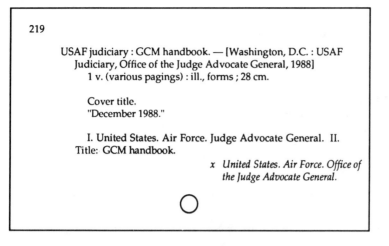

219

USAF judiciary : GCM handbook. — [Washington, D.C. : USAF
Judiciary, Office of the Judge Advocate General, 1988]
1 v. (various pagings) : ill., forms ; 28 cm.

Cover title.
"December 1988."

I. United States. Air Force. Judge Advocate General. II.
Title: GCM handbook.

x   *United States. Air Force. Office of
the Judge Advocate General.*

Rule 21.24A1
Armed force at the
national level

CHOICE OF ACCESS POINTS AND FORM OF ENTRY EXERCISE

Indicate the main entry, added entries, and cross references for each of the
following books. Record each entry in its correct form and into the order
appropriate for tracings, for example

World History, or, Why Things Are, by John Doe and Jane Smith-Jones.

Main entry: Doe, John
Added entries: Smith-Jones, Jane.
                 Title.
                 Title: Why things are.
References: x   Jones, Jane Smith-

For this assignment <u>don't</u> apply the optional addition Rule 21.0D1. You do not
need to add dates to names unless the dates for a person are supplied as
additional information about the work. Answers to this exercise appear in
Appendix C.

1. *World climate,* by John S. Herrold and Ruth Fairchild-Carruthers.
    [Originally published as: *Our Changing Climate*]

    x   Carruthers, Ruth Fairchild-

2. *Pamela in London & Pamela abroad,* by S. N. Rogers.
    [Two separate novels; author's forenames are Sidney Norris, although he
    usually writes under his surname using the initials S.N. rather than his
    forenames]

    x Rogers, Sidney Norris
    x Norris Rogers, Sidney

3.   *A bibliography on weather,* compiled by Roberta Jackson-Hunt. [A work in the Science bibliography series]

X Hunt , Roberta Jackson—

4.   *The weatherman! a book of cartoons,* drawn by E. Jay Stone with *An introduction to pictorial humor,* by Amanda Corselli. [Both titles are on the same title page]

NONE

5.   *Fifty years of impression,* by Robert Moser. [A catalog of a loan exhibition held in the Museum of Art, Fairfield, Conn., June, 1978]

x Fairfield , conn . Museum of Art .

6.   *Membership directory of the American Bar Association.* [Also referred to as the ABA within the text]

x A.B.A.

7.   *Charts of the past,* by Louis Brogan, Henrietta Larose, Joseph Ricardo and Florence W. Eames. [Part of the Paperback classics series]

NONE

8.   *Personnel handbook for the Cleveland Museum of Art,* compiled by Melissa Cranshaw.

x Cleveland Museum of Art

9.   *Petroleum, energy, and the state of mankind,* the Fifth Annual Conference on Energy held in Philadelphia, Pa., January 5-7, 1979. Edited by Thomas Fitzhugh.

10. *Mission to the stars,* by Veronica Estelle. [The name is the pseudonym of
     the 20th century author Emma Davis, born in 1918. Assume the library
     also has books in the collection written by the author under her real name]

xx Emma Davis

11. *Standards for air quality,* by the Air Quality Committee of the American
     Antipollution Society. [The Committee does not take a position on air
     quality standards but rather reports on existing standards.]

x Air Quality Committee

12. *Tragic hero : a novel,* by Peter Van Huven. Translated by Derek Smythe.
     [The author is Dutch. This is the only translation of the work into English]

x Van Huven, Peter

13. *Report on enrollment,* by the Curriculum Committee of the Graduate
     School of Business Administration, University of Western Idaho. [The
     Committee makes policy recommendations]

None

14. *The Anarchist Party program in Ohio,* by the Ohio Section of the
     Anarchist Party. [A statement of Party policy]

None

15. *Readings in ethics,* compiled by Louise Allenby and Kelly Bryant. Second
     Revised Edition by R. K. Smith. [R.K. Smith most frequently writes using
     his forename Robert]

x Smith, R.K.

16. *Three costume plays,* introduced and annotated by C. W. Guthrie.
     [Contents: Tintagel / A.J. Wilson — Summer in Cornwall / Tom Job — The
     Welsh highlands / W. Llewellyn]

None

17. *The message of President Theodore Roosevelt to the Congress, September 8, 1904.* [Dates in office, 1901-1909; dates of birth and death, 1858-1919]

None

18. *Annual Report of H. K. Lewisohn Company, Incorporated.*

x Lewisohn Company, Incorporated

19. *A country adventure — a play,* by Enid McFall. [A rewriting of the novel Weir of Hermiston by Robert Louis Stevenson]

20. *The complete poetry of Marianne M. Moore,* with an introduction by Simon Suggs. [Born in 1924 and died in 1957]

21. *The birds,* by Aristophanes. Translated into English by Robert Minton Blake. [This is the most recent of many translations of this work]

22. *The autobiography of Frodo,* as reported by Chela Ormond. Illustrated by Mary Ellen Chamberlain. [Frodo is a character in *The Lord of the Rings,* by J.R.R. Tolkien]

23. *Narcotics and the U. S. government,* prepared by the U. S. Bureau of Customs. [The Bureau of Customs is a part of the Department of the Treasury]

x U.S. Department of the Treasury

CHAPTER FIVE

Uniform Titles and References

Topic Outline

Rules

25.3   Works Created after 1500

25.4   Works Created before 1501

25.5   Additions

COLLECTIVE TITLES

25.9   Selections

25.10   Works in a Single Form

SPECIAL RULES FOR CERTAIN TYPES OF WORK

Laws, Treaties, Etc.

25.15   Laws

Sacred Scriptures

25.18   Parts of Sacred Scriptures and Additions

Readings: *Anglo-American Cataloguing Rules.* 2nd ed., 1988 revision
              Chapter 25, Uniform Titles, p. 480-512;
              Chapter 26, References, p. 557-562.

N.B. In the examples that follow, an indication is given at the bottom of the card of uniform title references that would be required for uniform title access points for that work. The references provided are not exhaustive, but rather, are those references likely to have been used in a typical catalog. In order to conserve space, only references for uniform titles and series are provided.

25.3   WORKS CREATED AFTER 1500

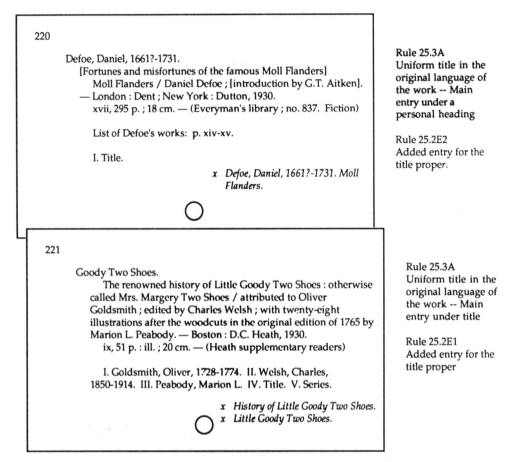

220

Defoe, Daniel, 1661?-1731.
   [Fortunes and misfortunes of the famous Moll Flanders]
   Moll Flanders / Daniel Defoe ; [introduction by G.T. Aitken].
— London : Dent ; New York : Dutton, 1930.
   xvii, 295 p. ; 18 cm. — (Everyman's library ; no. 837. Fiction)

List of Defoe's works: p. xiv-xv.

I. Title.

        *x   Defoe, Daniel, 1661?-1731. Moll
           Flanders.*

Rule 25.3A
Uniform title in the
original language of
the work -- Main
entry under a
personal heading

Rule 25.2E2
Added entry for the
title proper.

221

Goody Two Shoes.
   The renowned history of Little Goody Two Shoes : otherwise
called Mrs. Margery Two Shoes / attributed to Oliver
Goldsmith ; edited by Charles Welsh ; with twenty-eight
illustrations after the woodcuts in the original edition of 1765 by
Marion L. Peabody. — Boston : D.C. Heath, 1930.
   ix, 51 p. : ill. ; 20 cm. — (Heath supplementary readers)

I. Goldsmith, Oliver, 1728-1774. II. Welsh, Charles,
1850-1914. III. Peabody, Marion L. IV. Title. V. Series.

        x   History of Little Goody Two Shoes.
        x   Little Goody Two Shoes.

Rule 25.3A
Uniform title in the
original language of
the work -- Main
entry under title

Rule 25.2E1
Added entry for the
title proper

25.3C   Simultaneous publication under different titles

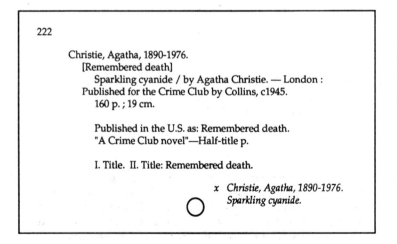

222

Christie, Agatha, 1890-1976.
   [Remembered death]
   Sparkling cyanide / by Agatha Christie. — London :
Published for the Crime Club by Collins, c1945.
   160 p. ; 19 cm.

Published in the U.S. as: Remembered death.
"A Crime Club novel"—Half-title p.

I. Title. II. Title: Remembered death.

        *x   Christie, Agatha, 1890-1976.
           Sparkling cyanide.*

Rule 25.3C1
Work published
simultaneously in
the same language
under different
titles

25.4 WORKS CREATED BEFORE 1501
25.4A General rule

223

Beowulf.
　　Beowulf : an edition with manuscript spacing notation and
graphotactic analyses / Robert D. Stevick. — New York :
Garland Pub. Co., 1975.
　　xxxix, 260 p. ; 22 cm.

　　Includes bibliographical references (p. xxxix) and index.
　　ISBN 0-8240-1090-6

　　I. Stevick, Robert D., 1928-　　II. Title.

Rule 25.4A1
Uniform title in the
language by which
the work is
identified in
modern sources

25.4B Classical and Byzantine Greek works

224

Homer.
　　[Iliad. English]
　　　The anger of Achilles : Homer's Iliad / translated by Robert
Graves ; illustrations by Ronald Searle. — Garden City, N.Y. :
Doubleday, c1959.
　　　383 p. : ill. ; 25 cm.

　　　I. Graves, Robert, 1895-　　II. Searle, Ronald, 1920-　　III.
Title.

　　　　　　　　x Homer. The anger of Achilles.

Rule 25.4B1
Uniform title in
English for a work
originally written in
classical Greek

25.5 ADDITIONS
25.5B Conflict resolution

225

Howard, Sidney Coe, 1891-1939.
　　GWTW : the screenplay / by Sidney Howard ; based on the
novel by Margaret Mitchell ; edited by Richard Harwell. —
New York : Macmillan, c1980.
　　　416 p. : ill. ; 23 cm.

　　Includes bibliographical references (p. 415-416).
　　ISBN 0-02-548660-8

　　I. Harwell, Richard Barksdale. II. Mitchell, Margaret,
1900-1949. Gone with the wind. III. Gone with the wind
(Motion picture) IV. Title.

Rule 25.5B1
Addition of a brief
phrase

Conflict resolution, cont'd.

226

Sonquist, John A.
 The detection of interaction effects : a report on a computer program for the selection of optimal combinations of explanatory variables / by John A. Sonquist, James N. Morgan. — 6th ed. — [Ann Arbor, Mich.] : Survey Research Center, Institute of Social Science, University of Michigan, 1970, c1964.
 xi, 296 p. : ill. ; 28 cm. — (Monograph / Survey Research Center, Institute for Social Research, The University of Michigan ; no. 35)
 Includes bibliographical references.
 I. Morgan, James N. II. Title. III. Series: Monograph (University of Michigan. Survey Research Center) ; no. 35.

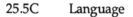   *x University of Michigan. Survey Research Center. Monograph.*

Rule 25.5B1
Addition of a
designation

[This method is used by the Library of Congress to resolve conflicts in series titles.]

25.5C Language

227

Gide, André, 1869-1951.
 [Porte étroite. English]
 Strait is the gate / André Gide ; translated from the French by Dorothy Bussy. — New York : Vintage Books, [1956?], c1924.
 148 p. ; 19 cm.

 Originally published in French as La porte étroite.

 I. Title.

    x Gide, André, 1869-1951. Strait is the gate.

Rule 25.5C1
Language of the
item differs from
that of the original

COLLECTIVE TITLES

25.9 SELECTIONS

228

Poe, Edgar Allan, 1809-1849.
 [Selections]
 Selected prose, poetry, and Eureka / Edgar Allan Poe ; edited with an introduction by W.H. Auden. — New York : Holt, Rinehart and Winston, [1968?]
 xxvi, 590 p. ; 21 cm. — (Rinehart editions ; 42)

 Originally published under the title: Selected prose and poetry.
 ISBN 0-03-084241-7

 I. Title.

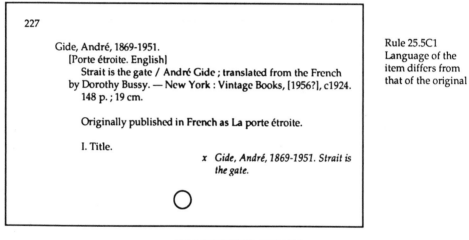   *x Poe, Edgar Allan, 1809-1849. Selected prose, poetry, and Eureka.*

Rule 25.9A
Selection of works
in various forms by
one person

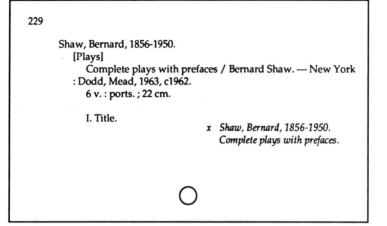

229

Shaw, Bernard, 1856-1950.
  [Plays]
    Complete plays with prefaces / Bernard Shaw. — New York
  : Dodd, Mead, 1963, c1962.
    6 v. : ports. ; 22 cm.

    I. Title.

                    x *Shaw, Bernard, 1856-1950.*
                       Complete plays with prefaces.

Rule 25.10A
Complete works of
a person in one
form

SPECIAL RULES FOR CERTAIN TYPES OF WORK

Laws, Treaties, Etc.

25.15   LAWS
25.15A   Modern laws, etc.

230

Wisconsin.
  [Laws, etc.]
    West's Wisconsin statutes annotated : under arrangement of
  the official Wisconsin statutes. — St. Paul, Minn. : West Pub.
  Co., c1957-
      v. : facsim., forms ; 27 cm.
    Kept up-to-date by revised volumes, pocket parts,
  supplementary and special pamphlets, West's Wisconsin
  legislative service, and interim annotation service.
    Includes unnumbered general index and constitution
  volumes.
    I. West Publishing Company. II. Title. III. Title: Wisconsin
  statutes annotated.   x *Wisconsin. West's Wisconsin*
                                statutes annotated.

Rule 25.15A1
Collection of the
laws of a
jurisdiction

231

California.
  [Unemployment insurance code]
    Unemployment insurance code, 1986 / compiled by Bion M.
  Gregory. — North Highlands : State of Calif., Dept. of General
  Services, Documents and Publications Section, [1986?]
    1 v. (various pagings) ; 23 cm.

    Includes bibliographical references and index.

    I. Gregory, Bion M. II. California. Documents and
  Publications Section. III. Title.

Rule 25.15A1
Compilation of the
laws of a
jurisdiction on a
specific subject that
has a citation title

232

Illinois.
 [Revenue act (1939)]
  The revenue act of 1939 : as enacted and amended by the 61st
General Assembly at its regular session, 1939, together with the
Revenue article of the Constitution, the Preadjudication act of
1939, the Rules of the Tax Commission and reference notes and
tables. — Springfield : Illinois Tax Commission, [1939]
  xiii, 238 p. ; 23 cm.

 Includes indexes.

 I. Illinois. Tax Commission. II. Title.

Rule 25.15A2
Different laws
having the same
title -- Addition
of the year of
promulgation

Sacred Scriptures

25.18 PARTS OF SACRED SCRIPTURES AND ADDITIONS
25.18A Bible

233

Bible. English. Authorized. 1948.
 Holy Bible : containing the Old and New Testaments,
authorized King James version, with notes especially adapted
for young Christians. — Pilgrim ed. — New York : Oxford
University Press, 1948.
  xxi, 1721 p. : ill., maps ; 28 cm.

 Editor-in-chief: E. Schuyler English.

 I. English, E. Schuyler (Eugene Schuyler), 1899- II. Title.

Rule 25.18A10
Language

Rule 25.18A11
Version

Rule 25.18A13
Year

234

Bible. N.T. English. New English. 1961.
 The New English Bible. New Testament. — [London?] :
Oxford University Press, 1961.
  xiii, 446 p. ; 24 cm.

 Translated under the supervision of the Joint Committee on
the New Translation of the Bible.

 I. Joint Committee on the New Translation of the Bible. II.
Title.

Rule 25.18A2
Testaments

Bible, cont'd.

235

Bible. O.T. Ezra. English. Myers. 1965.
　　　Ezra ; Nehemiah / introduction, translation, and notes by
Jacob M. Myers. — 1st ed. — Garden City, N.Y. : Doubleday,
1965.
　　　lxxxiii, 268 p. : ill. ; 25 cm. — (The Anchor Bible ; 14)

Includes bibliographical references (p. [lxxviii]-lxxxiii).

　　　I. Myers, Jacob M., 1904-　　II. Bible. O.T. Nehemiah. English.
Myers. 1965.　III. Title.　IV. Series: Bible. English. Anchor Bible.
1964 ; 14.

x　Bible. Ezra.
x　Ezra (Book of the Bible)

x　Bible. Nehemiah.
x　Nehemiah (Book of the Bible)

Rule 25.18A3
Books

Rule 25.18A8
Two selections

Part II

SUBJECT ANALYSIS

CHAPTER SIX

Dewey Decimal Classification

Topic Outline

A. History

B. Arrangement

   1. Order of Main Classes

   2. Summaries

   3. Schedules

   4. Tables

      a. Table 1. Standard subdivisions

      b. Table 2. Geographic areas, historical periods, persons

      c. Table 3. Subdivisions for individual literatures, for specific literary forms

         (1) Table 3-A. Subdivisions for works by or about individual authors

         (2) Table 3-B. Subdivisions for works by or about more than one author

         (3) Table 3-C. Notation to be added where instructed in Table 3-B and in 808-809

      d. Table 4. Subdivisions of individual languages

      e. Table 5. Racial, ethnic, national groups

      f. Table 6. Languages

      g. Table 7. Groups of persons

C. Techniques

   1. Centered headings

   2. Bracketed numbers

   3. "Add to" directions

Readings: Dewey, Melvil. *Dewey Decimal Classification and Relative Index.* Ed. 20. Albany, N.Y.: Forest Press, 1989.
"Introduction to Dewey Decimal Classification," p. xxv-l.

Comaromi, John P. *Book Numbers.* Littleton, Co.: Libraries Unlimited, 1981.
or
Lehnus, Donald J. *Book numbers: History, Principles, and Application.* Chicago: American Library Association, 1980.

Resources: Cutter, Charles A. *Cutter-Sanborn Three-Figure Author Table.* Swanson-Swift rev. Littleton, CO: Libraries Unlimited, 1969.

TECHNIQUES USED IN THE DEWEY DECIMAL CLASSIFICATION

Access to the Scheme. There are two methods for finding a specific subject within the Dewey Decimal Classification (DDC). One approach is through the use of the summaries located at the beginning of volume 2 (2:ix-xx), the other is the use of the index.

There are three summaries: the First Summary presents the class notation and headings for the "Ten Main Classes"; the Second Summary provides this information for the "Hundred Divisions"; while the Third Summary addresses the "Thousand Sections." It is possible to scan these summaries and identify an appropriate subclass as an entry point in the schedule for the further development of a class number.

In addition to the summaries for the schedule as a whole, DDC also provides two types of summaries for parts of a class. The first of this type of summary is the "single-level" summary used at the schedules and tables whenever classes are encountered whose subdivisions cover more than two pages. An example of this type of subdivision appears under Class 331.12 (Labor market) and Class 658.1 (Organization and finance). Also, DDC 20 provides a type of summary display not present in previous editions, a "multi-level summary." This type of summary, used for eight of the major divisions and the area tables for Europe and North America, incorporates two levels of structure to provide an overview of a class. Examples of this sort of summary appear under Class 330 (Economics), Class 370 (Education) and Class 780 (Music).

The use of the relative index is generally a more efficient and effective method of gaining access to the content of the DDC schedules when the notation for a topic is unknown. This index shows the distribution of subjects among the disciplines and provides the notation for these subjects in the schedule and in the tables. An example of an index presentation appears under "Soybeans"

Soybeans	583.322
Agricultural economics	338.175 655
Botany	583.322

Commercial processing	
economics	338.476 648 056 55
technology	664.805 655
cooking	641.656 55
field crop	633.34
food	641.356 55
garden crop	635.655

Here, notation is given for seven different classes in which works on soybeans might be classed depending upon the subject content of the book. Although not present in this example, the relative index also uses "see also" references to indicate related topics.

The Manual. The most striking change in DDC 20 is the presence of a manual to assist in its application. This manual (located following the relative index in volume 4) represents the core of a much larger body of notes first introduced in the *Manual on the Use of the Dewey Decimal Classification: Edition 19*, separately published in 1982. The current manual describes policies and practices of the Decimal Classification Division of the Library of Congress, offers advice on classification in difficult areas, and explains how to choose between related topics. The briefer notes in the 1982 Manual, and those that need to be used frequently are incorporated in the schedules and tables. These notes and the manual help classifiers resolve problems and use the DDC with greater consistency.

Call Numbers. Call numbers for the Dewey Decimal Classification generally consist of two elements: the classification number and the book number (often referred to as a "Cutter" number after individual, C. A. Cutter, who developed a means of systematically assigning an alpha-numeric code for the names of individuals). The following call number would be assigned to the book *The Bethesda Weight Loser Diet*, by Marilyn Lewis.

613.25	Classification number from DDC
L675b	Book number. "L625 represents the surname of the main entry "Lewis." The "b," called a "work mark," represents the first non-article word of the title.

Because the DDC is widely used in North America for shelf arrangement, hence, the subarrangement made possible by book numbers is an important consideration in the development of a final call number, although not as important as the arrangement made possible by the class number. The development of book numbers is discussed in detail later.

Classification Numbers. A Dewey Decimal Classification number uses a notation of Arabic numerals. The classification is based primarily on division by subject rather than form. Classification numbers may be expanded decimally to provide for special aspects of general subjects. One way to analyze the meaning of a class number is to analyze the meaning of its parts from the most basic element of the number to the most specific. An example of this type of analysis follows for the book *Sheltering Homeless Young Adult Crack Cocaine Abusers* assigned the class number 362.29883.

3	Social Sciences
36	Social problems and services; association
362	Social welfare problems and services
362.2	Mental and emotional illnesses and disturbances
362.29	Substance abuse
362.298	Cocaine
362.2988	Remedial measures services, forms of assistance
	[From 362-363]
362.29883	Provisions of food, shelter, household assistance, clothing, recreation

This method of presentation is will be used throughout this workbook in the development and analysis of DDC classification numbers.

TABLE 1

Standard Subdivisions. Standard subdivisions make it possible to specify more exactly the bibliographic form of the material being classified, i.e., dictionaries, serials, etc., or to indicate something about the treatment of the subject in the document, i.e., philosophy or history. If there is no range of numbers assigned or implied for the use of standard subdivisions, the notation is used as it appears in Table 1. The book *Mineralogy: an Outline* would be assigned the classification number 549.0202.

500	Natural sciences and mathematics
540	Chemistry and allied sciences
549	Mineralogy
549.0202	Synopses and outlines
	[From Table 1]
	-02 Miscellany
	-0202 Synopses and outlines

Sometimes a special range of numbers is supplied for use as standard subdivisions. One way this may be expressed is in a range of numbers specified within the schedules. For example, in Class 100 (Philosophy and Related Disciplines) standard subdivisions are indicated in the schedule as 101 through 109. These numbers may be further developed by adding the extensions of these numbers from Table 1. Thus, the book *An Outline of Philosophy* would be assigned the class number 102.02.

100	Philosophy, parapsychology and occultism, psychology
102	Miscellany of philosophy
102.02	Synopses and outlines
	[From Table 1]
	-02 Miscellany
	-0202 Synopses and outlines

Another way that the range of numbers for use as standard subdivisions is specified in the schedules appears in Class 361 (Social problems and social welfare in general.). In this class, the standard subdivisions are indicated by the allocation of the range ".001 - .008." A book that deals with social problems in an outline format would be assigned the class number 361.00202

300	Social sciences
360	Social problems and services; association
361	Social problems and social welfare in general
361.00202	Synopses and outlines
	[From Table 1]
	-02 Miscellany
	-0202 Synopses and outlines

Other tables. The other six tables may be used only when their use is directed either in the schedules or under a standard subdivision. When their use is directed, the user will always be provided with a base number to which the number from the table should be added. For example, under Class 374.4 (Correspondence schools and courses), one is directed to add to the base number 374.4, the number from Table 2 (Geographic areas, periods, persons). Thus, the book *Correspondence Schools in the United States* would be assigned the class number 374.473.

300	Social sciences
370	Education
374	Adult education
374.4	Correspondence schools and courses
374.473	United States
	[From Table 2]
	-7 North America
	-73 United States

"Add to" Directions. These directions are very similar to the number building operation used for Tables 2 through 7. The difference is that instead of adding from a table, the classifier is given a base number and instructed to add to that number from another part of the schedule. For example, under Class 359.1 to 359.2 (Naval life and resources), one is instructed to add the numbers following 355 in the range 355.1-355.2 to the base number 359. Following these instructions, the class number 359.1336 would be assigned to the book *Naval Etiquette.*

300	Social sciences
350	Public administration and military science
359	Sea (Naval) forces and warfare
359.1336	Naval etiquette
	[As instructed under "359.1-.2" the numbers following "355 for etiquette (1336) is added to the base number "359."]
	355.1336 Etiquette

In some cases, an "add to" direction provides for addition from the whole, or a large part, of the classification schedule (volumes 2 and 3). For example, under Class 016 (Bibliographies and catalogs of works on specific subjects or in specific disciplines) it is possible to provide a class number for a bibliography on any subject by following the "add to . . . 001-999" directions. For a bibliography of folklore, the class number 016.398 would be assigned.

010	Bibliography
016	Bibliographies and catalogs of specific disciplines and subjects
016.398	Folklore

[As instructed under "016," the number from the range "001-999" for folklore (398) is added to the base number "016."]

	3	Social sciences
	39	Customs, etiquette, folklore
	398	Folklore

Book or Cutter Numbers. Smaller libraries often use an alphabetic representation of the main entry as a way to subarrange works in the same class. An example of this approach is illustrated by the call number for the book *Air transportation* by Robert Bartlett.

> 387.7
> Bar

This type of arrangement works well for smaller collections. Problems arise when one encounters multiple works by the same person in the same class or works in the same class that have the same letters representing the main entry, for example, books on air transportation by Bartlett, Barnes, and Barrow. Generally, if a library anticipates growth beyond 50,000 titles or if many works are classified in a few classes because the library is specialized in its collection, an alphanumeric representation of the main entry should be used. Currently, there are three sources for this notation used by libraries using the Dewey Decimal Classification: *C. A. Cutter's Two-Figure Author Table*, *C. A. Cutter's Three-Figure Author Table* and the *Cutter-Sanborn Three-Figure Author Table*. Each of these tables, which provide an alphanumeric representation for the main entry, results in different notations for the same word. For example, the name Judith Watkins would be assigned the following book numbers from these cutter tables:

Cutter 2-Figure	Cutter 3-Figure	Cutter-Sanborn 3-Figure
W32	W325	W335

Examples of book numbers in this workbook have been derived from the *Cutter-Sanborn Three-Figure Author Table*. In addition to the notation derived from a Cutter table, most libraries use a letter of the alphabet in lower case to subarrange works by an author within a class. For the book *Organic Farming*, by Sheila Locke, the book number "L814o" would be assigned. The lowercase letter "o" represents the first non-article word of the title.

Special procedures for the assignment of books numbers for biographies, different editions, bibliographies, criticisms, translations, etc. are employed by libraries. The procedures followed may vary from library to library, although there are general principles for the assignment of these numbers. See the works by Comaromi and Lehnus for more detailed discussion of "cuttering" in these situations.

Location mark. A location mark is used to indicate the location of a particular work in a special collection of a library, for example, browsing, reference, oversized, or juvenile collections. The location mark is generally placed at the head of the call number. For the *Concordance to the Works of Sir Walter Scott* by John Kerry, the "R" is the location mark in the call number

R
823.6
S431k

DEWEY DECIMAL CLASSIFICATION EXERCISES

Answers to these exercises appear in Appendix D

A. The Relative Index. Indicate the appropriate classification number in the Relative Index for each of these titles.

1. *Seed pictures and other dried natural arrangements.*

    700

2. *The varieties of cheese and how they are produced.*

    641.306   637.3

3. *The decorative arts of primitive peoples.*

    700

4. *The tactics of aerial warfare.*

    355.02

5. *Beginning typewriting: tests and drills.*

    652.3   0204

6. *Book mending for libraries.*

    025.7

7. *Short-range weather forecasting.*

    551.6

8. *Doll furniture designs for the amateur craftsman.*

    745.592 3

B. <u>Analyzing DDC Numbers.</u> Indicate the hierarchical development for the classification number provided with each title.

9. *Library instruction in the elementary school.*

    027.8222   *General libraries*
              Elementary

10. *Cancer in Connecticut: incidence and characteristics.*

    616.994009746   *Specific diseases*
                    Tumors
                    Cancer
                    CT

11. *Spare part surgery: transplants, the surgical practice of the future.*

    617.95   *medicine*
             operative surgery
             Cosmetic "

12. *The farm beef herd.*

    636.213

13. *Collective bargaining in the U. S. lithographic industry.*

    331.8904168623150973   *lithography*   *09 = Histore*
                           Labor unions - collective bargaining + disputes
                           Specific groups

14. *Education for librarianship: the design of the curriculum of library schools in the United States.*

    020.71173

C.   Table 1: Standard Subdivisions. Classify the following document titles
      as specifically as possible.

15.   *The quarterly journal of technology.*

16.   *A short history of inventions.*

17.   *A dictionary of physics.*

18.   *Current methods used in adult education research.*

19.   *Technology during the thirteenth century: a history.*

20.   *The encyclopedia of religion.*

21.   *Bookbinding as a profession.*

22.   *A directory of mineralogists.*

23. *Biographies of 19th century mineralogists.*

D. <u>Table 2: Area Tables</u>. Classify the following document titles as specifically as possible.

24. *Patriotic societies of France.*

25. *Library schools in Germany: a description.*

26. *A bibliography of books published by the University of Chicago Press.* [Located in Chicago, Illinois)

27. *Folklore about the Lake Superior.*

E. <u>Tables 1 and 2</u>. Classify the following document titles as specifically as possible.

28. *A directory of lawyers in Italy.*

29. *A history of mining in 19th century Colorado.*

30. *Teaching engineering in Canadian universities.*

31. *A directory of engineers in Texas throughout the 20th century.*

F. Table 4: Subdivisions of Individual Languages. Classify the following document titles as specifically as possible.

32. *Language today.* [A Canadian English language periodical]

33. *Teaching the Romance languages.*

34. *Teaching French in American secondary schools.* [Coverage limited to the U.S.]

35. *A compilation of Spanish words incorporated into the English language.*

36. *The definitive French dictionary.*

37. *German-English, English-German dictionary.*

38. *German-Bulgarian, Bulgarian-German dictionary.*

39. *Papers of the East Slavic Languages Association.* [An international society]

G. 800s and Tables 3A, 3B, and 3C: Literature (Belles Lettres) and Subdivisions of Individual Literatures. Classify the following document titles as specifically as possible.

40. *The encyclopedia of English literature.*

41. *An anthology of English literature.*

42. *A collection of English fantasy.* [Do not treat fantasy as a literary form]

43. *English literature for boys.* [A collection]

44. *English literature of the pre-Elizabethan period: a criticism.*

45. *A critical study of English drama.*

46. *English drama of the Elizabethan period: a collection.*

47. *A collection of Welsh (Cymric) literature.*

48. *A collection of plays from modern Estonia.*

49. *A collection of 18th century French literature.*

50. *19th century French poetry: a collection.*

H. <u>900s: Geography, History and Auxiliary Disciplines.</u>

51. *Geography of Martha's Vineyard, Massachusetts.*

52. *Travel in the British Isles during the Roman occupation.*

53. *The exploration of Chile by Europeans.*

54. *A history of medieval Austria.*

55. *The Spanish-American War: the American perspective.*

56. *The history of Pawtucket, Rhode Island.*

57. *Outline of Eastern European history.*

58. *History of the Burmese in New Zealand.*

59. *World history of the Irish people.*

I. Other Tables and "Add To" Directions.

60. *Customs of the Huguenots.*

61. *The management of agricultural museums.*

62. *A guide to the Cobb Agriculture Museum, Butler County, Pennsylvania.*

63. *The manufacture of equipment for football.* [This is the American game of football]

64. *Congenital diseases of the scalp.*

65. *Cheerleading at Indiana University basketball games.* [Indiana University is located in Bloomington (Monroe County), Indiana]

66. *Materials for teaching science in elementary schools.*

67. *Stamps of Ghana: a collector's guide.*

68. *Atlas of France.*

69. *Seventeenth century bookbinding.*

70. *Ancient Roman coins: their description for collectors.*

71. *Photography as a hobby: a guide for the amateur.*

72. *Prospecting for gold in Colorado.*

73. *Flagstone sidewalks: illustrations of their design and construction.*

74. *A bibliography of folk literature.*

75. *Solar houses in Southern California.*

76. *A modern version of the Bible in Japanese.*

77. *The geography of Ethiopia.*

78. *Design of interior furnishings for Burroughs-Wellcome Company, Research Triangle Park, North Carolina.* [A pharmaceutical firm in Durham County, North Carolina]

79. *A programmed learning text for natural sciences.*

80. *The anatomy of snakes.*

81. *Research in toxicology.*

82. *Travel in Trinidad today.*

83. *The management of poplar forests.*

84. *Books written by adolescents: a bibliography.*

85. *Crime in Brazil.*

CHAPTER SEVEN

Library of Congress Classification

Topic Outline

A. History

B. Arrangement

    1. Order of Main classes

    2. Preface

    3. Synopses

    4. Outline

    5. Schedule

    6. Tables

    7. Index

    8. Adds and changes (A&C)

    9. Index to A&C

C. Relationship to LC subject headings

D. Techniques

    1. Class letter(s)/numbers

    2. Cutter numbers

        a. Double cutter numbers

        b. A-Z cutter numbers

        c. Reserve cutter numbers

        d. Reserve cutter number ranges

        e. Successive cutter numbers

    3. Arrange-like directions

    4. Tables

    5. Date

Readings: Immroth, John Phillip. *Immorth's Guide to the Library of Congress Classification*. 3rd ed. by Lois Mai Chan. Littleton, CO.: Libraries Unlimited, 1980.

Resources: Library of Congress. Subject Cataloging Division. *Subject Cataloging Manual: Shelflisting*. Washington, DC: Library of Congress, 1986. (SCM:S)

Library of Congress. *Classification*.
[See the "Introduction" of this workbook for a list of the current editions of the LC schedules that may have been used in the exercises in this chapter.]

TECHNIQUES USED IN THE
LIBRARY OF CONGRESS CLASSIFICATION

Call Numbers. Call numbers for the Library of Congress Classification generally consist of three elements: the classification number (using both letters of the alphabet and arabic numerals) , one or two cutter numbers and a date.

SB
435.52
.N6
S3
1989

Classification Numbers. The classification number represents the subject nature of a document. They are composed of from one to three uppercase letters and an arabic whole number of up to four digits (1-9999). This number may have decimal extensions.

Cutter Numbers. Following the class number is a cutter or book number. The cutter number, usually representing the first non-article word of the main entry, provides for the alphabetical subarrangement of works within a class and enables a library to develop a unique call number for each work. In some situations LC may use two cutters numbers in a call number. This is called "double cuttering." Its use is explained more fully later in this chapter.

A cutter number consists of a single letter of the alphabet preceded by a decimal point. The alphabetic character is followed by one or more arabic numerals. When a second cutter number is used, only the first is preceded by a decimal point.

The table issued by the Library of Congress for the development of cutter numbers appears on the next page. It has been taken from the *Subject Cataloging Manual: Shelflisting* (SCM:S), Instruction G 060. It should be noted that cutter numbers derived from this table are decimal in nature and relative. As such, they can be expanded to provide unique call numbers and locate any given document between two others. This process of adjusting cutter numbers is referred to as shelflisting. LC advises its catalogers when shelflisting to never end a cutter number with "0" or "1." The following examples illustrate how names within the C range in a given class might be assigned different cutter numbers:

Catton	.C3	Cox	.C69
Cecil	.C4	Crane	.C7
Cheever	.C44	Crider	.C75
Cicco	.C5	Cronin	.C76
Clint	.C55	Cullen	.C8
Corson	.C6	Cyert	.C9

Double cutter numbers. This technique is used throughout the classification scheme. It occurs most frequently when the first cutter number is used to indicate a topic, with the second cutter number used to alphabetize for the main entry. Usually no more than two cutter numbers are used in the LC classification to develop a call number. Double cutter numbers are used in some of the examples that follow.

Cutter Table

(1) After initial vowels

for the second letter:	b	d	l-m	n	p	r	s-t	u-y
use number:	2	3	4	5	6	7	8	9

(2) After the initial letter S

for the second letter:	a	ch	e	h-i	m-p	t	u	w-z
use number:	2	3	4	5	6	7	8	9

(3) After the initial letters Qu
for the second
[i.e., third] letter:

	a	e	i	o	r	t	y
use number:	3	4	5	6	7	8	9

For initial letters
Qa-Qt, use: 2-29

(4) After other initial consonants

for the second letter:	a	e	i	o	r	u	y
use number:	3	4	5	6	7	8	9

(5) For expansion

for the [third] letter:	a-d	e-h	i-l	m-o	p-s	t-v	u-z
use number:	3	4	5	6	7	8	9

A-Z Cutter Number Division. Cuttering is used throughout the the LC classification to specify and subarrange topics in alphabetical order that would otherwise be distributed alphabetically by main entry within a class. This technique incorporates a subject or topical arrangement function into the cutter element of a call number. When these topical elements are known, they are often listed in the schedule with their associated cutter number. The following use of A-Z cutter number divisions occurs in Class SF (Animal culture):

```
SF       Animal culture
             Feeds and feeding.  Animal nutrition
   98              Special components, A-Z
             .A2     Additives
             .A4     Amino acids
             .A44    Ammonia
             .A5     Antibiotics
             .A9     Azelaic acid
             .C45    Chromium
             . . . .
             .T7     Trace elements
             .U7     Urea
             .V5     Vitamins
```

Using this table of cuttered topics, the book *Amino acids in animal nutrition*, by Boone (1983) would be assigned the call number

> SF98
> .A4
> B6
> 1983

In this call number, ".A4" is derived from the topical cutter number list in the schedule. Should a document being classified have a special topic that is not included in this list, it could be provided for within this alphabetic array. Although it is not specified in the schedule, a cutter number for the main entry is used in the call number to subarrange within the the special topic and to provide a unique call number.

   The A-Z technique is also specified for even though specific cutter numbers have not been preassigned to topics. This approach is used frequently to subarrange subjects by country, state or other political divisions. For example, in Class S (Agriculture), the following appears:

```
S                    Agriculture (General)
                     Agricultural education.
                     Agricultural extension work.
   544                   General and United States.
   544.3                    By state, A-W.
   544.5                 Other regions or countries, A-Z
```

Using this schedule, the book *Agricultural Extension Activities in Canada*, by Lansing (1987) would be assigned the call number

> S544.5
> .C3
> L3
> 1987

The hierarchical breakdown for this call number is

```
S               Agriculture
  530-559          Agricultural education
    544-545          Agricultural extension work
      544.5            Other regions or countries, A-Z
        .C3              [Cutter number for "Canada" from SCM:S
                           Instruction G 300]
        L3               [Cutter number for "Lansing"]
          1987             [Date]
```

   Reserve cutter numbers. In some situations, a cutter number, or a range of
cutter numbers, may be reserved for special purposes. Usually the objective is to
indicate, and collocate, works in a particular form. For example, in subclass SB
(Plant Culture), the following array appears:

```
SB             Plant culture
                 Parks and public reservations
  481.A1A-Z       Periodicals. Societies. Serials
      .A2A-Z        Congresses
      .A4-Z         General works
```

The periodical *Parks Monthly* would be assigned the call number

```
                SB481
                .A1
                P3
```

The hierarchical structure of this call number is

```
S               Agriculture
  SB               Plant culture
    481-485          Parks and public reservations
      481.A1           Periodicals. Societies. Serials
        .P3              [Cutter number for "Plant," the first word of
                           the title main entry]
```

Note that for this work, no date is provided in the call number. This is because
the work in question is a periodical rather than a monograph. The LC practice
for the inclusion of dates in call numbers is limited to monographic works.

In another part of the same subclass the following array appears.

```
SB             Plant culture
                 Landscape gardening. Landscape architecture
  469             Periodicals. Societies. Serials
    .2              Collected works (nonserial)
    .23             Congresses
    .25             Dictionaries and encyclopedias
                    Directories
    .3              General works
                    By region or country
                      United States
    .33               General works
    .34               By region or state, A-Z
```

.35	Other regions or countries, A-Z
.37	Vocational guidance
.4	Study and teaching
	.A2A-Z, General works
	.A3-Z, By country

All general works on the study and teaching of landscape gardening would be assigned the reserve cutter number .A2 followed by a cutter number for the main entry of the book. Thus, the book *The Beginning Student's Text to Landscape Gardening*, by Jones (1973) would be assigned the call number

SB469.4
.A2
J6
1973

The hierarchical structure of this call number is

S		Agriculture
SB		Plant culture
469-476		Landscape gardening. Landscape architecture
469.4		Study and teaching
.A2		General works
J6		*[Cutter number for "Jones"]*
1973		[Date]

In this instance the classifier is directed to cutter for the main entry "A-Z" following the reserve cutter number "A2." In other instances an instruction to cutter for main entry may be unstated but the requirement to cutter for the main entry still exists providing two cutter numbers have not already been used.

Reserve cutter number ranges. In some classes a range of numbers is reserved for a specific purpose. For example, in Class SH (Aquaculture. Fisheries. Angling) the following array appears

SH	Aquaculture. Fisheries. Angling
1	Periodicals. Societies. Serials
3	Congresses
	Documents ....
	United States
11.A1-5	Federal
.A6-Z	State

The cutter number range ".A1-5" is a shelflisting device. There is no way to determine the appropriate subarrangement within ".A1-5" without referring to either the library's shelflist or searching the LC records in the *National Union Catalog*, etc. under appropriate headings to determine the arrangement used by the Library of Congress.

Successive cutter numbers. This is another technique for subarrangement that is used to designate a subject subclass, indicate the form of material, or signal further geographical subarrangement. In the schedules the use of successive cutter numbers is indicated by the use of numbers enclosed within parentheses, for example, "(1)", or as the use of a variable, for example, ".x3." It should be noted that not all numbers enclosed within parentheses in the schedules are successive cutter numbers. In Class SB (Plant Culture) the following table, utilizing successive cutter numbers, appears:

SB		Plant culture
		Documents ....
		United States
19		Federal
21		State, A-W
		Under each:
		State societies
	(1)	Reports, proceedings, transactions (Annual)
	(2)	Journal, bulletins, etc. (Weekly, monthly, quarterly)
	(3)	Committee reports
	(4)	Charters, constitutions, by-laws. By date
	(5)	Programs
	(6)	Addresses, history, etc., A-Z
		Laws. By date
		Other documents

The *Bulletin* of the Horticultural Society of New York would be assigned the call number

SB21
.N42

The hierarchical structure of this call number is

S		Agriculture
SB		Plant culture
19-29		Documents
19-21		United States
21		States, A-W
	.N4	*[Cutter number for "New York"]*
	.N42	*[Successive cutter number "2" for "Journal, bulletins, etc."]*

Successive cutter numbers are often used to provide geographic subarrangement. In Class SF (Animal Culture) the following provision for geographical subdivision is used:

SF	Animal culture
	Cats
	Shows. Showing
445	General works
.2	Juvenile works

.3	International. By place, A-Z
	National, state, and local
	By region or country
	United States
.32	General works
.33	By region or state, A-Z
	Under each state:
	x General works
	.x2 By place, A-Z

The book, *The Philadelphia cat show, 1960-1985,* compiled by Jenkins (1986) would be assigned the call number

SF445.33
.P42
P4
1986

The hierarchical structure of this call number is

S	Agriculture
SF	Animal culture
411-459	Pets
441-450	Cats
445-445.36	Shows. Showing
445.32-445.35	By region or country
445.32-445.33	United States
445.33	By region or state, A-Z
.P4	*[Cutter number for Pennsylvania from SCM:S Instruction G 302.]*
.P42	By place, A-Z *["2" is the successive cutter number]*
P4	*[Cutter number for Philadelphia]*
1986	[Date]

Date. Since 1982, the Library of Congress has added the date to all call numbers created for monographs. Prior to that year, a date was added only to call number for a monograph when it was needed to identify another edition of that work. Generally, the date used is the imprint date, although their are special situations where other dates are used. For complete instructions on the assignment of dates see the SCM:S Instruction G 140.

LIBRARY OF CONGRESS CLASSIFICATION EXERCISES

Answers to these exercises appear in Appendix E.

A.   Assign LC call numbers to each of the following titles. Indicate the hierarchy for each call number.

1. *How to catalog a rare book,* by Duncan. 1973.

2. *How to grow asparagus,* by Unwin. 1922.

3. *The conservation of museum collections,* by Sand. 1938.

4. *The folklore of holy wells and springs,* by Ash. 1956.

5. *How to train your homing pigeon,* by Walls. 1934.

6. *The first book of astronomy,* by Clark. 1985. [A book for children]

7. *The art of writing biographies,* by Queen. 1981. [A book of techniques]

8. *A manual of archeology for the amateur archaeologist,* by Biddle. 1979.

9. *The chemical analysis of rocks,* by Hruska. 1979.

10. *Photography for children,* by Lytton. 1953.

11. *Lawyers as characters in modern fiction,* by O'Rorke. 1980.

12. *Coins and coin collectors,* by Quiller. 1983.

13. *A survey of veterinary hospitals,* by Ivers. 1986.

14. *A history of 18th century astrology,* by Lewis. 1969.

15. *Vocational education for women,* by Tyrone. 1986.

16. *A dictionary of philosophy,* by Ludlow. 1976. [In English]

17. *Children's furniture building for the home craftsman,* by Twining. 1949.

B. A-Z directions. Assign LC call numbers to each of the following titles.

18. *Life on the stage: the biography of Helen Hayes* , by Loy. 1982. [The American actress born in 1900]

19. *The National League,* by Greg. 1922. [A history of the professional baseball league]

20. *Go Cubs! a history of the Chicago Cubs,* by Rogers. 1974. [The professional baseball team]

21. *School architecture in California,* by Salten. 1951.

22. *Witchcraft in Alabama,* by Shick. 1961.

23. *Cheesebox on a raft: the Union ironclad Monitor,* by Carr. 1919. [Centers on the activities of this ship during the Civil War]

24. *The Hogarth Press: the history of a great private press,* by Hull. 1966.

25. *Techniques of writing mystery and detective stories,* by Fry. 1971.

26. *A repair manual for the Buick automobile,* by Ferry. 1985.

27. *A bibliography of articles on motorcycles,* by Jansen. 1978.

28. *North American Indian embroidery,* by Llewellyn. 1947.

29. *Flowers in literature,* by Escher. 1949.

30. *How to win at the game Trivial Pursuit,* by Eastman. 1985.

31. *Modern paper manufacture in Japan,* by Ervin. 1980.

C. <u>Fixed Successive Cutter Numbers</u>. Assign LC call numbers to each of the following titles.

32. *The Newsletter of the Alpha Delta Phi.* [A general fraternity]

33. *A history of Alpha Delta Phi from 1900-1970*, by Bates. 1972.

34. *Past presidents of Delta Upsilon*, by Pry. 1981. [A general fraternity]

35. *A membership directory of Pi Kappa Alpha.* 1972. [A general fraternity]

36. *The constitution of Delta Tau Delta.* 1907. [A general fraternity]

37. *The by-laws of Beta Phi Mu.* 1965. [A library science honor society]

38. *A history of Phi Beta Kappa, 1890-1920*, by Olinger. 1923.

39. *A directory of the members of the Xi Chapter of Beta Phi Mu (University of Hawaii.)* 1984.

D. <u>Tables within the text. Double Cutter Numbers.</u> Assign LC call numbers to each of the following titles.

40. *A directory of school officials in Kentucky,* issued by the Kentucky Department of Education. 1977.

41. *A directory of school officials in Preston County, W. Va.,* issued by Preston County. 1980.

42. *An examination of the British drug scene,* by Hunter. 1971.

43. *Psychedelic drug use in Vancouver,* by Steele. 1982.

44. *A history of libraries in Brazil,* by Louis. 1955.

45. *Library statistics of Luxemburg,* by Astor. 1975.

46. *A history of libraries in the Tolna region, Hungary,* by Case. 1952.

47. *Caves in the United States,* by Edison. 1946.

48. *Arkansas caves,* by Lutz. 1981.

49. *Caves of Scotland,* by MacDonald. 1977.

50. *A handbook for publishers in France,* by La Mont. 1974.

51. *A history of publishing in Czechoslovakia,* by Zdarsky. 1984.

52. *A directory of publishers and booksellers in Turkey,* by Land. 1985.

E. <u>Tables within the text</u>. Assign LC call numbers to each of the following titles.

Use GV581+ (Sports : History).

53. *A history of sports in Texas,* by Loman. 1964.

54. *A history of sports in Baton Rouge, La.,* by Quentin. 1921.

55. *A history of sports in Ontario Province, Canada,* by Stone. 1932.

56.   *A history of sports in Mexico City, Mexico,* by Squires. 1970.

57.   *A history of sports in Bogota,* by Lares. 1968. [The city in Colombia, South America]

58.   *A history of sports in Ireland,* by O'Brien. 1949.

59.   *A history of sports in Dublin,* by McCaffrey. 1976.

F.   <u>Class H</u>. Assign LC call numbers to each of the following titles. Use HV 8157-8280.7 (Police).

60.   *The municipal police of Buenos Aires,* by Edwards. 1981.

61.   *The accountability of the English constable,* by Marshall. 1973.

62.   *The national police in Bulgaria,* by Raible. 1961.

Use HN101-940 (Social history and conditions. Social problems. Social reform).

63. *A century of social reform in India*, by Natira. 1949.

64. *A study of life in a Devonshire community*, by White. 1976.

65. *Social problems in the Arab countries: a statistical report*, by Azeno. 1983.

66. *A social history of 19th century Europe*, by Hill. 1935

67. *Power in Ica: the social structure of a Peruvian community*, by Lyle. 1966.

68. *Social mobility in Gibraltar*, by Wherry. 1981.

69. *The literature of social reform in China, 1830-1860*, compiled and translated by Ogden. 1927.

70. *Continuity and change: the social history of Spain since World War II*, by Ilian. 1978.

Use HG2701-3542.7 (Banking).

71. *A history of the Bank of England, 1640-1903*, by Andre. 1909.

72. *Banking and monetary control in South Africa*, by Koster. 1978.

73. *Annual report of the Banco de los Andes in Bogota, Colombia.*

74. *Banking in Barcelona, Spain from 1840 to 1920*, by Voltes. 1962.

G. Class P: Forty-Nine Number Author. Assign LC call numbers to each of the following titles.

75. *The writings of Mark Twain* (Samuel Langhorne Clemens). Autograph [unedited] edition. 1899.

76. *The adventures of Huckleberry Finn*, by Mark Twain. London. 1844.

77. *Le avventure di Tom Sawyer,* par Mark Twain ; traduzione di T. Orsi. 1930. [A translation into Italian]

78. *Interpretations of Adventures of Huckleberry Finn: a collection of essays,* edited by Abbott. 1938.

79. *Mark Twain's The mysterious stranger and the critics,* by Tuckey. 1968. [A criticism]

80. *Mark Twain: a profile,* by Kaplan. 1967. [A biography]

81. *Mark Twain's letters,* arranged with comment by Paine. 1917.

H. <u>Class P: Nineteen Number Author.</u> Assign LC call numbers to each of the following titles.

82. *The works of Herman Melville.* London, 1922-1924.

83. *Typee,* or *A peep at Polynesian life,* by Herman Melville. 1957.

84. *Typee,* roman traduit de L'anglois par Verdier, Paris. 1945. [A translation into French]

85. *Rebel genius, a life of Herman Melville,* by Bixby. 1970.

86. *Studies in the minor and later works of Melville,* by Hull. 1970.

87. *Melville's use of the Bible,* by Wright. 1949.

88. *Melville's Israel Potter,* by Keyssar. 1969. [A criticism]

89. *The letters of Herman Melville,* edited by Davis. 1960.

I.   Class P: Cutter Number Author. Assign LC call numbers to each of the following titles.

90. *The Faulkner reader: selections from the works of William Faulkner.* 1954.

91.   *The sound and the fury,* by William Faulkner. 1961.

92.   *Faulkner's The sound and the fury,* by Gold. 1964. [A criticism]

93.   *Requiem pour une Nonne,* by William Faulkner ; translated by Coindreau. 1957. [A translation into French.]

94.   *Four studies of Faulkner,* by Overton. 1980. [A criticism]

CHAPTER EIGHT

Library of Congress Subject Headings

Topic Outline

A. History

B. Word Forms

C. Format

D. Entry Elements

   1. Heading

   2. LC Classification Numbers

   3. Scope Notes

   4. Term Relationships

      a. "Use"

      b. "Used For" Terms

      c. "Broader" Terms

      d. "Narrower" Terms

      e. "Related" Terms

   5. Subdivisions

      a. Types

         (1) Topical

         (2) Form

         (3) Chronological

         (4) Geographical

      b. Free-Floating

         (1) Form and Topical

         (2) Persons, Corporate Bodies, Places, etc.

         (3) Pattern Headings

E. Headings Not Listed in the Controlled Vocabulary

Readings: Chan, Lois Mai. *Library of Congress Subject Headings: Principles and Application*. 2nd ed. Littleton, CO: Libraries Unlimited, 1986.

Library of Congress. Subject Cataloging Division. *Library of Congress Subject Headings*. 12th ed. Washington, DC: Library of Congress, 1989. "Introduction."

Resources: Library of Congress. Subject Cataloging Division. *Library of Congress Subject Headings*. 12th ed. Washington, DC: Library of Congress, 1989. (LCSH)

Library of Congress. Subject Cataloging Division. *Subject Cataloging Manual: Subject Headings*. 3rd ed. Washington, DC: Library of Congress, 1988. (SCM:SH)

TECHNIQUES USED IN
LIBRARY OF CONGRESS SUBJECT HEADINGS

Word Forms. Subject headings use a variety of word forms. A listing of the forms used by the Library of Congress, and some examples of each, appear below:

	Examples
Common nouns	Artillery
	Carols
Phrases	Artillery drill and tactics
	Carnival in art;
	Copper in the body
Inverted headings	Artillery, Field and mountain
	Artists, Blind
Glossed headings	Calypso (Game);
	Fire control (Gunnery)
Proper Nouns	Artistic Woodwork Strike, 1973
	Canada
	Canaan Mountain (W. Va.)

[Although there are few proper names in LCSH, they primarily serve as examples. Proper names are added by an individual library as needed in the appropriate form, i.e., AACR2R, for the entry of the name as a heading.]

Format. Subject added entries are traditionally the first added entries indicated in the tracings. The first letter of the first word of a subject heading as well as the first letter of proper nouns and proper adjectives are capitalized (see SCM:SH Instruction H 32). When multiple subject added entries are assigned to a document, they are assigned in order of decreasing importance. In many cases, the first subject heading is closely representative of the class number assigned the document (see SCM:SH Instruction H 80).

Each subject heading is preceded by an arabic numeral followed by a period and one space (see SCM:SH Instruction 30). The Library of Congress places a period after each subject heading with few exceptions. Two spaces separate the end of one subject heading from the number of another. Subject subdivisions are indicated by the placement of a dash (or two hyphens) before the subdivision.

When a subject heading is produced on the subject added entry card, it is generally typed in upper case. A variety of forms of representation of subject index terms are used in online catalogs. The following card represents a typical subject added entry catalog card

```
        SACCO-VANZETTI CASE.
KF224   Young, William, 1927-1980.
.S2           Postmortem : new evidence in the case of Sacco and Vanzetti
V68     / William Young and David E. Kaiser. — Amherst : University
1985    of Massachusetts Press, 1985.
              xiv, 186 p. : ill. ; 23 cm.

              Bibliography: p. [165]-184.
              Includes index.

              1. Sacco-Vanzetti case. 2. Trials (Murder)--
        Massachusetts--Dedham. I. Kaiser, David E., 1947-
        I. Title.
                         O
```

USE references. A direction under an unauthorized heading referring users of the subject heading list to the legal heading(s) for that concept.

>Contagious diseases
>   USE Communicable diseases

LC Classification number references. Following some subject headings and some subheadings are bracketed and italicized classification numbers derived from the Library of Congress Classification that represent an appropriate class for the material covered by that subject heading. These classification indications may be a single class number, a range of class numbers, or several class numbers, each followed by a term defining its scope. One use for these classification numbers is as a partial index to the classification scheme.

>Cardiac arrest
>   *[RC685.C173]*

>Deafness
>   *[RF290-RF310]*

Dreams
[BF1074-BF1099 (Parapsychology)]
[QP426 (Physiology)]
[RC499.D7 (Hypnosis)]

Scope notes. A scope note defines the coverage or meaning of a heading within a controlled vocabulary. Scope notes provide for consistency in the application of a subject heading for a particular concept. Consider the scope note below for "Ballistic missiles:"

Ballistic missiles
Here are entered works on high-altitude, high-speed atomic missiles which are self-propelled and guided in the first stage of flight only, after which the trajectory becomes natural and uncontrolled. Works on conventional missiles are entered under Projectiles. Works on powered and guided missiles are entered under Rockets (Ordnance) and Guided missiles.

Syndetic structure. The relationships among the terms in the subject heading list is indicated by its cross-reference or syndetic structure. Beginning with the 11th edition of LCSH, the Library of Congress changed the appearance of the syndetic structure to that of a thesaurus format. That format indicates broader, narrower, and related term relationships, as well as synonymous terms or concepts. For the subject heading "Communicable diseases" the following syndetic structure is given:

Communicable diseases
   UF Contagion and contagious diseases
       Contagious diseases
       Infectious diseases
       Microbial diseases in man
       Zymotic diseases
   BT Diseases
       Infection
       Medical microbiology
       Public health
   RT Diseases--Reporting
       Diseases--Transmission
       Epidemics
       Immunity
       Quarantine
   SA *names of communicable diseases, e.g. Q fever*
   NT Airborne infection
       Animals as carriers of disease
       Bacterial diseases
       Biological warfare
       Carrier state (Communicable diseases)
       Focal infection
       ....
       Vaccination
       Virus diseases
       Waterborne infection
       Zoonoses

For manual catalogs, references, either "see" or "see also," would be made from either the term used to one of the referenced terms, or from the referenced term to the term used. The use of these references is explained in greater detail under each type of reference. For online catalogs a variety of methods can be used to represent this reference structure to the user, including the provision of an online thesaurus and the automatic linking of some references, for example, the UF references.

"Used For" (UF) References. "Used for" references list unauthorized headings for the concept covered by the authorized term. These unauthorized terms are often synonyms or different word forms of the authorized heading. Prior to the 11th edition of LCSH "UF" references were called "see from" references and were identified in the list by the use of "x." In the example for "Communicable Diseases," documents that deal with the topics "contagion and contagious diseases" and "infectious diseases" would be represented in the catalog by the heading "Communicable diseases." In a card catalog, references would be made from the "UF" headings to the authorized subject heading.

> Contagion and contagious diseases
> see
> COMMUNICABLE DISEASES

> Infectious diseases
> see
> COMMUNICABLE DISEASES

"Broader Term" (BT) References. "Broader term" references indicate authorized headings that are broader in meaning than the heading under which they appear. Prior to the 11th edition of LCSH "BT" references were called "see also from" references and were identified in the list by "xx." For the subject heading "Communicable diseases," the headings "Diseases" and "Infections" are broader in meaning than the heading "Communicable diseases." In a card catalog, references would be made from the "BT" headings to the authorized heading.

> DISEASES   INFECTIONS
> see also   see also
> COMMUNICABLE DISEASES   COMMUNICABLE DISEASES

"Narrower Term" (NT) References. "Narrower term" references indicate authorized headings that are narrower in meaning than the heading under which they appear. Prior to the 11th edition of LCSH, "NT" references were called "see also to" references and were identified in the list by "sa." For the subject heading "Communicable diseases," the headings "Airborne infection" and "Animals as carriers of disease" are two of the headings considered more narrow in meaning than the heading "Communicable diseases." In a card catalog, references would be made from the authorized heading to the "NT" headings.

COMMUNICABLE DISEASES
       see also
AIRBORNE INFECTION
ANIMALS AS CARRIERS OF DISEASE
BACTERIAL DISEASES
BIOLOGICAL WARFARE
       etc.

When "NT" references are made, the cataloger must ensure that the references refer to headings that exist in the catalog. If an entry does not exist in the catalog, that term should be excluded from the "see also" list. The excluded terms can be added later if the library acquires documents that are assigned that subject heading.

"Related Term" (RT) References. "Related term" references provide links between terms that are related in other than a hierarchical way. "RT" references are new to the thesaurus format of LCSH. This relationship was expressed previously in LCSH through the treatment of an associated term as both a "see also to" and as a "see also from" reference. For the subject heading "Communicable diseases," the headings "Diseases--Reporting" and "Diseases--Transmission" are considered neither broader nor narrower than the heading "Communicable diseases."
        For each of the five "RT" headings under "Communicable diseases," that heading appears as a "RT" heading under the heading of each of the five terms. Thus, in a card catalog, references would be made from the "RT" heading to the authorized heading and from the authorized heading to the RT heading.

"See also" (SA) Instructions. "See also" instruction refer from a general heading to a more specific type of heading. This is different from the "NT" reference which refers from a general heading to a more specific heading. In a card catalog, a general reference can be made for these situations.

COMMUNICABLE DISEASES
       see also the names of communicable diseases, e.g., Q fever

When examples are provided for these reference, the cataloger should ensure that entries exist in the catalog for the headings given as examples.

Free-floating subdivisions. These are subdivisions that can be used, with limitations, with many subject headings to further specify the form or content of the document. LC has identified five types of free floating subdivisions: (1) form and topical subdivisions of general applicability; (2) subdivisions under classes of persons and ethnic groups; (3) subdivisions under name of individual corporate bodies, persons, and families; (4) subdivisions under place names; and (5) subdivisions controlled by pattern headings. Usually only one free-floating subdivision is added to a heading and it is generally the final element in the heading.

Form and Topical Subdivisions of General Applicability. This type of free-floating subdivision is the most frequently used. The following list identifies some of the more commonly assigned free-floating subdivisions.

–Abstracting and indexing
–Amateurs' manuals
–Automation
–Bibliography
–Biography
–Dictionaries
–Directories
–Fiction

–Handbooks, manuals, etc.
–History
–Juvenile literature
–Maintenance and repair
–Periodicals
–Popular works
--Statistics
--Study and teaching

Other more specialized form and topical free-floating subdivisions include:

–Ability testing
–Defense measures
–Foreign influences
–Lighting

–Moisture
–Psychological aspects
–Toxicology
–Transportation

A complete listing of the free-floating subdivisions is given in SCM:SH Instruction H 1095.

Other Free-Floating Subdivisions. The other types of free-floating subdivisions are similar to form and topical free-floating subdivisions in their use except that they are more limited in the situations in which they can be applied. See the following SCM:SH Instructions for specific guidance in using these specialized free-floating subdivisions:

H 1100	Subdivision under classes of persons
H 1103	Subdivision under ethnic groups
H 1105	Subdivision under names of corporate bodies
H 1110	Subdivision under name of persons
H 1140	Subdivision under names of places
H 1145.5	Subdivision under names of bodies of water, streams, etc.

SCM:SH Instructions H 1146 to H 1200 cover use of free-floating subdivisions for headings controlled by pattern headings. Pattern headings are standardized sets of topical and form divisions for certain categories of subject headings. Rather than repeat these subdivisions under all headings covered by these categories, representative or "pattern" subdivisions are developed under a few headings for each category. These subdivisions can be applied to any heading falling under the category. Some examples of pattern headings are the following:

Category	Pattern Heading
Chemicals	Copper; Insulin
Diseases	Cancer; Tuberculosis
Domestic animals	Cattle
Individual literary authors	Shakespeare, William, 1564-1616.
Industries	Construction industry
Land vehicles	Automobiles
Musical instruments	Piano
Plants and crops	Corn
Sports	Soccer
Types of educational institutions	Universities and colleges

Geographic subdivision. "May Subd Geog" is a parenthesized and italicized, statement immediately following a main heading or subdivision that indicates that further geographic subdivision is permitted. Unless this direction appears, names of geographic areas and political divisions cannot be added to a heading or subdivision.

Geographic subdivision is done indirectly. This means that the larger political jurisdiction, i.e., country, is interposed between the heading or subheading and specific place name. For example, for a book on the artisans of Paris the subject heading assigned would be

ARTISANS--FRANCE--PARIS

while a book on their political activity would be assigned the subject heading

ARTISANS--FRANCE--PARIS--POLITICAL ACTIVITY

In this latter situation, the geographical subdivision is placed before the topical subdivision because the instruction to subdivide geographically appears in the heading list after Artisans" and not after "Political activity." When the indication to subdivide geographically appears after another subdivision, that instruction takes precedence over any instruction to subdivide geographically after the main subject heading. Thus, a book on the taxation of artisans in Paris would be assigned the following subject heading:

ARTISANS--TAXATION--FRANCE--PARIS

For some countries (the United States, Canada, Great Britain, and the Soviet Union), first-level political divisions (states, provinces, constituent countries and republics, respectively) are assigned directly without the interposition of the country name. These subdivisions may be further subdivided by the names of counties, cities, and other subordinate units.

CAMPUS PARKING--OHIO--COLUMBUS
CAMPING-NOVA SCOTIA--HALIFAX
CLOTHING WORKERS--ENGLAND--LONDON
CONSTRUCTION WORKERS--UKRAINE--ODESSA

See SCM:SH Instructions H 690-1050 for additional information on the use of geographic headings and subdivisions.

Multiple Headings. The heading "Carols, Czech [Dutch, English, etc.]" is a multiple heading. This type of heading, using bracketed information and "etc.," is used to indicate that other terms can be provided for the the varying element. The example above, indicates that the adjectival form of any national name for can be used with the subject heading "Carols."

CAROLS, DANISH
CAROLS, FRENCH
CAROLS, HUNGARIAN

See SCM:SH Instruction H 1090 for further information on the use of multiple headings.

LIBRARY OF CONGRESS SUBJECT HEADINGS EXERCISES

Use 12th Edition

Answers to these exercises appear in Appendix F.

A. <u>Simple Headings</u>. Assign the most appropriate subject heading(s) for the following titles.

1. *Plea Bargaining: is it fair?*

2. *An introduction to machine-shop mathematics.*

3. *Water-borne power projection: naval policy and a nation's destiny.*

4. *Ocean drilling vessels.*

5. *What are the effects of agricultural chemicals on plants?*

6. *Windmills: the clean, free power source.*

7. *Your solar heated home.*

8. *An introduction to industrial psychology.*

9. *The story of orchestration.*

10. *The Sopwith Camel.* [A type of fighter plane]

11. *Danish Christmas hymns.*

12. *Rats and the diseases they carry.*

13. *The Battle for Guadalcanal.* [A World War Two battle]

14. *Requirements for controlled atmospheres in space.*

15. *Infant welfare.*

B. <u>Topical Subdivision Headings</u>. Assign the most appropriate subject heading(s) for the following titles.

16. *The 1956 Anglo-French intervention in Egypt.*

17. *Ride down that road again: recycling road building materials.*

18. *How to breed roses.*

19. *When did Buddha die? The controversy continues.*

20. *Gasoline pipelines.*

21. *Light filters in photography.*

22. *Crabgrass, dandelions, and other green lawn disasters: weed control in the lawns of suburbia.*

23. *Aircraft collision avoidance systems: the state of the art.*

24. *Darkroom techniques for top quality photos.*

25. *Operation Overlord: D-Day, 1944.* [Accounts of the invasion]

C. Geographical Subdivision Headings. Assign the most appropriate subject heading(s) for the following titles.

26. *The courts of Scotland.*

27. *The taxation of artists in Ireland: the laws and commentary.*

28. *The children of working parents in Minneapolis.*

29. *Crack abuse in Cleveland: the report of the 1989 survey.*

30. *Diamond smuggling in South Africa.*

31. *Labor unions in the tire industry of Akron, Ohio.*

32. *The political activities of artisans in Mexico City.*

33. *The pre-Lenten carnival in Baton Rouge, Louisiana.*

34. *Dog laws of Portland, Maine.*

35. *Bog men of England and Denmark.*

36. *A new way to get the job done in the U.S.: contracting for services.*

37. *Nineteenth century magazine illustration in Great Britain.*

38.   *A history of costume in 17th and 18th century France.*

39.   *Mandatory retirement laws in Georgia.*

40.   *Depression glass of East Liverpool, Ohio.*

41.   *The problem of family abandonment in Indiana.*

D.   <u>Form and Topical Free-Floating Subdivision Headings</u>. Assign the most appropriate subject heading(s) for the following titles.

42.   *The history of the Dewey Decimal Classification.*

43.   *Soil density in Zurich Switzerland: a bibliography.*

44.   *The effects of drugs on the newborn: a compilation of essays.*

45. *Minority employment in the states of California and New York: a comparative statistical report.*

46. *U. S. copyright law for musical works: abstracts.*

47. *A history of fox hunting in Albemarle County, Virginia.*

48. *Fire towers and fire spotters of North and South Carolina: a directory.*

49. *Physics: a basic textbook.*

50. *Macroeconomics for the layman.*

51. *Railroad accidents in late 19th century Pennsylvania.*

52. *Zeppelins: a photographic history.* [Over half of this book consists of pictures]

53. *Yearbook of industrial psychiatry.*

54. *Campsites in Tennessee: a directory.*

55. *Nursing home care and the Federal commitment*

56. *Japanese history, 1919 to 1945: a sourcebook.*

57. *House repair for the homeowner.*

E.   Pattern and Other Free-Floating Subdivision Headings. Assign the most appropriate subject heading(s) for the titles that follow.

58. *Thomas Alva Edison: a definitive biography.*

59. *The travelers' guide to Peru.*

60. *Genealogy of the Carpenter family of Massachusetts.*

61. *Control of the color fading of apples.*

62. *Edgar Allan Poe as a character in mystery novels: a review.*

63. *Camping and backpacking in the Great Lakes area.*

64. *The foreign relations of Japan and France.*

65. *The Strait of Magellan along the Chilean coast.* [A general geography text]

66. *They fell for the Union: a listing of Pennsylvanian's who died for their country in the Civil War.*

67. *Lord Peter: English dilettante or true detective?* [A character created by Dorothy L. Sayers]

68. *Tunnel vision: retinitis pigmentosa research in the United States.*

69. *Diseases of lambs in Greene County, Pennsylvania: a statistical evaluation.*

70. *Lost with the Titanic.* [A novel about the loss of the steamship Titanic in 1912]

71. *Henry Ford's contributions to the automobile industry.*

72. *The West Virginia University: pictorial views of the campus.*

73. *Women in the fiction of Ernest Hemingway.*

74. *Recruiting practices of the Central Intelligence Agency.*

F. The titles that follow are the same ones encountered previously in the
    Library of Congress classification exercise (Titles 1-31). Assign the most
    appropriate subject heading(s) for each title. You might want to compare
    the subject indication provided by the call number you had developed
    with the subject access points provided by the Library of Congress subject
    headings.

75. *How to catalog a rare book.*

76. *How to grow asparagus.*

77. *The conservation of museum collections.*

78. *The folklore of holy wells and springs in Europe.*

79. *How to train your homing pigeon.*

80. *The first book of astronomy.* [A book for children]

81. *The art of writing biographies.* [A book of techniques]

82.   *A manual of archeology for the amateur archaeologist.*

83.   *The chemical analysis of rocks.*

84.   *Photography for children.*

85.   *Lawyers as characters in modern fiction.*

86.   *Coins and coin collectors.*

87.   *A survey of veterinary hospitals.*

88.   *A history of 18th century astrology.*

89.   *Vocational education for women.*

90. *A dictionary of philosophy.* [In English]

91. *Children's furniture building for the home craftsman.*

92. *Life on the stage: the biography of Helen Hayes.* [The American actress born in 1900]

93. *The National League.* [A history of the professional baseball league]

94. *Go Cubs! a history of the Chicago Cubs.* [The professional baseball team]

95. *School architecture in California.*

96. *Witchcraft in Alabama.*

97. *Cheesebox on a raft: the Union ironclad Monitor.* [Centers on the activities of this ship during the Civil War]

98. *The Hogarth Press: the history of a great private press.*

99. *Techniques of writing mystery and detective stories.*

100. *A repair manual for the Buick automobile.*

101. *A bibliography of articles on motorcycles.*

102. *North American Indian embroidery.*

103. *Flowers in literature.*

104. *How to win at the game Trivial Pursuit.*

105. *Modern paper manufacture in Japan.*

APPENDICES:
ANSWERS TO THE EXERCISES

APPENDIX A

Answers to the
Descriptive Cataloging Exercise

1.

House design for modern living / Robert Grogan ; with
illustrations by Patty Brown. — 3rd ed. — New York : Albatross
Press, c1977.
xii, 306 p., [12] p. of plates : ill. (some col.) ; 22 cm.

ISBN 0-9876-4321-0

Area 1
  Title proper   Rule 1.1B1
                                     [The wording, order and spelling of the title
                                       proper are retained, but not the capitalization.]
  Statement of responsibility   Rule 1.1F1
                                       Rule 1.1F6
                                       [The individuals perform different functions.]

Area 2
  Edition statement   Rule 1.2B1
                                       Rule C.8A
                                       [Numbered editions are recorded as ordinal
                                       numbers in this form.]
                                       Rule B.9
                                       [Abbreviations must be used when available.]

Area 4
  Place   Rule 1.4C1
                                           [Only the 1st named place in the country of the
                                       cataloging agency is recorded.]
  Publisher   Rule 1.4D1 & Rule 1.4D2
                                         [In recording the "shortest form" possible, terms
                                       of incorporation are usually not recorded.]

Date	Rule 1.4F6
	[The date on the title page is the date of the 2nd printing. With no known date of publication, a copyright date in recorded instead. The Library of Congress does not treat a 1st printing as a known date of publication.]
Area 5	
Pagination	Rule 2.5B1 & Rule 2.5B2
	[The last numbered page of each numbered sequence is recorded. This book has 2 sequences, i-xii and 1-306.]
Plates	Rule 2.5B10
	[Because the plates are unnumbered, the number is enclosed within square brackets.]
Illustrative matter	Rule 2.5C1 & Rule 2.5C3
	["Ill. (some col.)" is recorded to account for both the colored plates and the black and white photographs.]
	Rule B.9
	[Abbreviations must be used when available.]
Dimensions	Rule 2.5D1
	[Generally, only the height of a book is recorded.]
Area 8	
Standard number	Rule 1.8B1

2.

Environmental effects of the use of asbestos / Horace Lemper, Justine McCabe ; introduction by J. Wells Sinclair ; photographs by Ann Reed & Ella Julianno. — 2nd rev. ed. — London ; New York : Osgood Pub. Co., 1969.
398 p. : ill. ; 23 cm.

Includes bibliographical references (p. [361]-388) and index.
ISBN 0-683-49361-2

○

Area 1	
Title proper	Rule 1.1B1
	[The wording, order and spelling of the title proper are retained, but not the capitalization.]
Statement of responsibility	Rule 1.1F1
	[In transcribing the statement of responsibility, the statement is recorded in the form in which it appears in the item, including ampersands, etc.]
	Rule 1.1F6
	[The individuals perform different functions].
	Rule 1.1F7
	[Qualifications, i.e., degrees, are not recorded.]

Area 2
   Edition statement

Rule 1.2B1
[Brackets are not used because the edition statement is taken from a prescribed source of information for Area 2, i.e., a preliminary -- the title page verso.]
Rule C.8A
[Numbered editions are recorded as ordinal numbers in this form.]
Rule B.9
[Abbreviations must be used when available.]

Area 4
   Place

Rule 1.4C4
[Only the first named place not in the country of the cataloging agency, and a later named place in that country, are recorded.]

   Publisher

Rule 1.4D1 & Rule 1.4D2
Rule B.9
[Abbreviations must be used when available.]

   Date

Rule 1.4F1
[The date of publication of the 2nd rev. ed. is recorded. The date on the title page corresponds with the date of reprinting.]

   Place of manufacture

Rule 1.4G1 or Rule 1.4G4
[This information is only recorded as an option only when the place of manufacture and name of the manufacturer are known. In this case, only the place of manufacture is known.]

Area 5
   Pagination

Rule 2.5B1 & Rule 2.5B2
[The last numbered page of each numbered sequence is recorded. Although both roman and arabic numerals are used, there is only one numbering sequence, i [i.e., 1] to 398.]

   Illustrative matter

Rule 2.5C1
[Tables are considered text, not illustrations.]
Rule B.9
[Abbreviations must be used when available.]

   Dimensions

Rule 2.5D1
[Height is recorded to the next whole centimeter.]

Area 7
   Contents

Rule 2.7B18
[Informal contents note using the style of the Library of Congress. Pagination of a single bibliography is enclosed within parentheses. Because the 1st page of the bibliography is unnumbered, the number is enclosed in square brackets. Generally, the pagination of an index is not recorded.]

Area 8
   Standard number

Rule 1.8B1
[A SBN is converted to an ISBN as per LC policy by the addition of an initial "0" for works published in the United States, Canada, or the United Kingdom.]

3.

> The problems of earth : readings in ecology / by Adam Smith ... [et al.]. — Bloomington, Ind. : Ecology Association Press, 1969, c1968.
> 296 p. : maps ; 24 cm. — (Series on the environmental sciences ; no. 9)
>
> Maps on lining papers.
> Includes bibliographical references.
> ISBN 0-2345-9870-1. — ISBN 0-2345-9871-2 (pbk.)
>
> ○

Area 1	
Title proper	Rule 1.1B1
	[The wording, order and spelling of the title proper are retained, but not the capitalization.]
Other title information	Rule 1.1E1
Statement of responsibility	Rule 1.1F1
	Rule 1.1F5
	[With more than 3 persons performing the same function, only the first named is recorded. The others are represented by the mark of omission and "[et al.]".]
Area 4	
Place	Rule 1.4C1
Publisher	Rule 1.4D1
Date	Rule 1.4F1
	[The date on the title page is the date of the 3rd printing. The publication date, 1969, is recorded.]
	Rule 1.4F5
	[The "optional addition" of recording the latest copyright date, if it is different from the publication date, was exercised.]
Area 5	
Pagination	Rule 2.5B1 & Rule 2.5B2
	[The last numbered page of each numbered sequence was recorded. This book has 1 numbered sequence.]
	Rule 2.5B3
	[The unnumbered preliminary pages were not recorded because they do not constitute a "substantial part" of the work.]
Illustrative matter	Rule 2.5C2
	[The illustrations are of only 1 type -- maps.]
Dimensions	Rule 2.5D1
Area 6	
Title proper of series	Rule 1.6B1
Statement of responsibility	Rule 1.6E1

relating to the series	*[The statement was not recorded because it was not necessary for the identification of the series.]*
Numbering within the series	Rule 1.6G1
	Rule B.9
	[Abbreviations must be used when available.]
	Rule C.2B1
	[Arabic numerals are substituted for roman numerals in the Series Area.]

Area 7

Physical description	Rule 2.7B10
	[All of the illustrations appear on the lining papers. See also Rule 2.5C4.]
Contents	Rule 2.7B18
	[Informal contents note using the style of the Library of Congress. LC policy does not call for recording page numbers if the work has multiple bibliographies.]

Area 8

Standard number	Rule 1.8B1
	Rule 1.8B2
	[With multiple ISBNs, the one pertaining to the item being described must be recorded. Applying the option to this rule allows for recording the other ISBN along with a qualification. When recording multiple ISBNs, LC policy calls for recording the ISBN for the item being described first.]
Qualification	Rule 1.8E2
	Rule B.9
	[Abbreviations must be used when available.]

4.

American book illustrators : a bibliography / by Karen Gale.
American binders : a bibliography / by Hugo Trees. —
Pittsburgh, Pa. : Gambit Press, c1987.
2 v. in 1 ; 28 cm. + 120 slides (col.). — (Books for collectors)

Spine title: American book illustrators and binders.
Slides in pockets.
Includes index.
ISBN 0-5678-9012-3

O

Area 1

Title proper	Rule 1.1B1
	[The wording, order and spelling of the title proper are retained, but not the capitalization.]
	Rule 1.1G2 and Rule 1.1G3
	[When an item, (1) lacks a collective title, (2) neither work predominates, and (3) the work is described as a unit, the titles are recorded in the order in which they appear on the title page.]

Statement of responsibility	Rule 1.1F1
	Rule 1.1G3
	[When an item lacks a collective title, neither work predominates, and the work is described as a unit, the statements of responsibility are recorded following the work with which they are associated.]
Area 4	
Place	Rule 1.4C1
	Rule B.9
	[Abbreviations must be used when available.]
Publisher	Rule 1.4D1 & Rule 1.4D2
Date	Rule 1.4F7
	[With no known date of publication, the copyright date is recorded instead.]
Area 5	
Pagination	Rule 2.5B19
	[This work contains 2 bibliographical works in 1 physical volume.]
Dimensions	Rule 2.5D1
Area 6	
Title proper of series	Rule 1.6B1
Area 7	
Variations in title	Rule 2.7B4
Accompanying material	Rule 2.7B11
	[Location of the accompanying material.]
Contents	Rule 2.7B18
	[Informal contents note using the style of the Library of Congress.
Area 8	
Standard number	Rule 1.8B1

5.

The official guide to post-service employment opportunities / Department of the Navy, Office of the Judge Advocate General. — [United States] : The Office, [1989]
96 p. ; 22 cm.

Cover title.
Compiled by Nelson F. Halleck.
Revision of: The reference guide to post-service employment opportunities for naval personnel.
"May 1989."
Includes bibliographical references and index.
"JAG P-19913." ○

Area 1	
Title proper	Rule 1.1B1
	[The wording, order and spelling of the title proper are retained, but not the capitalization.]

Statement of responsibility	Rule 1.1F1
	[The statement of responsibility is recorded as it appears on the title page substitute. Halleck cannot be recorded here as a statement of responsibility, even if enclosed in square brackets, because the statement does not come from a prescribed source of information for either Area 1 or 2, i.e., title page, other preliminaries, or colophon. If transcribed at all, it must be in a note.]
	Rule 1.1F3
	[In the description, the statement of responsibility is transposed to follow the title proper.]
Area 4	
Place	Rule 1.4C6
	[No place of publication is known. The country of publication is assumed with confidence.]
Publisher	Rule 1.4D1
	[Often with corporate works, statements of responsibility and statements of publication are stated only once, but serve a dual purpose.]
	Rule 1.4D4
	[Because the name of the publisher appears in a recognizable form in the title proper, it is given here in the shortest form possible.]
Date	Rule 1.4F6
	[The date on the title page is a transmittal date. These dates are most often associated with works from corporate bodies and contain the month and sometimes day of the month, in addition to the year. The Library of Congress does not consider a transmittal date as the date of publication. A transmittal date can be recorded as a probable date of publication, enclosed in square brackets. The transmittal date itself, is recorded as a quoted note.]
Area 5	
Pagination	Rule 2.5B1 & Rule 2.5B2
	[The last numbered page of each numbered sequence is recorded. This book has 1 numbered sequence.
	Rule 2.5B3
	[The unnumbered preliminary pages were not recorded because they do not constitute a "substantial part" of the work.]
Dimensions	Rule 2.5D1
Area 7	
Source of title proper	Rule 2.7B3
	[The cover was used as the chief source of information. See also rule 1.1B1.]
Statement of responsibility	Rule 2.7B6
Edition and history	Rule 2.7B7

Publication, distribution, etc. Rule 2.7B9
                                  *[The Library of Congress records a transmittal
                                  date as a quoted note.]*
Contents   Rule 2.7B18
                                  *[Informal contents note using the style of the
                                  Library of Congress.]*
Numbers   Rule 2.7B19
                                  *[This number is not a standard number, but
                                  could be useful in identifying the item.]*

6.

The right of women : our struggle for the vote / by Alice
Faberman. — 1st ed. — Philadelphia : Feminist Press, 1990.
xiii, 389 p., [1] leaf of plates : port. ; 23 cm. — (The Feminist
struggle series ; v. 7)

Reprint. Originally published: Philadelphia : Lippincott,
1911.
"Limited to 500 copies"—T.p. verso.
"A Susan Ebert/Karen Norris book."
"Copy 173"—T.p. verso.
ISBN 0-361-45927-5

Area 1
  Title proper   Rule 1.1B1
                                  *[The wording, order and spelling of the title
                                  proper are retained, but not the capitalization.]*
  Statement of responsibility   Rule 1.1F1
Area 2
  Edition statement   Rule 1.2B1
                                  Rule 1.2B1
                                  *[Brackets are not used because the edition
                                  statement is taken from a prescribed source of
                                  information for Area 2, i.e., a preliminary -- the
                                  title page verso.]*
                                  Rule C.8A
                                  *[Numbered editions are recorded as ordinal
                                  numbers in this form.]*
                                  Rule B.9
                                  [Abbreviations must be used when available.]
Area 4
  Place   Rule 1.4C1
  Publisher   Rule 1.4D1 & Rule 1.4D2
                                  *[In recording the "shortest form" possible, initial
                                  articles are usually not recorded.]*
  Date   Rule 1.4F6
                                  *[The date on the title page is the date of
                                  publication.]*

Area 5
  Pagination

Rule 2.5B1 & Rule 2.5B2
[The last numbered page of each numbered sequence is recorded. This book has 2 sequences, i-xiii and 1-389.]

  Plates

Rule 2.5B10
[The frontispiece is a plate. Because it is printed on only 1 side, it is referred to as a leaf.]

  Illustrative matter

Rule 2.5C2
[The frontispiece is the only illustration in the work. It is of one type -- a portrait.]

Rule B.9
[Abbreviations must be used when available.]

  Dimensions

Rule 2.5D1

Area 6
  Title proper of series

Rule 1.6B1

Rule 1.6B2
[Because series title on the title page differs from the series title on the series title page, the form that appeared on the 1st of the prescribed sources of information for Series Area (the series title page) was transcribed.]

Rule A.9A1
[When the first word of a series title is an article, the second word is also capitalized. See Rule A.4F -- a series title is treated like a title proper for a work with a title main entry.]

  Numbering within series

Rule 1.6G1

Rule B.9

Rule C.2B1
{Numbers represented by words are converted to numerals.]

Area 7
  Edition and history

Rule 2.7B7
[This is the style used by the Library of Congress for this note.]

Rule 1.7A3
[The order for data in a note should correspond to the ISBD order and punctuation used in the area related to those data.]
{The location of the original copy is generally not mentioned in the description.]

Rule 2.7B7
[A limited production statement is considered a form of edition statement and is generally given as a quoted note by the Library of Congress.]

Rule 1.7A3
[The source of a quoted note must be given if that source is other than the chief source of information.]

  Series

Rule 2.7B12
[It is Library of Congress policy to reject as a series, a phrase naming in-house editors or another official of the firm. This information is recorded instead, as a quoted series note.]

Copy being described	Rule 2.7B21
	[This number is unique to the library's copy.]
Area 8	
Standard number	Rule 1.8B1

7.

Wilson's history of computer processing. — 3rd ed. / revised
by B. Cameron. — New York : McGraw-Hill, 1990-
v. : ill. ; 27 cm.

Includes bibliographical references and index.
ISBN 0-513-64399-1 (v. 1)

○

Area 1
Title proper   Rule 1.1B1
                                [The wording, order and spelling of the title
                                proper are retained, but not the capitalization.]
                                Rule 1.1B2
                                [The statement of responsibility is an integral
                                part of this title proper.]
Statement of responsibility   Rule 1.1F1
                                [Generally, a person responsible for design of
                                the cover is not transcribed in the statement of
                                responsibility.]
                                Rule 1.1F13
                                [When the name associated with responsibility
                                for the item has been named in the title proper,
                                a statement of responsibility is recorded for that
                                name only if there is a separate responsibility
                                statement on the chief source of information.]
Area 2
Edition statement   Rule 1.2B1
                                Rule C.8A
                                [Numbered editions are recorded as ordinal
                                numbers in this form.]
                                Rule B.9
                                [Abbreviations must be used when available.]
Statement of responsibility ·   Rule 1.2C1
relating to the edition

                                Rule 1.1F7
                                [Qualifications are not transcribed.]
                                Rule B.4A
                                [Abbreviations in a statement of responsibility
                                are limited to those found in the prescribed
                                sources of information and the abbreviations
                                "i.e." and ""et al.". The other abbreviations in
                                Rule B.9 cannot be used.]

Area 4	
Place	Rule 1.4C1
Publisher	Rule 1.4D1 & Rule 1.4D2
Date	Rule 1.4F8
	[The date on the title page is the publication date. For multipart works not yet complete, the earliest date of publication is recorded followed by a hyphen.]
Place of manufacture and name of manufacturer	Rule 1.4G4
	[The "optional addition" of recording the place of manufacture and name of the manufacturer, when that name differs from the name of the publisher, has not been exercised.]
Area 5	
Extent of item	Rule 1.5B5
	[For multipart works not yet complete, three spaces are recorded, followed by "v.".]
Pagination	Rule 2.5B20 or Rule 2.5B21
	[The pagination of multivolume works is not recorded if the work is incomplete because the final pagination is unknown.]
Plates	Rule 2.5B10
	[Plates are not recorded for multivolume works. Rule 2.5B10 comes under the heading for "single volumes" (see p. 72 in AACR2R). The physical description rules for multivolume works begin on p. 75.]
Illustrative matter	Rule 2.5C1
	[The plates are the illustrations.]
	Rule B.9
	[Abbreviations must be used when available.]
Dimensions	Rule 2.5D1
Area 7	
Contents	Rule 2.7B18
	[Informal contents note using the style of the Library of Congress.]
Numbers	Rule 2.7B19
	[Generally, LC card order numbers are not recorded in a note.]
Area 8	
Standard number	Rule 1.8B1
Qualification	Rule 1.8B2
	[Qualifications are given if there are 2 or more standard numbers. In this case, the other volumes will have ISBNs.]

173

APPENDIX B

Answers to the
Access Points Exercise

In the answers that follow, rather than repeat the same rule each time, unless otherwise stated, entry under personal authorship involves the use of Rule 21.1A2 in addition to the rule cited in the answers, Rule 21.4A1. Similarly, title access points were derived from the instructions stated in Rule 21.30J1 while the provision of access points for series were based on the criteria stated in Rule 21.30L1.

1. *Of whales and men.*

      Main entry: Robertson, R. B.   *[Rule 21.4A1]*
      Added entries: Title.

2. *From plantation to ghetto.*

      Main entry: Meier, August.   *[Rule 21.6C1]*
      Added entries: Rudwick, Elliott.   *[Rule 21.6C1]*
                      Title.
                      Series.

3. *Carnegie Library of Pittsburgh: a brief history and description.*

      Main entry: Munn, Ralph.   *[Rule 21.4A1]*
      Added entries: Title.

4. *Isn't that just like a man! Oh, well, you know how women are.*

      Main entry: Rinehart, Mary Roberts.   *[Rule 21.7C1]*
      Added entries: Cobb, Irvin S. Oh, well, you know *[Rule 21.7C1]*
                   how women are.
                      Title.

5. *Nothing could be finer than a crisis that is minor in the morning.*

    Main entry: Osgood, Charles.   *[Rule 21.4A1]*
    Added entries: Title.

6. *Deutsch für Amerikaner.*

    Main entry: Goedsche, C. R.   *[Rule 21.6C1]*
    Added entries: Spann, Meno.   *[Rule 21.6C1]*
                    Title.

7. *Decimal classification and relativ index.*

    Main entry: Dewey, Melvil.   *[Rule 21.4A1]*
    Added entries: Title.
                    Title: Decimal classification and
                       relative index.
                    *[No access points were
                    provided for the editors
                    because they are not named
                    prominently in the work, i.e.,
                    they were named in the
                    foreword. See Rule 21.30D1.]*

8. *Slaughterhouse-five, or, the children's crusade: a duty dance with death.*

    Main entry: Vonnegut, Kurt, Jr.   *[Rule 21.4A1]*
    Added entries: Title.
                    Title: Slaughterhouse-five.
                    Title: Slaughterhouse 5.
                    Title: The children's crusade.

9. *Chaucer's major poetry.*

    Main entry: Chaucer.   *[Rule 21.4A1]*
    Added entries: Baugh, Albert C.   *[Rule 21.30D1]*
                    Title.

10. *Ronald Brunlees McKerrow: a selection of essays.*

    Main entry: McKerrow, Ronald Brunlees. *[Rule 21.4A1]*
    Added entries: Immroth, John Phillip.   *[Rule 21.30D1]*
                    Title.
                    Series.

11. *Three from the 87th.*

Main entry:	McBain, Ed.	[Rule 21.4A1]
Added entries:	Title.	
	Title: 3 from the 87th.	
	[In the interest of brevity, it was assumed that no user would expect "87th" to have been spelled-out.]	
	Title: Hail, hail, the gang's all here.	
	Title: Jigsaw.	
	Title: Fuzz.	
	[The provision of access points for the individual titles is a local library option.]	

12. *Simon and Schuster's international dictionary, English/Spanish, Spanish/English = Diccionario internacional Simon and Schuster, Inglés/Espanol, Espanol/Inglés.*

Main entry:	*[Title main entry]*	[Rule 21.7B1]
Added entries:	Gámez, Tana de.	[Rule 21.7B1]
	Title: Diccionario internacional Simon and Schuster, Inglés/ Espanol, Espanol/Inglés.	

13. *Murallas de San Juan = Forts of San Juan.*

Main entry:	*[Title main entry]*	[Rule 21.5A]
Added entries:	Title: Forts of San Juan.	

14. *The wild boy of Burundi: a study of an outcast child.*

Main entry:	Lane, Harlan.	[Rule 21.6C1]
Added entries:	Pillard, Richard.	[Rule 21.6C1]
	Title.	
	[Generally, no access point would be provided for the author of a foreword.]	

15. *Birds of North America: a guide to field identification.*

Main entry:	Robbins, Chandler S.	[Rules 21.6C1 & 21.11A1]
Added entries:	Bruun, Bertel.	[Rule 21.6C1]
	Zim, Herbert S.	[Rule 21.6C1]
	Singer, Arthur.	[Rules 21.11A1 & 21.30K2]
	[The illustrations were considered an important feature of this work.]	
	Title.	
	Series.	

16. *Gray lady down: original title, Event 1000: a novel.*

    Main entry: Lavallee, David.   *[Rule 21.4A1]*
    Added entries: Title.
                    Title: Event 1000.
                    Title: Event one thousand.
                    [The provision of these 2 access
                    points is a local library option.]

17. *1066 and all that: a memorable history of England.*

    Main entry: Sellar, Walter Carruthers.   *[Rules 21.6C1 & 21.11A1]*
    Added entries: Yeatman, Robert Julian.   *[Rule 21.6C1]*
                    Title.
                    [For a single year written in
                    arabic numerals, LC policy calls
                    for no additional added entry
                    for the date in spelled-out form.
                    No access point was provided
                    for the illustrator. The illustrations
                    were not considered an important
                    feature of this work. See Rule
                    21.30K2.]

18. *Lake Wobegon days.*

    Main entry: Keillor, Garrison.   *[Rule 21.4A1]*
    Added entries: Title.

19. *Pictorial treasury of U.S. stamps.*

    Main entry: *[Title main entry]*   *[Rules 21.1B3 & 21.7B1]*
    Added entries: Marzulla, Elena.   *[Rule 21.30D1]*
                    Collectors Institute.   *[Rule 21.30E1]*
                    Series.

20. *The American scene: a reader.*

    Main entry: Mencken, H. L.   *[Rule 21.4A1]*
    Added entries: Cairns, Huntington.   *[Rule 21.30D1]*
                    Title.

21. *Digging up the past.*

    Main entry: Woolley, Leonard.   *[Rule 21.4A1]*
    Added entries: Title.
                    [Usually no access point would
                    be provided for this series -- it is
                    format related.]

22. *"And I was there.": Pearl Harbor and Midway--breaking the secrets.*

    Main entry: Layton, Edwin T.   *[Rule 21.6B1]*
    Added entries: Pineau, Roger.   *[Rule 21.6B1]*
                   Costello, John.   *[Rule 21.6B1]*
                   Title.

23. *Famous speeches of the eight Chicago anarchists.*

    Main entry: *[Title main entry]*   *[Rule 21.7B1]*
    Added entries: Parsons, Lucy.   *[Rule 21.7B1]*
                   Spies, August.   *[Rule 21.7B1]*
                   Title: Speeches of the eight
                       Chicago anarchists.
                   Series.
                   [In the interest of brevity, it was
                   assumed that no user would expect
                   "eight" to have been in numerals.]

24. *Outdoor education.*

    Main entry: *[Title main entry]*   *[Rule 21.6C2]*
    Added entries: Smith, Julian W.   *[Rule 21.6C2]*

25. *Irving Wallace: a writer's profile.*

    Main entry: Leverence, John.   *[Rule 21.4A1]*
    Added entries: Title.
                   Series.
                   [The contributions of
                   Weidman, Grogg and Browne
                   were not considered significant
                   enough to warrant the provision
                   of access points for them.]

26. *From Anne to Victoria.*

    Main entry: *[Title main entry]*   *[Rule 21.7B1]*
    Added entries: Dobrée, Bonamy.   *[Rule 21.7B1]*

27. *The diary of Samuel Sewall.*

    Main entry: Sewall, Samuel.   *[Rule 21.12A1]*
    Added entries: Wish, Harvey.   *[Rule 21.12A1]*
                   Title.

28. *Cobb's spelling book: being a just standard for pronouncing the English language* . . .

Main entry:	Cobb, Lyman.	[Rule 21.4A1]
Added entries:	Walker, J.	[Rule 21.30F1]
	Title.	
	Title: Spelling book.	

29. *Solitaire & Double solitaire.*

Main entry:	Anderson, Robert.	[Rule 21.4A1]
Added entries:	Title.	
	Title: Solitaire.	
	Title: Double solitaire.	

30. *An introduction to historical bibliography.*

Main entry:	Binns, Norman E.	[Rule 21.4A1]
Added entries:	Title.	

31. *Two thousand years of science: the wonders of nature and their discoverers.*

Main entry:	Harvey-Gibson, R. J.	[Rule 21.12A1]
Added entries:	Titherley, A. W.	[Rule 21.12A1]
	Title.	
	Title: 2000 years of science.	

32. *Spas, hot tubs & home saunas.*

Main entry:	[Title main entry]	[Rule 21.5A]
Added entries:	Watson, Susan.	[Rule 21.30C1]
	Spring, Paul.	[Rule 21.30C1]
	Sunset Books.	[Rule 21.30E1]

33. *The happy critic and other essays.*

Main entry:	Van Doren, Mark.	[Rule 21.4A1]
Added entries:	Title.	

34. *Brian Friel.*

Main entry:	Maxwell, D. E. S.	[Rule 21.4A1]
Added entries:	Title.	
	Series.	

35. *Strictly speaking: will America be the death of English?*

      Main entry: Newman, Edwin.   *[Rule 21.4A1]*
      Added entries: Title.

36. *The 13th valley: a novel.*

      Main entry: Del Vecchio, John M.   *[Rule 21.4A1]*
      Added entries: Title.
                      Title: The thirteenth valley.

37. *Proceedings: Southern Soybean Disease Workers ninth annual meeting . . .*

      Main entry: *[Title main entry]*   *[Rules 21.1B3 & 21.1C1c]*
      Added entries: Southern Soybean Disease   *[Rule 21.30E1]*
                      Workers.

38. *Kennedy and Roosevelt: the uneasy alliance.*

      Main entry: Beschloss, Michael R.   *[Rule 21.4A1]*
      Added entries: Title.
                      [Generally, no access point would be provided for the writer of a foreword.]

39. *Printed books, 1481-1900, in the Horticultural Society of New York: a listing.*

      Main entry: Horticultural Society of New York.   *[Rules 21.1B2a & 21.4B1]*
      Added entries: Hall, Elizabeth Cornelia.   *[Rule 21.30C1]*
                      Title.
                      [For a span of years written in arabic numerals, LC policy calls for no additional added entry for the dates in spelled-out form.]

40. *Secrecy and power: the life of J. Edgar Hoover.*

      Main entry: Powers, Richard Gid.   *[Rule 21.4A1]*
      Added entries: Title.

41. *Raising laboratory animals: a handbook for biological and behavioral research.*

Main entry:	Silvan, James.	*[Rules 21.1B3 & 21.4A1]*
Added entries:	American Museum of Natural History.	*[Rule 21.30E1]*
	Title.	

42. *Rare, vanishing & lost British birds.*

Main entry:	Hudson, W. H.	*[Rule 21.12A1]*
Added entries:	Gardiner, Linda.	*[Rule 21.12A1]*
	Gronvold, H.	*[Rule 21.30K2]*
	[The illustrations were considered an important feature of this work.]	
	Title: Rare, vanishing and lost British birds	

43. *Shipwrecks in Puerto Rico's history.*

Main entry:	Cardona Bonet, Walter A.	*[Rule 21.4A1]*
Added entries:	Title.	

44. *Perjury: the Hiss-Chambers case.*

Main entry:	Weinstein, Allen.	*[Rule 21.4A1]*
Added entries:	Title.	

45. *The printed word: professional word processing with Microsoft Word on the Apple Macintosh.*

Main entry:	Kater, David A.	*[Rule 21.6C1]*
Added entries:	Kater, Richard L.	*[Rule 21.6C1]*
	Title.	

46. *Tunnel war.*

Main entry:	Poyer, Joe.	*[Rule 21.4A1]*
Added entries:	Title.	

47. *Down the rabbit hole: adventures & misadventures in the realm of children's literature.*

Main entry:	Lanes, Selma G.	*[Rule 21.4A1]*
Added entries:	Title.	

48. *Five hundred years of printing.*

    Main entry: Steinberg, S. H.   *[Rule 21.4A1]*
    Added entries: Title.
                    Title: 500 years of printing.
                    *[Generally, no access point
                    would be provided for the writer
                    of a foreword. Similarly, no
                    access point would be provided
                    for this series -- it is format
                    related.]*

49. *Petticoat rule.*

    Main entry: Orczy, Baroness.   *[Rule 21.4A1]*
    Added entries: Title.

50. *Golden mists.*

    Main entry: Author of Poppet.   *[Rule 21.5C]*
                    *[Assumes the identity of this
                    person is unknown]*
    Added entries: Title.
                    Series.

51. *A history of book publishing in the United States.*

    Main entry: Tebbel, John.   *[Rule 21.4A1]*
    Added entries: Title.
                    Title: The creation of an industry,
                      1630-1865.
                    Title: The expansion of an industry,
                      1865-1919.
                    Title: The golden age between two
                      wars, 1920-1940.
                    Title: The great change, 1940-1980.
                    *[The provision of access points
                    for the titles of the individual
                    volumes is a local library
                    option.]*

52. *Whose broad stripes and bright stars: the trivial pursuit of the
Presidency, 1988.*

    Main entry: Germond, Jack W.   *[Rule 21.6C1]*
    Added entries: Witcover, Jules.   *[Rule 21.6C1]*
                    Title.

53. *Technical services: a syllabus for training leading to certification of library assistants.*

Main entry: [Title main entry]   [Rules 21.1B3 & 21.1C1c]
Added entries: Pennsylvania State Library.   [Rule 21.30E1]
                Bureau of Library Development.

54. *Daniel Deronda.*

Main entry: Eliot, George.   [Rule 21.4A1]
Added entries: Handley, Graham.   [Rule 21.30D1]
                Title.
                Series.
                [Usually no access point would be provided for the second series -- it is format related.]

55. *Certainly, Carrie, cut the cake: poems A-Z.*

Main entry: Moore, Margaret.   [Rules 21.24A1 & 21.6C1]
Added entries: Moore, John Travers.   [Rule 21.6C1]
                Anderson, Laurie.   [Rule 21.24A1]
                Title.

56. *The Doonesbury chronicles.*

Main entry: Trudeau, G. B.   [Rule 21.4A1]
Added entries: Title.
                [Generally, no access point would be provided for the writer of an introduction.]

57. *Trees, shrubs and vines: a pictorial guide to the ornamental woody plants of the Northern United States exclusive of conifers.*

Main entry: Viertel, Arthur T.   [Rule 21.4A1]
Added entries: Title.

58. *Compressible flow manual: a handbook for the design of compressible flow piping systems and a complete source of gas properties.*

Main entry: Coulter, Bailey M., Jr.   [Rule 21.4A1]
Added entries: Title.

59. *Library of Congress rule interpretations.*

Main entry: [Title main entry]   [Rules 21.1B3 & 21.1C1c]
[The Library of Congress does not consider this to be an administrative work although one can see how others might, and thus make the Library of Congress the main entry.]

Added entries: Library of Congress. Office for   [Rule 21.30E1]
Descriptive Cataloging Policy.
[No access point would be provided for the editor because he is not named prominently in the work, i.e., he was named in the preface. See Rule 21.30D1.]

60. *Lucy: the beginnings of humankind.*

Main entry: Johanson, Donald C.   [Rule 21.6C1]
Added entries: Edey, Maitland A.   [Rule 21.6C1]
Title.

61. *The makers of Florence: Dante, Giotto, Savonarola, and their city.*

Main entry: Oliphant, Mrs.   [Rule 21.11A1]
Added entries: Title.
[No access point would be provided for the illustrator because the illustrations were not considered an important feature of this work. See Rule 21.30K2.]

62. *Was this Camelot?: excavations at Cadbury Castle, 1966-1970.*

Main entry: Alcock, Leslie.   [Rule 21.4A1]
Added entries: Camelot Research Committee.   [Rule 21.30E1]
Title.
Series.

63. *The complete works of O. Henry.*

Main entry: Henry, O.   [Rule 21.4A1]
Added entries: Title.

64. *The organic chemistry of palladium.*

    Main entry: Maitlis, Peter M.   *[Rule 21.4A1]*
    Added entries: Title.
                     Title: Metal complexes.
                     Title: Catalytic reactions.
                     [The provision of access points for the titles of the individual volumes is a local library option.]
                     Series.

65. *West's New York digest, 4th.*

    Main entry: *[Title main entry]*   *[Rule 21.34C]*
    Added entries: West Publishing Company.   *[Rule 21.34C]*
                     [It was assumed that no user would expect "4th" to have been spelled-out.]
                     Title: New York digest, 4th.

66. *The best of Henny Youngman: three volumes in one.*

    Main entry: Youngman, Henny.   *[Rule 21.4A1]*
    Added entries: Title.
                     Title: How do you like me so far?
                     Title: 400 traveling salesmen's jokes.
                     Title: Four hundred traveling salesmen's jokes.
                     Title: Henny Youngman's bar bets, bar jokes, bar tricks.
                     Title: Bar bets, bar jokes, bar tricks.
                     [The provision of access points for the individual titles is a local library option. No access point would be provided for the illustrator because the illustrations were not considered an important feature of this work. See Rule 21.30K2.]

67. *Strong poison.*

    Main entry: Sayers, Dorothy L.   *[Rule 21.4A1]*
    Added entries: Title.

68. *Burning down the house: MOVE and the tragedy of Philadelphia.*

    Main entry: Anderson, John.   *[Rule 21.6C1]*
    Added entries: Hevenor, Hilary.   *[Rule 21.6C1]*
                     Title.

69. *Why Wisconsin.*

    Main entry: Bowman, Francis Favill.   *[Rule 21.4A1]*
    Added entries: Title.

70. *Pittsburgh: the story of an American city.*

    Main entry: Lorant, Stefan.   *[Rule 21.6B1]*
    Added entries: Title.
                   [No access point would be provided for the 1st named contributor (Comanger) because there are more than two other contributors. See the Animal motivation example under Rule 21.6B1.]

71. *The secret life of Walter Kitty.*

    Main entry: Goodman, Joan Elizabeth.   *[Rule 21.4A1]*
    Added entries: Title.
                 Series.
                 [A series access point would be provided because this series is limited to a special audience -- children.]

72. *Greek art.*

    Main entry: Boardman, John.   *[Rule 21.4A1]*
    Added entries: Title.
                 Series.

73. *Riding the Iron Rooster: by train through China.*

    Main entry: Theroux, Paul.   *[Rule 21.4A1]*
    Added entries: Title.

74. *Gods' man: a novel in woodcuts.*

    Main entry: Ward, Lynd.   *[Rule 21.4A1]*
    Added entries: Title.

75. *Men of Dunwich: the story of a vanished town.*

    Main entry: Parker, Rowland.   *[Rule 21.4A1]*
    Added entries: Title.

76. *Reader's Digest complete do-it-yourself manual.*

    Main entry: [Title main entry]   *[Rules 21.1B3 & 21.1C1c]*
    Added entries: Reader's Digest Association.   *[Rule 21.30E1]*
                  Title: Complete do-it-yourself
                  manual.

77. *Records management: controlling business information.*

    Main entry: Place, Irene.   *[Rule 21.6C1]*
    Added entries: Hyslop, David J.   *[Rule 21.6C1]*
                  Title.

78. *Victorian bookbindings: a pictorial survey.*

    Main entry: Allen, Sue.   *[Rule 21.4A1]*
    Added entries: Title.
                  [Usually no access point would
                  be provided for this series -- it is
                  format related.]

79. *Ladies and gentlemen, Easy Aces.*

    Main entry: Ace, Goodman.   *[Rule 21.4A1]*
    Added entries: Title.

80. *Doors and windows.*

    Main entry: [Title main entry]   *[Rules 21.1B3 & 21.5A]*
    Added entries: Time-Life Books.   *[Rule 21.30E1]*
                  Series.

81. *Accounting for costs of capacity.*

    Main entry: National Association of   *[Rules 21.1B2c & 21.4B1]*
                  Accountants.
                  [Assumes that this is a
                  statement of policy.]
    Added entries: Title.
                  Series: National Association of
                  Accountants. Research report ;
                  no. 39.
                  [This is a name-title series entry
                  because it falls under the
                  provisions of Rule 21.1B2c
                  assuming that all of the Research
                  reports are statements of policy.
                  The series number was recorded
                  if the option to Rule 21.30L1 was
                  exercised.]

82. *The perils of prosperity, 1914-32.*

Main entry: Leuchtenburg, William E.   *[Rule 21.4A1]*
Added entries: Title.
[For a span of years written in arabic numerals, LC policy calls for no additional added entry for the dates in spelled-out form.]
Series.

83. *Fort Sumter National Monument, South Carolina.*

Main entry: Barnes, Frank.   *[Rules 21.1B3 & 21.4A1]*
Added entries: National Park Service.   *[Rule 21.30E1]*
Title.
Series.

84. *The creation of an industry, 1630-1865.*

Main entry: Tebbel, John.   *[Rule 21.4A1]*
Added entries: Title.
[For a span of years written in arabic numerals, LC policy calls for no additional added entry for the dates in spelled-out form.]
Series: Tebbel, John. A history of book publishing in the United States ; v.1.
[This is a name-title series entry because the personal author is responsible for all the works in the series. See Card 51.]

85. *The quintessence of Irving Langmuir.*

Main entry: Rosenfeld, Albert.   *[Rule 21.4A1]*
Added entries: Title.
Series.
Series: The Commonwealth and international library. Selected readings in physics.
[When two series are traced, the second series is stated explicitly.]

86. *What Mrs. McGillicuddy saw!*

Main entry: Christie, Agatha.   *[Rule 21.4A1]*
Added entries: Title.
[Usually no access point would be provided for this series.]

87. *The education of Henry Adams.*

     Main entry: Adams, Henry.   *[Rule 21.4A1]*
     Added entries: Samuels, Ernest.   *[Rule 21.30D1]*
                    Samuels, Jane N.   *[Rule 21.30D1]*
                    Title.
                    [Usually no access point would be provided for this series.]

88. *The name of the rose.*

     Main entry: Eco, Umberto.   *[Rules 21.4A1 & 21.14A]*
     Added entries: Title.
                    [No access point would be provided for the translator. See Rule 21.30K1. Generally, no access point would be provided for the Italian title.]

89. *Defense Intelligence Agency organization, mission and key personnel.*

     Main entry: Defense Intelligence Agency.   *[Rules 21.1B2a & 21.4B1]*
     Added entries: Title.
                    [The Directorate for Human Resources is part of the Defense Intelligence Agency.]

90. *What you should know about selling and salesmanship.*

     Main entry: Burstein, Milton B.   *[Rule 21.4A1]*
     Added entries: Title.
                    Title: Selling and salesmanship.
                    Series.

91. *Great men of American popular song.*

     Main entry: Ewen, David.   *[Rule 21.4A1]*
     Added entries: Title.

92. *Classification. Class KJ-KKZ, law of Europe.*

     Main entry: Library of Congress. Processing   *[Rules 21.1B2a & 21.4B1]*
                    Services. Subject Cataloging Division.
     Added entries: Title.
                    Title: Law of Europe.
                    [No access point would be provided for Goldberg because she was not named prominently in the work. See Rule 21.30D1.]

93. *A journal of the plague year: being observations or memorials . . .*

Main entry:	Defoe, Daniel.	*[Rule 21.4A1]*
Added entries:	Title.	
	Series: Defoe, Daniel. The Shakespeare Head edition of the novels & selected writings of Daniel Defoe.	
	[This is a name-title series entry because the personal author is responsible for all the works in the series.]	

94. *Quotations from Chairman Mao Tse-Tung.*

Main entry:	Tse-Tung, Mao.	*[Rule 21.4A1]*
Added entries:	Title.	

95. *Report to Topmakers III.*

Main entry:	*[Title main entry]*	*[Rule 21.6C2]*
Added entries:	Eley, J. R.	*[Rule 21.6C2]*
	Commonwealth Scientific and Industrial Research Organization.	
	Title: Report to Topmakers 3.	
	Title: Report to Topmakers three.	
	Series.	

96. *Origins of modern art, 1905-1914.*

Main entry:	Galloway, John.	*[Rule 21.4A1]*
Added entries:	Title.	
	[For a span of years written in arabic numerals, LC policy calls for no additional added entry for the dates in spelled-out form.]	
	Series.	

97. *Death of a schoolboy.*

Main entry:	Koning, Hans.	*[Rule 21.4A1]*
Added entries:	Title.	

98. *A fistful of fig newtons.*

Main entry:	Shepherd, Jean.	*[Rule 21.4A1]*
Added entries:	Title.	

99. *Alexander and the terrible, horrible, no good, very bad day.*

Main entry:	Viorst, Judith.	*[Rule 21.24A]*
Added entries:	Cruz, Ray.	*[Rule 21.24A]*
	Title.	

100. *Rumpole and the age of miracles.*

Main entry:	Mortimer, John.	*[Rule 21.4A1]*
Added entries:	Title.	
	[No access points were provided for the titles in the contents note -- they are short stories.]	

101. *Shakespeare: lectures on five plays.*

Main entry:	*[Title main entry]*	*[Rule 21.7B1]*
Added entries:	Sochatoff, A. Fred.	*[Rule 21.7B1]*
	Series.	
	[No access points were provided for the titles in the contents note -- they are essays.]	

102. *A descriptive finding list of unstamped British periodicals, 1830-1836.*

Main entry:	Wiener, Joel H.	*[Rules 21.1B3 & 21.4A1]*
Added entries:	Bibliographical Society	*[Rule 21.30E1]*
	[The provision of an access point for the Society would depend upon its responsibility to, or association with, the work.]	
	Title.	

103. *Useful information for newly commissioned officers.*

Main entry:	Galanides, Antonio M.	*[Rules 21.1B3 & 21.12B1]*
Added entries:	Naval Education and Training Program Development Center.	*[Rule 21.30E1]*
	Title.	

104. *Elvis is dead and I don't feel so good myself.*

| Main entry: | Grizzard, Lewis. | *[Rule 21.4A1]* |
| Added entries: | Title. | |

105. *Edgar-Hilaire-Germain Degas.*

Main entry:	Rich, Daniel Catton.	*[Rule 21.17B1]*
Added entries:	Degas, Edgar-Hilaire-Germain.	*[Rule 21.17B1]*
	Title.	
	Series.	

106. *Andrew Carnegie.*

Main entry:	Wall, Joseph Frazier.	*[Rule 21.4A1]*
Added entries:	Title.	

APPENDIX C

Answers to the
Access Points and Forms of Headings Exercise

In the answers that follow, rather than repeat the same rule each time, unless otherwise stated, title access points were derived from the instructions stated in Rule 21.30J1. Similarly, decisions on the provision of an access point for series were based on the criteria stated in Rule 21.30L1.

1. *World climate*, by John S. Herrold and Ruth Fairchild-Carruthers. [Originally published as: *Our Changing Climate*]

Main entry:	Herrold, John S.	*[Rules 21.6C1 & 22.1A]*
Added entries:	Fairchild-Carruthers, Ruth.	*[Rules 21.6C1 & 22.5C3]*
	Title.	
	Title: Our changing climate.	
	[The provision of this access point is a local library option.]	
References:	x Carruthers, Ruth Fairchild-	

2. *Pamela in London & Pamela abroad*, by S. N. Rogers. [Two separate novels; author's forenames are Sidney Norris, although he usually writes under his surname using the initials S.N. rather than his forenames]

Main entry:	Rogers, S. N. (Sidney Norris)	*[Rules 21.4A1 & 22.18A]*
Added entries:	Title.	
	Title: Pamela in London.	
	Title:: Pamela abroad.	
	[These multiple title access points follow LC policy for this situation.]	
References:	x Rogers, Sidney Norris	

3. *A bibliography on weather*, compiled by Roberta Jackson-Hunt. [A work in the Science bibliography series]

Main entry:	Jackson-Hunt, Roberta.	*[Rules 21.4A1 & 22.5C3]*
Added entries:	Title.	
	Series	
References:	x Hunt, Roberta Jackson	

4. *The weatherman! a book of cartoons,* drawn by E. Jay Stone with *An introduction to pictorial humor,* by Amanda Corselli. [Both titles are on the same title page]

Main entry:	Stone. E. Jay.	*[Rules 21.7C1, 21.4A1, & 22.1A]*
Added entires:	Corselli, Amanda. An introduction to pictorial humor. Title.	*[Rules 21.7C1, 21.4A1, & 22.1A]*
References:	*[No references are needed],*	

5. *Fifty years of impression,* by Robert Moser. [A catalog of a loan exhibition held in the Museum of Art, Fairfield, Conn., June, 1978]

Main entry:	Moser, Robert.	*[Rules 21.1B3, 21.4A1, & 22.1A]*
Added entires:	Museum of Art (Fairfield, Conn.) *The main entry for this work is not this corporate body because the work is not a catalog of the resources of the body but rather a loan collection.]* Title.	*[Rules 21.30E1 & 24.4C4]*
References:	x Fairfield, Conn. Museum of Art.	

6. *Membership directory of the American Bar Association.* [Also referred to as the ABA within the text]

Main entry:	American Bar Association.	*[Rules 21.1B2a, 21.4B1, & 24.1A]*
Added entires:	Title.	
References:	x A.B.A.	
	x ABA.	

7. *Charts of the past,* by Louis Brogan, Henrietta Larose, Joseph Ricardo and Florence W. Eames. [Part of the Paperback classics series]

Main entry:	*[Title main entry]*	*[Rule 21.6C2]*
Added entires:	Brogan, Louis. *[No access point would be provided for the series because it is based on physical characteristics.]*	*[Rules 21.6C2 & 22.1A]*
References:	*[No references are needed]*	

8. *Personnel handbook for the Cleveland Museum of Art,* compiled by Melissa Cranshaw.

Main entry:	Cleveland Museum of Art.	*[Rules 21.1B2a, 21.4B1, & 24.1A]*

Added entires: Cranshaw, Melissa.   *[Rules 21.30D1 & 22.1A]*
                   Title.
References: x Cleveland, Ohio. Museum of Art.

9.   *Petroleum, energy, and the state of mankind,* the Fifth Annual Conference on Energy held in Philadelphia, Pa., January 5-7, 1979. Edited by Thomas Fitzhugh.

     Main entry: Conference on Energy   *[Rules 21.1B2d, 21.4B1,*
                      (5th : 1979 : Philadelphia, Pa.)   *24.7A1, & 24.7B2-B4]*
     Added entires: Fitzhugh, Thómas.   *[Rules 21.30D1 & 22.1A]*
                      Title.
     References: *[No references are needed]*

10.   *Mission to the stars,* by Veronica Estelle. [The name is the pseudonym of the 20th century author Emma Davis, born in 1918. Assume the library also has books in the collection written by the author under her real name]

     Main entry: Estelle, Veronica, 1918-   *[Rules 21.4A1, 22.2B1, &*
                                               22.17A]

     Added entries: Title
     References: xx Davis, Emma, 1918-

11.   *Standards for air quality,* by the Air Quality Committee of the American Antipollution Society. [The Committee does not take a position on air quality standards but rather reports on existing standards.]

     Main entry: *[Title main entry]*   *[Rules 21.1B3 & 21.1C1c]*
     Added entires: American Antipollution Society.   *[Rules 21.30E1, &*
                      Air Quality Committee.   *24.14A]*
     References: x Air Quality Committee (American
                         Antipollution Society)

12.   *Tragic hero: a novel,* by Peter Van Huven. Translated by Derek Smythe. [The author is Dutch. This is the only translation of the work into English]

     Main entry: Huven, Peter van.   *[Rules 21.4A1 & 22.5D1]*
     Added entries: Title.
                     [No access point would be
                     provided for the translator. See
                     Rule 21.30K1.]
     References: x Van Huven, Peter.

13. *Report on enrollment*, by the Curriculum Committee of the Graduate School of Business Administration, University of Western Idaho. [The Committee makes policy recommendations]

Main entry:	University of Western Idaho. Graduate School of Business Administration. Curriculum Committee.	*[Rules 21.1B2c, 21.4B1, & 24.14A]*
Added entires:	Title.	
References:	*[No references are needed]*	

14. *The Anarchist Party program in Ohio*, by the Ohio Section of the Anarchist Party. [A statement of Party policy]

Main entry:	Anarchist Party (Ohio)	*[Rules 21.1B2c, 21.4B1, & 24.4C2]*
Added entires:	Title.	
References:	*[No references are needed]*	

15. *Readings in ethics*, compiled by Louise Allenby and Kelly Bryant. Second Revised Edition by R. K. Smith. [R.K. Smith most frequently writes using his forename Robert]

Main entry:	*[Title main entry]*	*[Rule 21.7B1]*
Added entires:	Allenby, Louise.	*[Rules 21.12A1, 21.7B1, & 22.1A]*
	Bryant, Kelly.	*[Rules 21.7B1 & 22.1A]*
	Smith, Robert K.	*[Rules 21.12A1 & 22.1A]*
References:	x Smith, R. K. (Robert K.)	

16. *Three costume plays*, introduced and annotated by C. W. Guthrie. [Contents: Tintagel / A.J. Wilson — Summer in Cornwall / Tom Job — The Welsh highlands / W. Llewellyn]

Main entry:	*[Main entry under collective title]*	*[Rule 21.7B1]*
Added entires:	Guthrie, C. W.	*[Rules 21.7B1 & 22.1A]*
	Wilson, A. J. Tintagel.	*[Rules 21.30M1 & 22.1A]*
	Job, Tom. Summer in Cornwall.	*[Rules 21.30M1 & 22.1A]*
	Llewellyn, W. The Welsh highlands.	*[Rules 21.30M1 & 22.1A]*
References:	*[No references are needed]*	

17. *The message of President Theodore Roosevelt to the Congress, September 8, 1904.* [Dates in office, 1901-1909; dates of birth and death, 1858-1919]

Main entry:	United States. President (1901-1909 : Roosevelt)	*[Rules 21.4D1 & 24.20B1]*

Added entires: Roosevelt, Theodore, 1858-1919.   *[Rules 21.4D1, 22.1A, & 22.17A]*

    Title.
References: *[No references are needed]*

18.   *Annual Report of H. K. Lewisohn Company, Incorporated.*

    Main entry: H. K. Lewisohn Company.   *[Rules 21.1B2a, 21.4B1, 24.1A, & 24.5C1]*

    Added entires: Title.
    References: x Lewisohn (H. K.) Company.
                   x Lewisohn Company.

19.   *A country adventure — a play,* by Enid McFall. [A rewriting of the novel Weir of Hermiston by Robert Louis Stevenson]

    Main entry: McFall, Enid.   *[Rules 21.10A & 22.1A]*
    Added entires: Stevenson, Robert Louis. Weir   *[Rules 21.10A& 22.1A]*
                       of Hermiston.
                   Title.
    References: *[No references are needed]*

20.   *The complete poetry of Marianne M. Moore,* with an introduction by Simon Suggs. [Born in 1924 and died in 1957]

    Main entry: Moore, Marianne M., 1924-1957.   *[Rules 21.4A1, 22.1A, & 22.17A]*

    Added entires: Title.
                   *[Generally no access point
                   would be provided for the writer
                   of an introduction.]*
    References: *[No references are needed]*

21.   *The birds,* by Aristophanes. Translated into English by Robert Minton Blake. [This is the most recent of many translations of this work]

    Main entry: Aristophanes.   *[Rules 21.14A & 22.8A1]*
    Added entires: Blake, Robert Minton.   *[Rules 21.14A , 21.30K1, & 22.1A]*

                   Title.
    References: *[No references are needed]*

22.   *The autobiography of Frodo,* as reported by Chela Ormond. Illustrated by Mary Ellen Chamberlain. [Frodo is a character in *The Lord of the Rings,* by J.R.R. Tolkien]

    Main entry: Ormond, Chela.   *[Rules 21.28B1, 21.11A1, 21.4A1, & 22.1A]*

197

Added entires: Chamberlain, Mary Ellen.   *[Rules 22.11A1, 21.30K2, & 22.1A]*

Title.

Tolkien, J. R. R. The Lord of the   *[Rules 21.28B1 & 22.1A]*
Rings.

References: *[No references are needed]*

23.   *Narcotics and the U. S. government,* prepared by the U. S. Bureau of Customs. [The Bureau of Customs is a part of the Department of the Treasury]

Main entry: *[Title main entry]*   *[Rules 21.1B3 & 21.1C1c]*
Added entries: United States. Bureau   *[Rules 21.1B3, 21.30E1,*
         of Customs.   *24.18A Type 2 & 24.19A]*
References: x   United States. Department of
         the Treasury. Bureau of Customs.

APPENDIX D

Answers to the
Dewey Decimal Classification Exercise

In the sections that follow, information enclosed within square brackets indicates that it was not derived directly from the classification schedules. In the hierarchical development of the answers, number ranges and centered headings have been not been included in the hierarchies. For example, for title 9, range "026-027" for specific kinds of institutions was not indicated in the hierarchical development. Similarly, to aid readability, if a numbered added to a base number has its own hierarchical development, that development is shown under the full number added to the base number.

A. The Index. [The number is square brackets is the fully developed class number]

1. *Seed pictures and other dried natural arrangements.*

    745.928   *[Search under: Seed arrangements. decorative arts]*   [745.928]

2. *The varieties of cheese and how they are produced.*

    637.3   *[Search under: Cheese. processing]*   [637.35]

3. *The decorative arts of primitive peoples.*

    745   *[Search under: Decorative arts]*   [745.441]

4. *The tactics of aerial warfare.*

    358.4   *[Search under: Aerial warfare]*   [358.4142]

5. *Beginning typewriting: tests and drills.*

    652.3   *[Search under: Typewriting]*   [652.3024]

6. *Book mending for libraries.*

   025.7   *[Search under: Book restoration. library science]*   [025.7]

7. *Short-range weather forecasting.*

   551.63   *[Search under: Weather forecasting]*   [551.6263]

8. Doll furniture designs for the amateur craftsman.

   745.5923   *[Search under: Doll furniture. handicrafts]*   [745.5923]

B.   <u>Analyzing DDC Numbers.</u>

9. *Library instruction in the elementary school.*

   027.8222

02	Library and information sciences
027	General libraries, archives, information centers
027.8	School libraries
027.82	Specific levels and specific libraries
027.822	Specific levels
027.8222	Elementary level

10. *Cancer in Connecticut: incidence and characteristics.*

   616.994009746

6	Technology (Applied sciences)
61	Medical sciences. Medicine
616	Diseases
616.9	Other diseases
616.99	Tumors and miscellaneous communicable diseases
616.994	Cancers (Malignant tumors [neoplasms])
616.994009	Historical, geographical, persons treatment *[Standard subdivision derived from instructions under "618.1-618.8"]*
616.994009746	Connecticut *[From Table 2]*
	-7 North America
	-74 Northeastern United States (New England and Middle Atlantic states)
	-746 Connecticut

11. *Spare part surgery: transplants, the surgical practice of the future.*

617.95

6	Technology (Applied sciences)	
61	Medical sciences. Medicine	
617	Miscellaneous branches of medicine. Surgery	
617.9	Operative surgery and special fields of surgery	
617.95	Cosmetic and restorative plastic surgery, transplantation of tissue and organs, implantation of artificial organs	

12. *The farm beef herd.*

636.213

6	Technology (Applied sciences)
63	Agriculture and related technologies
636	Animal husbandry
636.2	Ruminants and Tylopoda. Bovines. Cattle
636.21	Cattle for specific purposes
636.213	Food animals
	[As instructed under "636.21," the number following "636.088" for food animals (3) is added to the base number "636.21."]

13. *Collective bargaining in the U. S. lithographic industry.*

331.8904168623150973

3	Social sciences
33	Economics
331	Labor economics
331.8	Labor unions (Trade unions), labor-management (collective) bargaining and disputes
331.89	Labor-management (Collective) bargaining and disputes
331.8904	In specific industries and occupations and specific groups of industries and occupations
331.89041	In industries and occupations other than extractive, manufacturing, construction
331.890416862315	Planographic (Flat-surface)
	[As instructed under "331.89041," the number from "001-999" for lithography (686.2315) is added to the base number "331.89041."]

      6 Technology (Applied sciences)

      68 Manufacture of products for specific uses

      686 Printing and related activities

	686.2 Printing
	686.23 Presswork (Impression)
	686.231 Mechanical techniques
	686.2315 Planographic (Flat-surface)
331.89041686231509	Historical, geographical, persons treatment
	[From Table 1]
331.8904168623150973	United States
	[From Table 2]
	-7 North America
	-73 United States

14. *Education for librarianship: the design of the curriculum of library schools in the United States.*

020.71173

02	Library and information sciences
020.711	In higher education
	[From Table 1]
	-07 Education, research, related topics
	-071 School and courses
	-0711 In higher education
020.71173	United States
	[As instructed under standard subdivision "-0711," the number From Table 2 for the United States (-73) is added to the base number "-0711."]
	-7 North America
	-73 United States

C.   Table 1: Standard Subdivisions.

15. *The quarterly journal of technology.*

605

6	Technology (Applied sciences)
605	Serial publications
	[Although taken from the schedule, this is a standard subdivision equivalent to "-05" in Table 1.]

16. *A short history of inventions.*

609

6	Technology (Applied sciences)
609	Historical, geographical, persons treatment
	[Although taken from the schedule, this is a standard subdivision equivalent to "-09" in Table 1.]

17. *A dictionary of physics.*

530.03

5	Science
53	Physics
530.03	Dictionaries, encyclopedias, concordances
	[From Table 1. In the schedule, the range ".03-09" is given for standard subdivisions.

18. *Current methods used in adult education research.*

374.0072

3	Social sciences
37	Education
374	Adult education
374.0072	Research
	[From Table 1. In the schedule, the range ".001-008" is given for standard subdivisions.]
	-07 Education, research, related topics
	-072 Research

19. *Technology during the thirteenth century: a history.*

609.022

6	Technology (Applied sciences)
609	Historical geographical, persons treatment
	[Although taken from the schedule, this is a standard subdivision equivalent to "-09" in Table 1.]
609.022	13th century, 1200-1299
	[From Table 1]
	-0902 6th-15th centuries, 500-1499
	-09022 13th century, 1200-1299

20. *The encyclopedia of religion.*

200.3

2	Religion
200.3	Dictionaries, encyclopedias, concordances
	[From Table 1. In the schedule, the range ".2-.6" is given for standard subdivisions.]

21. *Bookbinding as a profession.*

686.30023

6	Technology (Applied sciences)
68	Manufacture of products for specific uses

686	Printing and related activities
686.3	Bookbinding
686.30023	The subject as a profession, occupation, hobby

[From Table 1. In the schedule the range "686.3001-686.3009" is given for standard subdivisions.]

-02 Miscellany
-023 The subject as a profession, occupation, hobby

22. *A directory of mineralogists.*

549.025

5	Natural sciences and mathematics
54	Chemistry and allied sciences
549	Mineralogy
549.025	Directories of persons and organizations

[From Table 1]

-02 Miscellany
-025 Directories of persons and organizations

23. *Biographies of 19th century mineralogists.*

549.0922

5	Natural sciences and mathematics
54	Chemistry and allied sciences
549	Mineralogy
549.0922	Collected treatment

[From Table 1. Note table of precedence on 1:3.]

-09 Historical, geographical, persons treatment
-092 Persons
-0922 Collected treatment

D. Table 2: Area Tables.

24. *Patriotic societies of France.*

369.244

3	Social sciences
36	Social problems and social welfare in general
369	Miscellaneous kinds of associations
369.2	Hereditary, military, patriotic societies
369.244	France and Monaco

[As instructed under "369.2," the number from Table 2 for France (-44) is added to the base number "369.2."]

-4 Europe. Western Europe
-44 France and Monaco

25. *Library schools in Germany: a description.*

020.71143

02	Library and information science
020.711	In higher education
	[From Table 1]
	-07 Education, research, related topics
	-071 Schools and courses
	-0711 In higher education
020.71143	Central Europe. Germany
	[As instructed under standard subdivision "-0711,"
	the number from Table 2 for Germany (-43) is added
	to be base number "-0711."]
	-4 Europe. Western Europe
	-43 Central Europe. Germany

26. *A bibliography of books published by the University of Chicago Press.*
[Located in Chicago, Illinois)

015.77311054

01	Bibliography
015	Bibliographies and catalogs of works from specific places
015.77311	Chicago
	[As instructed under "015," the number from Table 2
	for Chicago (-77311) is added to the base number
	"015."]
	-7 North America
	-77 North Central United Sates. Lake states
	-773 Illinois
	-7731 Cook County
	-77311 Chicago
015.77311054	Publications of university and college presses
	[As instructed under "015," a "0" is added following
	"015.77311." Then, the number following "011" for
	publications of university and college presses (54)
	is added to "015.773110"]
	5 General bibliographies of works issued by specific kinds of publishers
	54 Publications of university and college presses

27. *Folklore about the Lake Superior.*

398.3297749

3	Social sciences
39	Customs, etiquette, folklore
398	Folklore

398.3	Natural and physical phenomena as subjects of folklore
398.32	Places
398.329	Specific places
398.3297749	Upper Peninsula

[*As instructed under "398.329," the number from Table 2 for the Upper Peninsula of Michigan which includes Lake Superior (-7749) is added to the base number "398.329."*]

	-7	North America
	-77	North central United States. Lake states
	-774	Michigan
	-7749	Upper Peninsula

E.   Tables 1 and 2.

28.   *A directory of lawyers in Italy.*

340.02545

3	Social sciences
34	Law
340.025	Directories of persons and organizations

[*From Table 1*]

-02 Miscellany of law

[*Although taken from the schedule, "340.02" is a standard subdivision equivalent to "-02" in Table 1.*]

-025 Directories of persons and organizations

340.02545   Italian peninsula and adjacent islands. Italy

[*As instructed under standard subdivision "-025," the number from Table 2 for Italy (-45) is added to the base number "-025."*]

	-4	Europe
	-45	Italian peninsula and adjacent islands. Italy

29.   *A history of mining in 19th century Colorado.*

622.0978809034

6	Technology (Applied sciences)
62	Engineering and allied operations
622	Mining and related operations
622.09	Historical, geographical, persons treatment

[*From Table 1*]

622.09788   Colorado

[*From Table 2*]

	-7	North America
	-78	Western United States
	-788	Colorado

622.0978809034   19th century, 1800-1899
[From Table 1, see the note under "-093-099"
that allows for the use of "09 Historical and
geographic treatment."]

    09   Historical and geographic treatment
    0903   Modern period, 1500-
    09034   19th century, 1800-1899

30.   *Teaching engineering in Canadian universities.*

620.0071171

6	Technology (Applied sciences)
62	Engineering and allied operations
620.00711	In higher education

[From Table 1. In the schedule, the range ".005-.008"
is given for standard subdivisions.]

    -07 Education, research, related topics
    -071   Schools and courses
    -0711   In higher education

620.0071171   Canada

[As instructed under standard subdivision "-0711,'
the number from Table 2 for Canada (-71) is
added to the base number "-0711.']

    -7   North America
    -71   Canada

31.   *A directory of engineers in Texas throughout the 20th century.*

620.0025764

6	Technology (Applied sciences)
62	Engineering and allied operations
620.0025	Directories of persons and organizations

[From Table 1]

    -02 Miscellany
        [Although taken from the schedule,
        "620.002," is a standard subdivision
        equivalent to "-02" in Table 1.]
    -025   Directories
        [From Table 1]

620.0025764   Texas

[As instructed under the standard subdivision "-
025," the number from Table 2 for Texas (-764) is
added to the base number "-025."]

    -7   North America
    -76   South Central United States. Gulf
        Coast states
    -764   Texas

F.   Table 4: Subdivisions of Individual Languages.

32. *Language today.* [A Canadian English language periodical]

420.5

4	Language
42	English and Old English (Anglo-Saxon)
	["42" is the base number for the English language.]
420.5	Serial publications
	[From Table 1. The range for standard subdivisions ("-05-09") is taken from Table 4.]

33. *Teaching the Romance languages.*

440.07

4	Language
44	Romance languages. French
	["44" is the base number for the Romance languages.]
440.07	Education, research, related topics
	[From Table 1. In the schedule, the range ".01-.09" is given for the standard subdivisions of Romance languages.]

34. *Teaching French in American secondary schools.* [Coverage limited to the U.S.]

440.71273

4	Language
44	Romance languages. French
	["44" is the base number for the French language.]
440.712	In secondary education
	[From Table 1. In the schedule, the range "440.1-440.6" is given for the standard subdivisions of the French language.]
	-7 Education, research, related topics
	-71 Schools and courses
	-712 In secondary education
440.71273	United States
	[As instructed under standard subdivision "-0712," the number from Table 2 for the United States (-73) is added to the base number "-0712."]
	-7 North America
	-73 United States

35. *A compilation of Spanish words incorporated into the English language.*

422.461

4	Language
42	English and Old English (Anglo-Saxon)
	["42" is the base number for the English language.]
422	Etymology of the standard form of the language
	[From Table 4. The number from Table 4 for etymology (-2) is added to the base number for the English language.]
422.4	Foreign elements
422.461	Spanish
	[From Table 6. As instructed under "-24" in Table 4, the number in Table 6 for the language of the foreign element (Spanish, (-61)) is added to "-24."]

-6   Spanish and Portuguese
-61   Spanish

36. *The definitive French dictionary.*

443

4	Language
44	Romance languages. French
	["44" is the base number for the French language.]
443	Dictionaries of the standard form of the language
	[From Table 4. The number from Table 4 for dictionaries (-3) is added to the base number for the French language. The standard subdivision "-03" should not be used in this situation.]

37. *German-English, English-German dictionary.*

433.21

4	Language
43	Germanic (Teutonic languages). German
	[Classify a bilingual dictionary "with the language in which it will be the more useful."—1:418. "44" is the base number for the German language.]
433	Dictionaries of the standard form of the language
	[From Table 4. The number from Table 4 for dictionaries (-3) is added to the base number for the German language. The standard subdivision "-03" should not be used in this situation.]
433.21	English
	[As instructed under "-32-39" in Table 4, the number In Table 6 for English (-21) is added to "3."]

-2   English and Old English (Anglo-Saxon)
-21   English

209

38. *German-Bulgarian, Bulgarian-German dictionary.*

491.81331

4	Language
49	Other languages
491	East Indo-European and Celtic languages

[Classify a bilingual dictionary "with the language in which it will be the more useful .... if classification with either language is equally useful, give priority to the language coming later in the sequence 420-490."—1:418.]

491.8	Slavic languages
491.81	South Slavic languages. Bulgarian

["491.81" is the base number for the Bulgarian language.]

491.813	Dictionaries of the standard form of the language

[From Table 4. The number from Table 4 for dictionaries (-3) is added to the base number for the Bulgarian language. The standard subdivision "-03" should not be used in this situation.]

491.81331	German

[As instructed under "-32-39" in Table 4, the number for German in Table 6 (-31) is added to "3."]

-3   Germanic (Teutonic) languages
-31   German

39. *Papers of the East Slavic Languages Association.* [An international society]

491.700601

4	Language
49	Other languages
491	East Indo-European and Celtic languages
491.7	East Slavic languages. Russian
491.700601	International organization

[From Table 1. The standard subdivision for international organizations was assigned rather than the standard subdivision for serials because the former has a higher position in the table of precedence for standard subdivisions (see 1:3).]

-006   Organizations and management
-00601   International organization

G. 800s and Tables 3A, 3B, and 3C: Literature (Belles Lettres) and
    Subdivisions of Individual Literatures.

    For titles 40-46 the following initial hierarchy applies:

8	Literature (Belles-lettres) and rhetoric
82	English and Old English (Anglo-Saxon) literatures
	["82" is the base number for English literature.]

40. *The encyclopedia of English literature.*

    820.3

        820.3   Dictionaries, encyclopedias, concordances
[From Table 1. The range for standard subdivisions (-01-07) is given in Table 3B. As instructed at the beginning of Table 3, the number from that table for dictionaries (-03) is added to the base number "82."]

41. *An anthology of English literature.*

    820.8

        820.8   Collections of literary texts in more than one form
[From Table 3B. As instructed at the beginning of Table 3, the number from that table for collections (-08) is added to the base number "82."]

42. *A collection of English fantasy.* [Do not treat fantasy as a literary form]

    820.8015

        820.8   Collections of literary texts in more than one form
[From Table 3B. As instructed at the beginning of Table 3, the number from that table for collections (-08) is added to the base number "82."]

        820.8015   Symbolism, allegory, fantasy, myth
[From Table 3C. As instructed under "-08" in Table 3B, a "0" is added following "-08" followed by he number from Table 3C for fantasy (-015).]
                -01 Literature displaying specific qualities of style, mood, perspective
                -015 Symbolism, allegory, fantasy, myth

43.   *English literature for boys.* [A collection]

820.8092826

820.8   Collections of literary texts in more than one form
*[From Table 3B. As instructed at the beginning of
Table 3, the number from that table for collections (-
08) is added to the base number "82."]*

820.8092826   Boys
*[From Table 3C. As instructed under "-08" in Table
3B, a "0" is added to "-08" followed by he number
from Table 3C for boys (-92826.]*

    -9   Literature for and by other specific kinds
of persons
    -92   For and by persons of specific classes
    -928   Of specific age groups and sexes
    -9282 ·   Children
    -92826   Boys

44.   *English literature of the pre-Elizabethan period: a criticism.*

820.9002

820.9   History, description, critical appraisal of works in
more than one form
*[From Table 3B. As instructed at the beginning of
Table 3, the number from that table for critical
appraisal (-09) is added to the base number "82."]*

820.9002   Pre-Elizabethan period, 1400-1558
*[As instructed in Table 3B, the number for the
Pre-Elizabethan period from the period table for
Great Britain and Ireland in the schedule (2) (see
3:657), is added to "-0900."]*

45.   *A critical study of English drama.*

822.009

822   Drama
*[From Table 3B. As instructed at the beginning of
Table 3, the number from that table for drama (-2) is
added to the base number "82."]*

822.009   History, description, critical appraisal
*[As instructed in Table 3B under "-2001-2009," the
number for critical appraisal under "-1-8" (see
1:396) (9) is added to "-200."]*

46. *English drama of the Elizabethan period: a collection.*

822.308

822	Drama
	[From Table 3B. As instructed at the beginning of Table 3, the number from that table for drama (-2) is added to the base number "82."]
822.3	Elizabethan period, 1558-1625
	[As instructed in Table 3B, the number for the Elizabethan period from the period table for Great Britain and Ireland in the schedule (-3) is added to "-2."]
822.308	Collections of literary texts
	[As instructed in Table 3B under "-2001-2009," the number for collections under "-1-8" (see 1:398) (8) is added to "-200."]

47. *A collection of Welsh (Cymric) literature.*

891.6608

8	Literature (Belles-lettres) and rhetoric
89	Literatures of other languages
891	East Indo-European and Celtic literatures
891.6	Celtic literatures
891.66	Welsh (Cymric)
	[Base number for Welsh literature is "891.66"]
891.6608	Collections of literary texts in more than one form
	[From Table 3B. As instructed at the beginning of Table 3, the number (from that table for collections (-08) is added to the base number "891.66."]

48. *A collection of plays from modern Estonia.*

894.5452208

8	Literature (Belles-lettres) and rhetoric
89	Literatures of other languages
894	Ural-Altaic, Paleosiberian, Dravidian literatures
894.5	Finno-Ugric literatures
894.54	Finnic literatures
894.545	Estonian
	[Base number for Estonian literature is "894.545"]
894.5452	Drama
	[From Table 3B. As instructed at the beginning of Table 3, the number from that table for drama (-2) is added to the base number "894.545."]

894.54522	Modern Period, 1861- *[As instructed in Table 3B, the number for the modern period from the period table for Estonian literature in the schedule (2) (see 3:686), is added to "-2."]*
894.5452208	Collections of literary texts *[From Table 3B. As instructed under "-21-29" the number for collections under "-1-8" at the beginning of Table 3B (8) is added to "-0." The result is then added to "2."]*

49.   *A collection of 18th century French literature.*

840.8005

8	Literature (Belles-lettres) and rhetoric
84	Literatures of Romance languages. French literature *[Base number for French literature is "84"]*
840.8	Collections of literary texts *[From Table 3B. As instructed at the beginning of Table 3, the number from that table (-08) is added to the base number "84."]*
840.8005	1715-1789 *[As instructed under "08" in Table 3B, a "0" is added after "-08" followed by a number from Table 3C. For time periods of literature, a "0" precedes the number for the time period of the specific literature. Time period for 18th century French literature in the schedule (5) is used (see 3:666).]*

50.   *19th century French poetry: a collection.*

841.708

8	Literature (Belles-lettres) and rhetoric
84	Literatures of Romance languages. French literature *[Base number for French literature is "84"]*
841	Poetry *[From Table 3B. As instructed at the beginning of Table 3, the number from that table for poetry (-1) is added to the base number for French literature.]*
841.7	Constitutional monarchy, 1815-1848 *[As instructed in Table 3B, the number from for the 19th century (note the "class here" note) from the period table for French literature in the schedule (7), is added to "-1" (see 3:666).]*
841.708	Collections of literary texts *[From Table 3B. As instructed under "-11-19" the number for collections under "-1-8" at the beginning of Table 3B (8) is added to "0." The result is then added to the period number for the literature.]*

51.   *Geography of Martha's Vineyard, Massachusetts.*

917.4494

9	Geography, history, and auxiliary disciplines
91	Geography and travel
917.4494	Dukes County

[As instructed under "913-919," the number from Table 2 (-74494) is added to the base number "91."]

-7	Geography of and travel in North America
-74	Northeastern United States (New England and Middle Atlantic states)
-744	Massachusetts
-7449	Counties bordering Nantucket Sound
-74494	Dukes County

52.   *Travel in the British Isles during the Roman occupation.*

913.61044

9	Geography, history, and auxiliary disciplines
91	Geography and travel
913.61	British Isles. Northern Britain and Ireland

[As instructed under "913-919," the number from Table 2 for the British Isles in the ancient world (-3) is added to the base number "91."]

-3	Geography of and travel in ancient world
-36	Europe north and west of Italian Peninsula
-361	British Isles. Northern Britain and Ireland

913.6104	Travel

[As instructed under "913-919," a number from that table for travel (04) is added to "913.61."]

913.61044	Roman period, 43-410

[As instructed under "04," the number following "0" for the historical period for the British Isles (936.204) (i.e., 4) is added to "913.6104."]

53.   *The exploration of Chile by Europeans.*

918.3042

9	Geography, history, and auxiliary disciplines
91	Geography and travel
918.3	Chile

[As instructed under "913-919," the number from Table 2 for Chile (-8) is added to the base number "91."]

8   Geography of and travel in South America
83   Chile

918.304   Travel
[As instructed under "913-919," a number from that table (04) is added to "918.3."]

918.3042   Period of European discovery and conquest, 1535-1560
[As instructed under "04," the number following "0" for the historical period for Chile (982.02) (i.e., 2) is added to "918.304."]

54.   *A history of medieval Austria.*

943.602

9	Geography, history, and auxiliary disciplines
94	General history of Europe. Western Europe
943	Central Europe. Germany
943.6	Austria and Liechtenstein
943.602	Medieval period, 481-1500

55.   *The Spanish-American War: the American perspective.*

973.89

9	Geography, history, and auxiliary disciplines
97	General history of North America
973	United States
973.8	Reconstruction period, 1865-1900
973.89	Spanish-American War, 1898

56.   *The history of Pawtucket, Rhode Island.*

974.51

9	Geography, history, and auxiliary disciplines
974.51	Providence County

[As instructed under "930-990," the number from Table 2 for Providence County (-7451) is added to the base number "9."]

-7   North America
-74   Northeastern United States (New England and Middle Atlantic states)
-745   Rhode Island
-7451   Providence County

57. *Outline of Eastern European history.*

947.000202

9	Geography, history, and auxiliary disciplines
94	General history of Europe. Western Europe
947	Eastern Europe. Union of Soviet Socialist Republics (Soviet Union)
947.000202	Synopses and outlines

[From Table 1. In the schedule, the range ".0001-.0009" is given for the standard subdivisions of Eastern Europe.]

-02 Miscellany
-0202 Synopses and outlines

58. *History of the Burmese in New Zealand.*

993.004958

9	Geography, history and auxiliary disciplines
99	General history of other parts of world, of extraterrestrial worlds. Pacific Ocean islands
993	New Zealand
993.004	Racial, ethnic, national groups

[From the instructions under "930-990"]

993.004958	Burmese

[As instructed under "930-990," the number from Table 5 for Burmese (-958) is added to "004."]

-9 Other Indo-European peoples
-95 East and Southeast Asian peoples; Mundas
-958 Burmese

59. *World history of the Irish people.*

909.049162

9	Geography, history and auxiliary disciplines
909	World history
909.04	History with respect to racial, ethnic, national groups
909.049162	Irish

[From Table 5 as instructed under "909"]

-9 Other racial, ethnic, national groups
-91 Other Indo-European peoples
-916 Celts
-9162 Irish

I. Other Tables and "Add To" Directions.

60. *Customs of the Huguenots.*

390.088245

3	Social sciences
39	Customs, etiquette, folklore
390.088	Occupational and religious groups
	[From Table 1. In the schedule, the range "390.00-390.009" is given for standard subdivisions.]
	-08 History and description with respect to kinds of persons
	-088 Occupational and religious groups
390.088245	Huguenot churches
	[From Table 7. As instructed under '08809-08899," the number from Table 7 for Huguenot churches (-245) is added to "088."]
	-2 Persons occupied with or adherent to religion
	-24 With Protestant churches of Continental origin and related bodies
	-245 Huguenot churches

61. *The management of agricultural museums.*

630.75

6	Technology (Applied sciences)
63	Agriculture and related technologies
630.75	Museum activities and services. Collecting
	[From Table 1. Tange for standard subdivisions of "630" is shown by the presence of some standard subdivisions in the schedule, i.e., 630.2, 630.71.]
	-7 Education, research, related topics
	-75 Museum activities and services. Collecting

62. *A guide to the Cobb Agriculture Museum, Butler County, Pennsylvania.*

630.7474891

6	Technology (Applied sciences)
63	Agriculture and related technologies
630.74	Museums, collections, exhibits
	[From Table 1. Range for standard subdivisions of "630" shown by the presence of some standard subdivisions in the schedule, e.g., 630.2, 630.71.]
	-07 Education, research, related topics
	-074 Museums, collections, exhibits

218

630.7474891	Butler County

[From Table 2. As instructed under "-0741- -0749" the number from Table 2 for Butler County (-74891) is added to standard subdivision "-074."]

-7		North America
-74		Northeastern United States (New England and Middle Atlantic states)
-748		Pennsylvania
-7489		Northwestern counties
-74891		Butler County

63. *The manufacture of equipment for football.* [This is the American game of football]

688.76332

6	Technology (Applied sciences)
68	Manufacture of products for specific uses
688	Other final products, and packaging technology
688.7	Recreational equipment
688.76	Equipment for outdoor sports and games
688.76332	American football

[As instructed under "688.763," the number following "796" for football (332) is added to the the base number "688.76." Although there is further development for Apparatus, equipment, materials (796.332028), it is not used because equipment is already expressed in an earlier part of the class number "688.76."]

3	Ball games
33	Inflated ball driven by foot
332	American football

64. *Congenital diseases of the scalp.*

616.546043

6	Technology (Applied sciences)
61	Medical sciences. Medicine
616	Diseases
616.5	Diseases of the integument, hair, nails
616.54	Skin, hypertrophies, scalp diseases, related disorders
616.546	Diseases of scalp, hair, hair follicles
616.546043	Congenital diseases

[As instructed under "616.1-616.9," the number from the table for congenital diseases (043) is added to "616.54."]

04	Special classes of diseases
043	Congenital diseases

219

65. *Cheerleading at Indiana University basketball games.* [Indiana University is located in Bloomington (Monroe County), Indiana]

791.642309772255

7	The arts. Fine and decorative arts
79	Recreational and performing arts
791	Public performances
791.6	Pageantry
791.64	Cheerleading
791.6423	Basketball

[*As instructed under "791.64," the number following "796.3" for basketball (23) is added to the base number "791.64."*]

2   Inflated ball thrown or hit by hand
23   Basketball

791.642309	Historical, geographical, persons treatment

[*From Table 1*]

791.642309772255	Monroe County

[*From Table 2. As instructed under "-093-099," the number from Table 2 for Monroe County (-772255) is added to standard subdivision "-09."*]

-7   North America
-77   North Central United States. Lake states
-772   Indiana
-7722   South central counties
-77225   Brown and Monroe Counties
-772255   Monroe County

66. *Materials for teaching science in elementary schools.*

372.35044

3	Social sciences
37	Education
372	Elementary education
372.3	Science, technology, health
372.35	Science and technology
372.35044	Teaching

[*As instructed under "372.3-372.8," the number from the table for teaching (044) is added to "372.35."*]

04   Special topics
044   Teaching

67. *Stamps of Ghana: a collector's guide.*

769.569667

7	The arts. Fine and decorative arts
76	Graphic arts. Printmaking and prints

769	Prints
769.5	Forms of prints
769.56	Postage stamps and related devices
769.569	Historical, geographical, persons treatment
769.569667	Ghana

[As instructed under "769.5696," the number from Table 2 for Ghana (-667) is added to the base number "769.569."]

-6 Africa
-66 West Africa and offshore islands
-667 Ghana

68. *Atlas of France.*

912.44

9	Geography, history, and auxiliary disciplines
91	Geography and travel
912	Graphic representation of surface of earth and of extraterrestrial worlds
912.44	France and Monaco

[As instructed under "912," the number from Table 2 for France (-44) is added to the base number "912."]

-4 Europe. Western Europe
-44 France and Monaco

69. *Seventeenth century bookbinding.*

686.3009032

6	Technology (Applied sciences)
68	Manufacture of products for specific uses
686	Printing and related activities
686.3	Bookbinding
686.3009032	17th century, 1600-1699

[From Table 1. In the schedule, the range "686.3001-686.3009" is given for standard subdivisions.]

-09 Historical, geographical, persons treatment
-0903 Modern period, 1500
-09032 17th century, 1600-1699

70. *Ancient Roman coins: their description for collectors.*

737.4937

7	The arts. Fine and decorative arts
73	Plastic arts. Sculpture
737	Numismatics and sigillography

737.4	Coins
737.49	Of specific countries
737.4937	Italian Peninsula and adjacent territories

[As instructed under "737.49," the number from Table 2 for ancient Rome (-37) is added to the base number "737.49."]

-3	The ancient world
-37	Italian Peninsula and adjacent territories

71. *Photography as a hobby: a guide for the amateur.*

770.233

7	The arts. Fine and decorative arts
77	Photography and photographs
770.2	Miscellany

[Although taken from the schedule, this is a standard subdivision equivalent to "02" in Table 1.]

770.23	Photography as a profession, occupation, hobby
770.233	Photography as a hobby

72. *Prospecting for gold in Colorado.*

622.184109788

6	Technology (Applied sciences)
62	Engineering and allied operations
622	Mining and related operations
622.1	Prospecting and exploratory operations
622.18	Prospecting for specific materials
622.1841	Gold

[As instructed under "622.184," the number following "553" for gold (41) is added to the base number "622.18."]

4	Metals and semimetals
41	Gold

622.184109	Historical, geographical, persons treatment
	[From Table 1]
622.184109788	Colorado

[From Table 2. As instructed under "-093-099," the number from Table 2 for Colorado (-788) is added to standard subdivision "-09."]

-7	North America
-78	Western United States
-788	Colorado

73. *Flagstone sidewalks: illustrations of their design and construction.*

625.8810222

6	Technology (Applied sciences)
62	Engineering and allied operations
625	Engineering of railroads, roads, highways
625.8	Artificial road surfaces
625.88	Sidewalks and auxiliary pavements
625.881	Flagstones

[As instructed under "625.881-.886," the number following "625.8" for flagstones (1) is added to the base number "625.88."]

625.8810222   Pictures and related illustrations

[From Table 2]

-02 Miscellany
-022   Illustrations, models, miniatures
-0222   Pictures and related illustrations

74. *A bibliography of folk literature.*

016.3982

01	Bibliography
016	Bibliographies and catalogs of works on specific subjects or in specific disciplines
016.3982	Folk literature

[As instructed under "016," the number from the range "001-999" for folk literature (398.2) is added to the base number "016."]

3   Social sciences
39   Customs, etiquette, folklore
398   Folklore
398.2   Folk literature

75. *Solar houses in Southern California.*

728.370472097949

7	The arts. Fine and decorative arts
72	Architecture
728	Residential and related buildings
728.3	Specific kinds of conventional housing
728.37	Separate houses
728.3704	Special topics

[As instructed under "721-729," the number for special topics (04) is added to "728.37."]

728.370472   Energy resources

[As instructed under "04," the number following "720.4" for energy resources (72) is added to "04."]

| | | 7 | Architecture and the environment |
| | | 72 | Energy resources |

728.37047209   Historical, geographical, persons treatment
[From Table 1]

728.370472097949   Southern counties (Southern California)
[From Table 2. As instructed under "--093-099," the number from Table 2 for Southern California (-7949) is added to standard subdivision "-09."]

    -7   North America
    -79   Great Basin and Pacific Slope region of United States. Pacific Coast states
    -794   California
    -7949   Southern counties (Southern California)

76.   *A modern version of the Bible in Japanese.*

220.5956

2	Religion
22	Bible
220.5	Modern versions and translations
220.5956	Japanese

[From Table 6. As instructed under "220.53-220.59," the number for Japanese (-956) is added to the base number "220.5."]

    -9   East Indo-European and Celtic languages
    -95   Languages of East and Southeast Asia. Sino-Tibetan languages
    -956   Japanese

77.   *The geography of Ethiopia.*

916.3

9	Geography, history, and auxiliary disciplines
91	Geography and travel
916.3	Ethiopia

[As instructed under "913-919," the number from Table 2 for Ethiopia (-63) is added to the base number "91."]

    -6   Africa
    -63   Ethiopia

78. *Design of interior furnishings for Burroughs-Wellcome Company, Research Triangle Park, North Carolina.* [A pharmaceutical firm in Durham County, North Carolina]

747.87561509756563

7	The arts. Fine and decorative arts
74	Drawing and decorative arts
747	Interior decoration
747.8	Decoration of specific types of buildings
747.875	Research buildings

[As instructed under "747.85-747.87," the number in the range "725-728" for research buildings (75) is added to the base number "747.8."]

> 7 Buildings for educational and research purposes
> 75 Research buildings

747.875615	Pharmacology and therapeutics

[As instructed under "727.5", the number from the range "001"-"999" for pharmacology and therapeutics (615) is added to the base number "727.5."]

> 6 Technology (Applied sciences)
> 61 Medical sciences. Medicine
> 615 Pharmacology and therapeutics

747.87561509	Historical, geographical, persons treatment

[From Table 1]

747.87561509756563	Durham County

[From Table 2. As instructed under "-093-099," the number from Table 2 for Durham County (-756563) is added to standard subdivision "-09."]

> -7 North America
> -75 Southeastern United States (South Atlantic states)
> -756 North Carolina
> -7565 Northeast Piedmont counties
> -75656 Durham and Orange Counties
> -756563 Durham County

79. *A programmed learning text for natural sciences.*

507.7

5	Natural sciences and mathematics
507	Education, research, related topics

[Although taken from the schedule, this is a standard subdivision equivalent to "-07" in Table 1.]

507.7	Programmed texts

[From Table 1]

80. *The anatomy of snakes.*

597.96044

5	Natural sciences and mathematics
59	Zoological sciences
597	Cold-blooded vertebrates. Pisces (Fishes)
597.9	Reptilia
597.96	Serpentes (Snakes)
597.9604	Processes and parts

[As instructed under "592-599," the number for processes and parts (04) is added to "597.96."]

597.96044	Anatomy and morphology of animals

[As instructed under "04," the number following 591 for anatomy and morphology (4) is added to "04."]

81. *Research in toxicology.*

615.90072

6	Technology (Applied sciences)
61	Medical sciences. Medicine
615	Pharmacology and therapeutics
615.9	Toxicology
615.90072	Research

[From Table 1. In the schedule, the range ".9001-.9009" is given for standard subdivisions.]

-07 Education, research, related topics
-072 Research

82. *Travel in Trinidad today.*

917.298304

9	Geography, history, and auxiliary disciplines
91	Geography and travel
917.2983	Trinidad and Tobago

[As instructed under "913-919," the number from Table 2 for Trinidad (72983) is added to the base number "91."]

-7 North America
-72 Middle America. Mexico
-729 West Indies (Antilles) and Bermuda
-7298 Windward and other southern islands
-72983 Trinidad and Tobago

917.298304	Travel

[As instructed under "913-919," the number "04" is added to "917.2983."

83.   *The management of poplar forests.*

634.97232

6	Technology (Applied sciences)
63	Agriculture and related technologies
634	Orchards, fruits, forestry
634.9	Forestry
634.97	Kinds of trees
634.972	Dicotyledons
634.9723	Poplar
634.97232	Forest management

[As instructed under "634.97," the number following "634.9" for forest management (2) is added to "634.9723."]

84.   *Books written by adolescents: a bibliography.*

013.055

01	Bibliography
013	Bibliographies and catalogs of works by specific classes of authors
013.055	Young adults

[As instructed under "013," the number from Table 7 for young adults (055) is added to the base number "013."]

-05 Persons by age
-055   Young adults

85.   *Crime in Brazil.*

364.981

3	Social sciences
36	Social problems and services; association
364	Criminology
364.9	Historical, geographical, persons treatment of crime and its alleviation
364.981	Brazil

[As instructed under "364.9," the number from Table 2 for Brazil (-81) is added to the base number "364.9."]

-8   South America
-81   Brazil

Answers to the
Library of Congress Classification Exercise

In the sections that follow, information enclosed within square brackets indicates that it was not derived directly from the classification schedules.

A.

1. *How to catalog a rare book,* by Duncan. 1973.

    Z695.74 .D8 1973

Z	Bibliography and Library science
662-1000.5	Libraries
665-718.8	Library science. Information science
687-718.8	The collections. The books
693-695.83	Cataloging
695.2-695.83	By form
695.74	Rare books
.D8	*[Cutter number for 'Duncan"]*
1973	[Date]

2. *How to grow asparagus,* by Unwin. 1922.

    SB325 .U5 1922

S	Agriculture
SB	Plant culture
320-353.5	Vegetables
325-351	Culture of individual vegetables
325	Asparagus
.U5	*[Cutter number for "Unwin"]*
1922	[Date]

3. *The conservation of museum collections*, by Sand. 1938.

    AM141 .S2 1938

A		General works
	AM	Museums. Collectors and collecting
	111-157	Museology, Museum methods, technique, etc.
	141-145	Preparation and preservation
	141	General works
	.S2	*[Cutter number for "Sand"]*
	1938	[Date]

4. *The folklore of holy wells and springs*, by Ash. 1956.

    GR690 .A8 1956

G		Geography. Maps. Anthropology. Recreation
	GR	Folklore
	430-940	By subject
	650-690	Geographical topics
	678-690	Waters
	690	Springs. Wells
	.A8	*[Cutter number for "Ash"]*
	1956	[Date]

5. *How to train your homing pigeon*, by Walls. 1934.

    SF469 .W3 1934

S		Agriculture
	SF	Animal culture
	461-473	Birds
	465-472	Pigeons
	469	Homing, racing, and carrier pigeons
	.W3	*[Cutter number for "Walls"]*
	1934	[Date]

6. *The first book of astronomy*, by Clark. 1985. [A book for children]

    QB46 .C5 1985

Q		Science
	QB	Astronomy
	1-139	General
	46	Juvenile works
	.C5	*[Cutter number for "Clark"]*
	1985	[Date]

7.　*The art of writing biographies*, by Queen.　1981.　[A book of techniques]

CT22 .Q4 1981

C	Auxiliary sciences of history
CT	Biography
21-22	Biography as an art or literary form
22	Technique
.Q4	*[Cutter number for "Queen"]*
1981	[Date]

8.　*A manual of archeology for the amateur archaeologist*, by Biddle.　1979.

CC75.5 .B5 1979

C	Auxiliary sciences of history
CC	Archaeology (General)
73-80.6	Methodology
75.5	Amateurs' manuals
.B5	*[Cutter number for "Biddle"]*
1979	[Date]

9.　*The chemical analysis of rocks*, by Hruska.　1979.

QE438 .H7 1979

Q	Science
QE	Geology
420-499	Petrology
438	Chemical analysis of rocks
.H7	*[Cutter number for "Hruska"]*
1979	[Date]

10.　*Photography for children*, by Lytton.　1953.

TR149 .L9 1953

T	Technology
TR	Photography
1-195	[General]
149	Popular works. Juvenile works
.L9	*[Cutter number for "Lytton"]*
1953	[Date]

11.　*Lawyers as characters in modern fiction*, by O'Rorke.　1980.

PN 3426 .L37 O7 1980

P	[Language. Literature]
PN	Literature (General)
3311-3503	Prose. Prose fiction

3401-3426	Special topics
3418-3426	Special races, classes, types, etc., in fiction
3426	Other, A-Z
.L37	Lawyers
	[Cutter number from the list on p. 78]
O7	*[Cutter number for "O'Rorke"]*
1980	[Date]

12. *Coins and coin collectors*, by Quiller. 1983.

CJ76 .Q5 1983

C	Auxiliary sciences of history
CJ	Numismatics
1-4625	Coins
73-76	General works
76	1971-
.Q5	*[Cutter number for "Quiller"]*
1983	[Date]

13. *A survey of veterinary hospitals*, by Ivers. 1986.

SF604.5 .I9 1986

S	Agriculture
SF	Animal culture
600-1100	Veterinary medicine
604.5	Veterinary hospitals
.I9	*[Cutter number for "Ivers"]*
1986	[Date]

14. *A history of 18th century astrology*, by Lewis. 1969.

BF1679 .L4 1969

B	[Philosophy. Psychology. Religion]
BF	Psychology
1445-1891	Occult sciences
1651-1769	Astrology
1671-1679	History
1674-1679	By period
1679	Modern
.L4	*[Cutter number for "Lewis"]*
1969	[Date]

15. *Vocational education for women*, by Tyrone. 1986.

LC1500 .T9 1986

L	Education
LC	Special aspects of education
1390-5158	Education of special classes of persons

<pre>
            1401-2571   Women
            1500-1506   Vocational education
            1500   General works
            .T9   [Cutter number for "Tyrone"]
            1986   [Date]
</pre>

16. *A dictionary of philosophy,* by Ludlow. 1976. [In English]

B41 .L8 1976

<pre>
        B   [Philosophy. Psychology. Religion]
          B   Philosophy (General)
        40-48   Dictionaries
          41   English and American
          .L8   [Cutter number for "Ludlow"]
          1976   [Date]
</pre>

17. *Children's furniture building for the home craftsman,* by Twining. 1949.

TT197.5 .C5 T8 1949

<pre>
        T   Technology
          TT   Handicrafts. Arts and crafts
        180-200   Woodworking. Furniture making. Upholstering
        194-199.4   Furniture
        197.5   Special, A-Z
          .C5   Children's furniture
                               [Cutter no. from the list on p. 241]
          T8   [Cutter number for "Twining"]
          1949   [Date]
</pre>

B.   A-Z directions.

18. *Life on the stage : the biography of Helen Hayes* , by Loy. 1982. [The American actress born in 1900]

PN2287 .H3 L6 1982

<pre>
        P   [Language. Literature]
          PN   Literature (General)
        1600-3307   Drama
        2000-3307   Dramatic representation. Theater
        2219.3-3030   Special regions or countries
        2219.3-2554   America
        2219.3-2240   North America
        2220-2298   United States
        2285-2287   Biography
        2287   Individual, A-Z
          .H3   [Cutter number for "Hayes"]
          L6   [Cutter number for "Loy"]
          1982   [Date]
</pre>

19. *The National League,* by Greg. 1922. [A history of the professional baseball league]

GV875 .A3 G7 1922

G	Geography. Maps. Anthropology. Recreation
GV	Recreation. Leisure
561-1198.995	Sports
861-1017	Ball games
862-881	Baseball
875	Leagues, clubs, etc.
875.A3A-Z	National League of Professional Baseball Clubs
G7	*[Cutter number for "Greg"]*
1922	[Date]

20. *Go Cubs! a history of the Chicago Cubs,* by Rogers. 1974. [The professional baseball team]

GV875 .C6 R6 1974

G	Geography. Maps. Anthropology. Recreation
GV	Recreation. Leisure
561-1198.995	Sports
861-1017	Ball games
862-881	Baseball
875	Leagues, clubs, etc.
.A4-Z	Individual clubs. By name, A-Z
.C6	*[Cutter number for "Chicago" from the list on p. 353]*
R6	*[Cutter number for "Rogers"]*
1974	[Date]

21. *School architecture in California,* by Salten. 1951.

LB3218 .C2 S2 1951

L	Education
LB	Theory and practice of education
3201-3325	School architecture and equipment. School physical facilities. Campus planning
3218-3219	By region or country
3218	United States
.A5-Z	By state
.C2	*[Cutter number for "California" from SCM:S Instruction G 302]*
S2	*[Cutter number for "Salten"]*
1951	[Date]

22. *Witchcraft in Alabama*, by Shick. 1961.

BF1577 .A2 S5 1961

B		[Philosophy. Psychology. Religion]
BF		Psychology
1445-1891		Occult sciences
1562.5-1584		Witchcraft
1573-1584		By region or country
1573-1578		United States
1577		Other regions, A-Z
.A2		*[Cutter number for "Alabama" from SCM:S Instruction G 302]*
S5		*[Cutter number for "Shick"]*
1961		[Date]

23. *Cheesebox on a raft: the Union ironclad Monitor*, by Carr. 1919. [Centers on the activities of this ship during the Civil War]

E 595 .M7 C3 1919

E-F	History: America
E	[America and U.S. (non-local)]
151-839	United States
171-839	History
456-655	Civil War period, 1861-1865
461-655	The Civil War, 1861-1865
591-600	Naval history
591-595	General works. The Union Navy
595	Individual ships, A-Z
.M7	Monitor (Ironclad) *[Cutter number from the list on p. 114]*
C3	*[Cutter number for "Carr"]*
1919	[Date]

24. *The Hogarth Press: the history of a great private press*, by Hull. 1966.

Z232 .H6 H8 1966

Z	Bibliography and Library science
116-659	Book industries and trade
116.A5-265	Printing
231-232	Printers and printing establishments
232	Individual printers and establishments, A-Z
.H6	*[Cutter number for "Hogarth"]*
H8	*[Cutter number for "Hull"]*
1966	[Date]

25. *Techniques of writing mystery and detective stories,* by Fry. 1971.

PN3377.5 .D4 F7 1971

P	[Language. Literature]
PN	Literature (General)
3311-3503	Prose. Prose fiction
3355-3383	Technique. Authorship
3365-3377.5	Special forms, subjects, etc.
3377.5	Other, A-Z
.D4	Detective and mystery stories
	[Cutter number from the list on p. 77]
F7	*[Cutter number for "Fry"]*
1971	[Date]

26. *A repair manual for the Buick automobile,* by Ferry. 1985.

TL215. B8 F4 1985

T	Technology
TL	Motor vehicles. Aeronautics. Astronautics
1-480	Motor vehicles
200-229	Special automobiles, by power
205-229	Gasoline automobiles
215	Special makes, A-Z
.B8	*[Cutter number for "Buick"]*
F4	*[Cutter number for "Ferry"]*
1985	[Date]

27. *A bibliography of articles on motorcycles,* by Jansen. 1978.

Z5173 .M5 J3 1978

Z	Bibliography and Library science
1001-8999	Bibliography
5051-7999	Subject bibliography
5170-5173	Automobiles. Automobile travel. Motor vehicles
5173	Special topics, A-Z
.M5	*[Cutter for "motorcycles" to place it between ".M3, Maintenance and repair"; and ."M6, Motors"]*
J3	*[Cutter number for "Jansen"]*
1978	[Date]

28. *North American Indian embroidery,* by Llewellyn. 1947.

E98 .E5 L5 1947

E-F	History: America
E	[America and U.S. (non-local)]
77-99	Indians of North America

98	Other topics, A-Z
.E5	Embroidery
	[Cutter number from the list beginning on p. 10]
L5	*[Cutter number for "Llewellyn"]*
1947	[Date]

29. *Flowers in literature,* by Escher. 1949.

PN56 .F55 E8 1949

P	[Language. Literature]
PN	Literature (General)
45-57	Theory. Philosophy. Esthetics
46-57	Relation to and treatment of special elements, problems, and subjects
56-57	Other special
56	Topics, A-Z
.F55	Flowers
	[Cutter number from the list beginning on p. 2]
E8	*[Cutter number for "Escher"]*
1949	[Date]

30. *How to win at the game Trivial Pursuit,* by Eastman. 1985.

GV1469 .T7 E15 1985

G	Geography. Maps. Anthropology. Recreation
GV	Recreation. Leisure
1199-1570	Games and amusements
1221-1469	Indoor games and amusements
1312-1469	Board games. Move games
1469	Other board games, A-Z
.T7	*[Cutter number for "Trivial pursuit"]*
E15	*[Cutter number for "Eastman" developed by expanding on the decimal number .1. This was done because the cutter table provides for the use of ".E2" for words beginning with "Eb."]*
1985	[Date]

31. *Modern paper manufacture in Japan,* by Ervin. 1980.

TS1095 .J3 E7 1980

T	Technology
TS-TX	Composite group
TS	Manufactures
1080-1268	Paper manufacture and trade

1090-1096	History
1094-1096	Modern
1095	Special countries, A-Z
.J3	*[Cutter number for "Japan" from SCM:S Instruction G 300]*
E7	*[Cutter number for "Ervin"]*
1980	[Date]

C. Fixed Successive Cutter Numbers.

For titles 32-36 the following initial hierarchy applies:

L	Education
LJ	Student fraternities and societies, United States
75	General fraternities, A-Z

32. *The Newsletter of the Alpha Delta Phi.* [A general fraternity]

LJ75 .A5 N4

.A5	*[Cutter number for "Alpha.Delta Pi" taken from the examples given at the end of the table on p. 304. Because terminal zeros are not recorded in cutter numbers, the successive cutter number "0" for "Serials" is unstated but is reflected in the meaning of the cutter number.]*
N4	*[Cutter number for "Newsletter" the first word of the title main entry]* *[No dates are recorded for serials.]*

33. *A history of Alpha Delta Phi from 1900-1970,* by Bates. 1972.

LJ75 .A57 B3 1972

.A5	*[Cutter number for "Alpha Delta Pi" taken from the examples given at the end of the table on p. 304.]*
.A57	History, Modern, 1801- *[Successive cutter number "7" from the table on p. 304]*
B3	*[Cutter number for "Bates"]*
1972	[Date]

34. *Past presidents of Delta Upsilon*, by Pry. 1981. [A general fraternity]

LJ75 .D48 P7 1981

.D4	*[Cutter number for "Delta Upsilon"]*
.D48	Biography
	[Successive cutter number "5" from the table on p. 304]
P7	*[Cutter number for "Pry"]*
1981	[Date]

35. *A membership directory of Pi Kappa Alpha.* 1972. [A general fraternity]

LJ75 .P53 1972

.P5	*[Cutter number for "Pi Kappa Alpha"]*
.P53	Catalogs. Directories Nonserial. By date.
	[Successive cutter number "3" from the table on p. 304]
1972	[Date]

36. *The constitution of Delta Tau Delta.* 1907. [A general fraternity]

LJ75 .D503 1907

.D5	*[Cutter number for "Delta Tau Delta." Cutter number "4" modified to "5" to make it different from the cutter number previously used for Delta Upsilon]*
.D503	Charters. Constitutions. By date.
	[Successive cutter number "03" from the table on p. 304]
1907	[Date]

37. *The by-laws of Beta Phi Mu.* 1965. [A library science honor society]

LJ121 .B405 1965

L	Education
LJ	Student fraternities and societies, United States
91-121	Professional fraternities
121	Other professional fraternities, A-Z
.B4	*[Cutter number for "Beta Phi Mu"]*
.B405	Regulations. By Laws. By date
	[Successive cutter number "05" from the table on p. 304]
1965	[Date]

38. *A history of Phi Beta Kappa, 1890-1920,* by Olinger. 1923.

    LJ85 .P27 O4 1923

L	Education
LJ	Student fraternities and societies, United States
81-85	Honor societies and honorary fraternities
85	Individual fraternities, A-Z
.P2	[*Cutter number from the list on p. 305*]
.P27	History, Modern, 1801-
	[*Successive cutter number "7" from the table on p. 304*]
O4	[*Cutter number for "Olinger"*]
1923	[Date]

39. *A directory of the members of the Xi Chapter of Beta Phi Mu (University of Hawaii.)* 1984.

    LJ121 .B49 X5 1984

L	Education
LJ	Student fraternities and societies, United States
91-121	Professional fraternities
121	Other professional fraternities, A-Z
.B4	[*Cutter number for "Beta Phi Mu"*]
.B49	Local, A-Z
	[*Successive cutter number "9" from the table on p. 304*]
X5	[*Cutter number for "Xi"*]
1984	[Date]

D.   <u>Tables within the text. Double Cutter Numbers.</u>

40. *A directory of school officials in Kentucky,* issued by the Kentucky Department of Education. 1977.

    LB2803 .K4 K4 1977

L	Education
LB	Theory and practice of education
2801-3095	School administration and organization
2801-2865	General, and United States
2803	Directories and lists of school officials
A4-W	Regions or states
.K4	[*Cutter number for "Kentucky" from SCM:S Instruction G 302*]
	General
	[*Successive cutter number ".x" from the table on p. 101*]

239

K4   *[Cutter number for "Kentucky" (the main entry) from SCM:S Instruction G 302]*

1977   *[Date]*

41. *A directory of school officials in Preston County, W. Va.,* issued by Preston County. 1980.

LB2803 .W42 P7 1980

L	Education
LB	Theory and practice of education
2801-3095	School administration and organization
2801-2865	General, and United States
2803	Directories and lists of school officials
.W4	*[Cutter number for "West Virginia" from SCM:S Instruction G 302]*
.W42	Counties, A-Z *[Successive cutter number "2" from the table on p. 101]*
P7	*[Cutter number for "Preston County"]*
1980	*[Date]*

42. *An examination of the British drug scene,* by Hunter. 1971.

HV5840 .G7 H8 1971

H	Social sciences
HV	Social pathology. Social and public welfare. Criminology
5800-5840	Drug habits. Drug abuse
5825-5840	By region or country
5840	Other regions or countries, A-Z
.G7	*[Cutter number for "Great Britain" from the table on p. 145]*
H8	*[Cutter number for "Hunter"]*
1971	*[Date]*

43. *Psychedelic drug use in Vancouver,* by Steele. 1982.

HV5840 .C22 V3 1982

H	Social sciences
HV	Social pathology. Social and public welfare. Criminology
5800-5840	Drug habits. Drug abuse
5825-5840	By region or country
5840	Other regions or countries, A-Z
.C2	*[Cutter number for "Canada" from the table on p. 145]*

.C22	Local, A-Z
	[Successive cutter number "2" from the table on p. 101]
V3	*[Cutter number for "Vancouver"]*
1982	*[Date]*

44. *A history of libraries in Brazil*, by Louis. 1955.

Z769 .A1 L6 1955

Z	Bibliography and Library science
662-1000.5	Libraries
729-871	Library reports. History. Statistics
735-871	Other regions or countries
763-786	South America
769-770	Brazil
769.A1	General works. History
	[Using the column for 2 no. countries in the table on p. 46, the 1st number in the range (769) and the reserve cutter number ".A1" is used to express "General works. History."]
.L6	*[Cutter number for "Louis"]*
1955	*[Date]*

45. *Library statistics of Luxemburg*, by Astor. 1975.

Z816.3 .A1 A8 1975

Z	Bibliography and Library science
662-1000.5	Libraries
729-871	Library reports. History. Statistics
735-871	Other regions or countries
789-841.8	Europe
816.3	Luxemburg
.A1	General works. History
	[Using the column for 1 no. countries in the table on p. 46, the reserve cutter number ".A1" is used to express "General works. History."]
A8	*[Cutter number for "Astor"]*
1975	*[Date]*

46. *A history of libraries in the Tolna region, Hungary*, by Case. 1952.

Z794.3 .A2 T6 1952

Z	Bibliography and Library science
662-1000.5	Libraries
729-871	Library reports. History. Statistics

735-871	Other regions or countries
789-841.8	Europe
794.3	Hungary
.A2A-Z	By region, state or place
	[Using the column for 1 no. countries in the table on p. 46, the reserve cutter number ".A2" is used to express division "by region, state or place."]
.T6	*[Cutter number for "Tolna"]*
1952	*[Date]*

Note: No cutter number could be provided for Case because 2 cutter numbers were used as part of the subject classification.

47. *Caves in the United States*, by Edison. 1946.

GB604 .E3 1946

G	Geography. Maps. Anthropology. Recreation
GB	Physical geography
400-649	Geomorphology. Landforms. Terrain
561-649	Other natural landforms: Floodplains, caves, deserts, dunes, etc.
599-649	Karst landforms
601-649	Caves. Speleology
603-608	By region or country
603-606	America
604-606	United States
604	General works
.E3	*[Cutter number for "Edison"]*
1946	*[Date]*

48. *Arkansas caves*, by Lutz. 1981.

GB605 .A8 L8 1981

G	Geography. Maps. Anthropology. Recreation
GB	Physical geography
400-649	Geomorphology. Landforms. Terrain
561-649	Other natural landforms: Floodplains, caves, deserts, dunes, etc.
599-649	Karst landforms
601-649	Caves. Speleology
603-608	By region or country
604-606	United States
605	By region or state, A-Z
.A8	*[Cutter number for "Arkansas" from SCM:S Instruction G 302]*
L8	*[Cutter number for "Lutz"]*
1981	*[Date]*

49. *Caves of Scotland,* by MacDonald. 1977.

GB608.45 .M3 1977

G	Geography. Maps. Anthropology. Recreation
GB	Physical geography
400-649	Geomorphology. Landforms. Terrain
561-649	Other natural landforms: Floodplains, caves, deserts, dunes, etc.
599-649	Karst landforms
601-649	Caves. Speleology
603-608	By region or country
608	Other
608.45	Scotland
	[From Table I on p. 380]
.M3	*[Cutter number for "MacDonald"]*
1977	[Date]

50. *A handbook for publishers in France,* by La Mont. 1974.

Z308 .L3 1974

Z	Bibliography and Library science
116-659	Book industries and trade
278-549	Bookselling and publishing
287-550 [i.e., 549]	By region or country
291-444	Europe
303-310	France
308	*[Using the column for 8 no. countries in the table beginning on p. 17, the 6th number in the range (308) is used to express "Handbooks, manuals, etc."]*
.L3	*[Cutter number for "La Mont"]*
1974	[Date]

51. *A history of publishing in Czechoslovakia,* by Zdarsky. 1984.

Z301.3 .Z3 1984

Z	Bibliography and Library science
116-659	Book industries and trade
278-549	Bookselling and publishing
287-550 [i.e., 549]	By region or country
291-444	Europe
301	Czechoslovakia
301.3	History. Biography
	[Using the column for 1 no. countries in the table beginning on p. 17, the decimal extension ".3" is used to express "History. Biography."]
.Z3	*[Cutter number for "Zdarsky"]*
1984	[Date]

52. *A directory of publishers and booksellers in Turkey,* by Land. 1985.

Z464 .T895 L3 1985

Z	Bibliography and Library science
116-659	Book industries and trade
278-549	Bookselling and publishing
287-550 [i.e., 549]	By region or country
448-464	Asia
464	Other, A-Z
.T89	Turkey
.T895	Directories
	[Using the column for 1 no. countries in the table beginning on p. 17, the decimal extension ".5" is used to express "Directories."]
L3	*[Cutter number for "Land"]*
1985	[Date]

E.   Tables within the text.

For titles 53-59 the following initial hierarchy applies:

G	Geography. Maps. Anthropology. Recreation
GV	Recreation. Leisure
561-1198.995	Sports
571-688	History

53. *A history of sports in Texas,* by Loman. 1964.

GV584 .T4 L6 1964

581-601	America
583-584.5	United States
584	By state, A-W
.T4	*[Cutter number for Texas from SCM:S Instruction G 302]*
L6	*[Cutter number for "Loman"]*
1964	[Date]

54. *A history of sports in Baton Rouge, La.,* by Quentin. 1921.

GV584.5 .B3 Q4 1921

581-601	America
583-584.5	United States
584.5	By city, A-Z
.B3	*[Cutter number for "Baton Rouge"]*
Q4	*[Cutter number for "Quentin"]*
1921	[Date]

55. *A history of sports in Ontario Province, Canada,* by Stone. 1932.

GV585.3 .O6 S7 1932

581-601	America
585-585.5	Canada
585.3	By province, etc., A-Z
.O6	*[Cutter number for "Ontario" from SCM:S Instruction G 302]*
S7	*[Cutter number for "Stone"]*
1932	[Date]

56. *A history of sports in Mexico City, Mexico,* by Squires. 1970.

GV588.5 .M4 S6 1970

581-601	America
586-601	Latin America
587-588.5	Mexico
588.5	By city, A-Z *[Using the column for 2 no. countries in the table on p. 343, the 2.5th number in the range (588.5) is used to express "By city, A-Z."]*
.M4	*[Cutter number for "Mexico City"]*
S6	*[Cutter number for "Squires"]*
1970	[Date]

57. *A history of sports in Bogota,* by Lares. 1968. [The city in Colombia, South America]

GV601 .C75 B6 1968

581-601	America
586-601	Latin America
601	Other South American regions or countries, A-Z
.C7	*[Cutter number for "Columbia" from SCM:S Instruction G 300]*
.C75	By city, A-Z *[Using the column for Cutter no. countries in the table on p. 343, the successive cutter number ".x5" is used to express "By city, A-Z."]*
B6	*[Cutter number for "Bogota"]*
1968	[Date]

58. *A history of sports in Ireland*, by O'Brien. 1949.

GV606.5 .02 1949

605-648	Europe
606.5-606.55	Ireland
606.5	General works
	[Using the column for l no. countries in the table on p. 343, the 1st number in the range (606.5) is used to express "General works."]
.02	*[Cutter number for "O'Brien"]*
1949	[Date]

59. *A history of sports in Dublin*, by McCaffrey. 1976.

GV606.55 .D8 M3 1976

605-648	Europe
606.5-606.55	Ireland
606.55	By city, A-Z
	[Using the column for l no.countries in the table on p. 343, the 1.5th number (606.55) is used to express "By city, A-Z."]
.D8	*[Cutter number for "Dublin"]*
M3	*[Cutter number for "McCaffrey"]*
1976	[Date]

F.   Class H.

For titles 83-85 the following initial hierarchy applies:

H	Social Sciences
HV	Social pathology. Social and public welfare. Criminology
7231-9920.5	Penology
7551-8280.7	Police. Detectives. Constabulary
8130-8280.7	Police. By region or country
8157-8280.7	Other regions or countries

60. *The municipal police of Buenos Aires*, by Edwards. 1981.

HV8180 .B8 E3 1981

8180	Argentina.
	Local, by city, A-Z
	[In Table V Argentina's number range is 27-30. These numbers are

246

added to the base number 8150 (i.e., 8177-8180) as instructed by the footnote on p. 116 . Using the column for 4 nos. countries in the table on p. 116, the 4th number in the range for Argentina (8180) is used to express "Local, by city, A-Z."]

.B8   *[Cutter number for "Buenos Aires"]*
E3   *[Cutter number for "Edwards"]*
1981   [Date]

61.   *The accountability of the English constable,* by Marshall. 1973.

HV8196 .A2 M3 1973

8196   England and Wales
[In Table V England's number is 46. This number is added to the base number 8150 (i.e., 8196) as instructed by the footnote on p. 116.]

.A2   General works. History and description
[Using the column for 1 no. countries in the table on p. 116, the reserve cutter number ".A2" is used to express "General works. History and description."]

M3   *[Cutter number for "Marshall"]*
1973   [Date]

62.   *The national police in Bulgaria,* by Raible. 1961.

HV8241.5 .A2 R3 1961

8241.5   Bulgaria
[In Table V Bulgaria's number is 91.5. This number is added to the base number 8150 (i.e., 8241.5) as instructed by the footnote on p. 116.]

.A2   General works. History and description
[Using the column for 1 no. countries in the table on p. 116, the reserve cutter number ".A2" is used to express "General works. History and description."]

R3   *[Cutter number for "Raible"]*
1961   [Date]

For titles 63-70 the following hierarchy applies:

H	Social sciences
HN	Social history and conditions. Social problems. Social reform
50-980	By region or country
101-942.5	Other regions or countries

63. *A century of social reform in India*, by Natira. 1949.

HN683.N3 1949

683	India
	History and description
	[In Table VIII India's number range is
	581-590. These numbers are added to the
	base number 100 (i.e., 681-690) as
	instructed by the footnote on p. 6.Using
	the column for 10 no. countries in the
	table on p. 6, the 3rd number in the
	number range for India (683) is used to
	express "History and description."]
.N3	*[Cutter number for "Natira"]*
1949	[Date]

64. *A study of life in a Devonshire community*, by White. 1976.

HN398 .D4 W4 1976

398	Great Britain
	Local, A-Z
	[In Table VIII England's number range is
	281-300. These numbers are added to the
	base number 100 (i.e., 381-400) as
	instructed by the footnote on p. 6.Using
	the column for 20 no. countries in the
	table on p. 6, the 18th number in the
	number range for England (398) is used to
	express "Local, A-Z."]
.D4	*[Cutter number for "Devonshire"]*
W 4	*[Cutter number for "White"]*
1976	[Date]

65. *Social problems in the Arab countries: a statistical report*, by Azeno. 1983.

HN766 .A85 A9 1983

766	Arab countries (Collective)
	[In Table VIII the Arab countries are
	expressed by "666". This number is added to

248

the base number 100 (i.e., 766) as instructed
by the footnote on p. 6.]
    .A85   Statistics. Social indicators
*[Using the column for 1 no. countries in
the table on p. 7, the reserve cutter
number ".A85" is used to express
"Statistics. Social indicators."]*
    A9   *[Cutter number for "Azeno"]*
    1983   *[Date]*

66. *A social history of 19th century Europe,* by Hill. 1935

    HN373 .H5 1935

    373   Europe
History and description
*[In Table VIII Europe's number range is
271-280. These numbers are added to the
base number 100 (i.e., 371-380) as
instructed by the footnote on p. 6.Using
the column for 10 no. countries in the
table on p. 6, the 3rd number in the
number range for Europe (373) is used to
express "History and description."]*
    .H5   *[Cutter number for "Hill"]*
    1935   *[Date]*

67. *Power in Ica: the social structure of a Peruvian community,* by Lyle. 1966.

    HN350 .I2 L9 1966

    350   Peru
Local, A-Z
*[In Table VIII Peru's number range is
241-250. These numbers are added to the
base number 100 (i.e., 341-350) as
instructed by the footnote on p. 6.Using
the column for 10 no. countries in the
table on p. 6, the 10th number in the
number range for Peru (350) is used to
express "Local, A-Z."]*
    .I2   *[Cutter number for "Ica"]*
    L9   *[Cutter number for "Lyle"]*
    1966   *[Date]*

68. *Social mobility in Gibraltar,* by Wherry. 1981.

    HN590.5 .Z9 S65 1981

    590.5   Gibraltar
*[In Table VIII Gibraltar is expressed by the
number 590.5. This number is added to the
base number 100 (i.e., 590.5) as instructed
by the footnote on p. 6.]*

.Z9 Special topics (not otherwise provided
for), A-Z
*[Using the column or 1 no. countries in
the table on on p. 107, the reserve cutter
number ".Z9" is used to express "Special
topics."]*
S65 Social mobility
*[From the list of topics under
subdivisions 20, 10.29 and 5.2 in the
table on p. 6.]*
1981 [Date]

Note: No cutter number could be provided for Wherry because 2 cutter
numbers were used as part of the subject classification.

69. *The literature of social reform in China, 1830-1860,* compiled and
translated by Ogden. 1927.

HN735 .L5 1927

735 China
Social reform literature
Early through 1850
*[In Table VIII China's number range is
631-640. These numbers are added to
the base number 100 (i.e., 731-740) as
instructed by the footnote on p. 6.Using
the column for 10 no. countries in the
table on p. 6, the 5th number in the
number range for China (735) is used to
express "Social reform literature. Early
through 1850."]*
.L5 *[Cutter number for "Literature," the
first non-article word of the title main
entry]*
1927 [Date]

70. *Continuity and change: the social history of Spain since World War II* by
Ilian. 1978.

HN583.5 .I4 1978

583.5 Spain
History and description, 1945-
*[In Table VIII Spain's number range is
481-490. These numbers are added to the
base number 100 (i.e., 581-590) as
instructed by the footnote on p. 6.Using
the column for 10 no. countries in the
table on p. 6, the 3.5th number in the
number range for Spain (583.5) is used to
express "History and description, 1945- ."]*

250

.I4   [Cutter number for "Ilian"]
            1978   [Date]

For titles 94-97 the following initial hierarchy applies:

H   Social sciences
    HG   Finance
        1501-3550   Banking
            2401-3550   By region or country
                2701-3542.7   Other regions or countries

71. *A history of the Bank of England, 1640-1903*, by Andre. 1909.

   HG2994 .A5 1909

            2994   England and Wales.
                                    Central Bank. National Bank. Banks
                                    of issue.
                                       General Works. History and
                                       description
                                       *[In Table VIII England's number
                                       range is 281-300. These numbers are
                                       added to the base number 2700 (i.e.,
                                       2981-3000) as instructed by the
                                       footnote on p. 237.Using the column
                                       for 20 no. countries in the table on p.
                                       237, the 14th number in the number
                                       range for England (2994) is used to
                                       express "Central bank. National
                                       Bank. Banks of issue. General works.
                                       History and description."]*
            .A5   *[Cutter number for "Andre"]*
                1909   [Date]

72. *Banking and monetary control in South Africa*, by Koster. 1978.

   HG3401 .A6 K6 1978

            3401   South Africa
                                    *[In Table VIII South Africa is expressed
                                    by the number 701. This number is
                                    added to the base number 2700 (i.e., 3401)
                                    as instructed by the footnote on p. 237.]*
            .A6   History and policy
                                    *[Using the column for 1 no. countries in
                                    the table on p. 237, the reserve cutter
                                    number ".A6" is used to express
                                    "History and policy."]*
                K6   *[Cutter number for "Koster"]*
                    1978   [Date]

251

73. *Annual report of the Banco de los Andes in Bogota, Colombia.*

   HG2910 .B64 B3

2910	Colombia
	By city, A-Z5
	[In Table VIII Colombia's number range for is 201-210. These numbers are added to the base number 2700 (i.e., 2901-2910) as instructed by the footnote on p. 237.Using the column for 10 no. countries in the table on p. 237, the 10th number in the number range for Columbia (2910) is used to express "By city, A-Z5."]
.B6	*[Cutter number for "Bogota"]*
.B64	Individual banks, A-Z.
	[Successive cutter number ".x4" under subdivision 10 from the table on p. 237.]
B3	*[Cutter number for "Banco"]*

74. *Banking in Barcelona, Spain from 1840 to 1920,* by Voltes. 1962.

   HG3190 .B32 V6 1962

3190	By city, A-Z5
	[In Table VIII Spain's number range is 481-490. These numbers are added to the base number 2700 (i.e., 3181-3190) as instructed by the footnote on p. 237. Using the column for 10 no. countries in the table on p. 237, the 10th number in the number range for Spain (3190) is used to express "By city, A-Z5."]
.B3	*[Cutter number for "Barcelona"]*
.B32	General works
	[Successive cutter number ".x2" under subdivision 10 from the table on p. 237.]
V6	*[Cutter number for "Voltes"]*
1962	[Date]

G.   <u>Class P: Forty-Nine Number Author.</u>

For titles 75-81 the following initial hierarchy applies:

P	[Language. Literature]
PS	American literature
700-3576	Individual authors
991-3390	19th century

1300-1348	Clemens, Samuel Langhorne ("Mark Twain") *[Use Table XXXI (Authors with forty-nine numbers). The column headed "0" is used because the number range for Clemens ends in "00." If that range had ended in "50" the column headed "50" would have been used. The numbers from this table are added successively to the base number "13."]*

75. *The writings of Mark Twain* (Samuel Langhorne Clemens). Autograph [unedited] edition. 1899.

PS1300 .E99

1300	Collected works *[Number "0" from Table XXXI]*
.E00-E99	1800-1899 *[Date letter. "E" represents the 19th century]*
.E99	*[Date letter for 1899]*

76. *The adventures of Huckleberry Finn,* by Mark Twain. London. 1844.

PS1305 .A1 1844

1305-1322	Separate works
1305	Adventures of Huckleberry Finn
.A1-A3	Texts *[From Table XLI (Separate works with one number)]*
.A1	By date
1844	[Date]

77. *Le avventure di Tom Sawyer,* par Mark Twain ; traduzione di T. Orsi. 1930. [A translation into Italian]

PS1306 .A66 1930

1305-1322	Separate works
1306	Adventures of Tom Sawyer
.A31-69	Translations *[From Table XLI (Separate works with one number)]*
.A6-69	Other
.A66	[Italian] *[Represented by the second 6]*
1930	[Date]

78. *Interpretations of Adventures of Huckleberry Finn: a collection of essays,* edited by Abbott. 1938.

PS130 .I5 1938

1305-1322	Separate works
1305	Adventures of Huckleberry Finn
.A7-Z	Criticism
.I5	*[Cutter number for "Interpretations," the first word of the title main entry.]*
1938	[Date]

79. *Mark Twain's The mysterious stranger and the critics,* by Tuckey. 1968. [A criticism]

PS1322 .M93 T8 1968

1305-1322	Separate works
1322	Other, A-Z
.M9	*[Cutter number for "Mysterious"]*
.M93	Criticism
	[From Table XLIII (Separate works with successive Cutter numbers). The successive cutter number "3" expresses "criticism."]
T8	*[Cutter number for "Tuckey"]*
1968	[Date]

80. *Mark Twain: a profile,* by Kaplan. 1967. [A biography]

PS1331 .K3 1967

1329-1335	Biography, criticism, etc.
	[Numbers "29"-"35" from Table XXXI]
1331.A5-Z	General works
.K3	*[Cutter number for "Kaplan"]*
1967	[Date]

81. *Mark Twain's letters,* arranged with comment by Paine. 1917.

PS1331 .A4 1917

1329-1335	Biography, criticism, etc.
	[Numbers "29"-"35" From Table XXXI]
1331.A2-.A49	Autobiographical works
.A4	Letters (Collections). By date
1917	[Date]

H.   Class P: Nineteen Number Author.

For titles 82-89 the following initial hierarchy applies:

P	[Language. Literature]
PS	American literature
700-3576	Individual authors
991-3390	19th century
2380-2388	Melville, Herman
	[Use Table XXXIII (Authors with nine numbers)]

82.   *The works of Herman Melville.* London, 1922-1924.

PS2380 .F22

2380	Collected works. Bu date
	[The number "0" from Table XXXIII is added to the first number (2380) in Melville's range]
.F00-F99	1800-1899
	[Date letter "E" represents the 20th century]
.F22	*[Date letter for 1922]*

83.   *Typee,* or *A peep at Polynesian life,* by Herman Melville. 1957.

PS2384 .T91 1957

2384	Separate works. By title [A-Z]
	[The number "4" from Table XXXIII is added to the first number (2380) in Melville's range]
.T9	*[Cutter number for "Typee"]*
.T91	Text
	[From Table XLIII (Separate works with successive Cutter numbers). The successive cutter number "1" expresses "text."]
1957	[Date]

84.   *Typee,* roman traduit de L'anglois par Verdier, Paris. 1945. [A translation into French]

PS2384 .T91 F7 1945

2384	Separate works. By title [A-Z]
	[The number "4" from Table XXXIII is added to the first number (2380) in Melville's range]

.T9	[Cutter number for "Typee"]
.T91	Text
	[From Table XLIII (Separate works with successive Cutter numbers). The successive cutter number "1" expresses "text."]
A-Z	Translations. By language
F7	[Cutter number for "French"]
1945	[Date]

85.   *Rebel genius, a life of Herman Melville,* by Bixby. 1970.

PS2386 .B5 1970

2386	Biography, criticism, etc.
	[The number "6" from Table XXXIII is added to the first number (2380) in Melville's range]
.A5-Z	General works
.B5	[Cutter number for "Bixby"]
1970	[Date]

86.   *Studies in the minor and later works of Melville,* by Hull. 1970.

PS2387 .H8 1970

2387	Criticism
	[The number "7" from Table XXXIII is added to the first number (2380) in Melville's range]
	General works
.H8	[Cutter number for "Hull"]
1970	[Date]

87.   *Melville's use of the Bible,* by Wright. 1949.

PS2388 .B52 W7 1949

2388	Criticism
	Special
	Other, A-Z
	[The number "8" from Table XXXIII is added to the first number (2380) in Melville's range]
.B52	Bible
	[Cutter number from the list in Table XXXIII under the number "8."]
W 7	[Cutter number for "Wright"]
1949	[Date]

88. *Melville's Israel Potter*, by Keyssar. 1969. [A criticism]

PS2384 .I83 K4 1969

2384		Separate works. By title [A-Z]
		[The number "4" from Table XXXIII is added to the first number (2380) in Melville's range]
.I8		*[Cutter number for "Israel"]*
.I83		Criticism
		[From Table XLIII (Separate works with successive Cutter numbers]. The successive cutter number "3" expresses "criticism."]
	K4	*[Cutter number for "Keyssar"]*
	1969	[Date]

89. *The letters of Herman Melville*, edited by Davis. 1960.

PS2386 .A4 1960

2386		Biography, criticism, etc.
		[The number "6" from Table XXXIII is added to the first number (2380) in Melville's range]
.A4		Letters (Collections). By date
1960		[Date]

I.   Class P: Cutter Number Author.

For titles 90-93 the following initial hierarchy applies:

P	[Language. Literature]
PS	American literature
700-3576	Individual authors
3500-3549	1900-1960
3511	F
.A86	*[Cutter number for "aulkner." Using the LC cutter table this cutter would normally be ."A9." In order it fit Faulkner into its proper alphabetical location in the LC shelflist, LC uses the cutter number ".A86." This places Faulkner before "Faust, Frederick" (.87) a name that appears in the list of cuttered names under PS 3511.]*
	[Use Table XL Authors with [a] Cutter number.]

90. *The Faulkner reader: selections from the works of William Faulkner.* 1954.

PS3511 .A86 .A6 1954

.A6	Selected works. Selections. By date *[From Table XL]*
1954	[Date]

91. *The sound and the fury,* by William Faulkner. 1961.

PN3511 .A86 S61 1961

.xA61-Z458	Separate works. By title *[From Table XL]*
S6	*[Cutter number for "Sound and the fury"]*
S61	Text *[From Table XLIII (Separate works with cutter numbers). The successive cutter number "1" expresses "text." Usually LC does not record the "1" although text is implied. Thus, LC would have used the cutter number "S6" for this work.]*
1961	[Date]

92. *Faulkner's The sound and the fury,* by Gold. 1964. [A criticism]

PS3511 .A86 S633 1964

.xA61-Z458	Separate works. By title *[From Table XL]*
S6	*[Cutter number for "Sound and the fury"]*
S63	Criticism *[From Table XLIII (Separate works successive Cutter numbers). The successive cutter number "3" expresses "criticism."]*
S633	[Gold] *[A second successive cutter number is added to express the main entry of the criticism. Based on the range "1"-"9," the letter "g" for the main entry "Gold" is assigned the number "3." See SCM: SL Instruction G 340.]*
1964	[Date]

93. *Requiem pour une Nonne,* by William Faulkner ; translated by Coindreau. 1957. [A translation into French.]

PS3511 .A86 .R414 1957

.xA61-Z458	Separate works. By title	
	[From Table XL]	
R4	*[Cutter number for "Requiem pour une Nonne"]*	
R41	Texts	
	[From Table XLIII (Separate works with successive Cutter numbers]. The successive cutter number "1" expresses "text."]	
R414	Translations. By language .A4-Z	
	[Because two cutter numbers have already been used, the second "4" is used to express a translation into French. This number is derived from the Translation Table in SCM: SL Instruction G 150.]	
1957	[Date]	

94. *Four studies of Faulkner,* by Overton. 1980. [A criticism]

PN3511 .A86 Z78 1980

.xZ459-999	Biography and criticism	
	[From Table XL]	
.xZ5-999	Criticism	
Z78	*[Cutter number for "Overton"]*	
	[Because all criticisms of Faulkner are confined to the small cutter range of Z5-999 it is common in situations such as this to express the second letter of the name in the cutter number. In this case the "7" represents "O" and the "8" represents "v."]	
1980	[Date]	

APPENDIX F

Answers to the
Library of Congress Subject Headings Exercises

A.   Simple Headings.

1.   *Plea Bargaining: is it fair?*

    PLEA BARGAINING.

2.   *An introduction to machine-shop mathematics.*

    SHOP MATHEMATICS.

3.   *Water-borne power projection: naval policy and a nation's destiny.*

    SEA-POWER.

4.   *Ocean drilling vessels.*

    DEEP-SEA DRILLING SHIPS.

5.   *What are the effects of agricultural chemicals on plants?*

    PLANTS, EFFECT OF AGRICULTURAL CHEMICALS ON.

6.   *Windmills: the clean, free power source.*

    WINDMILLS.

7.   *Your solar heated home.*

    SOLAR HOUSES.

8. *An introduction to industrial psychology.*

   PSYCHOLOGY, INDUSTRIAL.

9. *The story of orchestration.*

   INSTRUMENTATION AND ORCHESTRATION.

10. *The Sopwith Camel.* [A type of fighter plane]

    CAMEL (FIGHTER PLANES)

11. *Danish Christmas hymns.*

    HYMNS, DANISH.

    CHRISTMAS MUSIC.

12. *Rats and the diseases they carry.*

    RATS AS CARRIERS OF DISEASE.

13. *The Battle for Guadalcanal.* [A World War Two battle]

    GUADALCANAL ISLAND (SOLOMON ISLANDS), BATTLE OF, 1942-1943.
    [See SCM:SH Instruction H 1285.]

14. *Requirements for controlled atmospheres in space.*

    ARTIFICIAL ATMOSPHERES (SPACE ENVIRONMENT)

15. *Infant welfare.*

    MATERNAL AND INFANT WELFARE.

B. Topical Subdivision Headings.

16. *The 1956 Anglo-French intervention in Egypt.*

    EGYPT--HISTORY--INTERVENTION, 1956.

261

17. *Ride down that road again: recycling road building materials.*

    ROAD MATERIALS--RECYCLING.

18. *How to breed roses.*

    ROSES--BREEDING.

19. *When did Buddha die? The controversy continues.*

    GAUTAMA BUDDHA–DATE OF DEATH.

20. *Gasoline pipelines.*

    GASOLINE–PIPE LINES.

21. *Light filters in photography.*

    PHOTOGRAPHY--LIGHT FILTERS.

22. *Crabgrass, dandelions, and other green lawn disasters: weed control in the lawns of suburbia.*

    LAWNS--WEED CONTROL.

23. *Aircraft collision avoidance systems: the state of the art.*

    AIRPLANES--COLLISON AVOIDANCE.

24. *Darkroom techniques for top quality photos.*

    PHOTOGRAPHY--PROCESSING.

25. *Operation Overlord: D-Day, 1944.* [Accounts of the invasion]

    WORLD WAR, 1939-1945--CAMPAIGNS--FRANCE--NORMANDY.
    [The subject heading"Operation Overlord" was not assigned because its use is limited by its scope note to documents that deal with the "military planning and diplomatic negotiations for the Normandy Invasion."]

C.   Geographical Subdivision Headings.

26.   *The courts of Scotland.*

COURTS--SCOTLAND.

27.   *The taxation of artists in Ireland: the laws and commentary.*

ARTISTS--TAXATION--LAW AND LEGISLATION--IRELAND.

28.   *The children of working parents in Minneapolis.*

CHILDREN OF WORKING PARENTS--MINNESOTA--MINNEAPOLIS.

29.   *Crack abuse in Cleveland: the report of the 1989 survey.*

CRACK (DRUG)--OHIO--CLEVELAND.
[The use of this subject heading is called for by the scope note under the subject heading "Drug abuse surveys."]

DRUG ABUSE SURVEYS--OHIO--CLEVELAND.

30.   *Diamond smuggling in South Africa.*

DIAMOND SMUGGLING.
[Geographical subdivision is not allowed for this subject heading.]

31.   *Labor unions in the tire industry of Akron Ohio.*

TRADE UNIONS--TIRE INDUSTRY WORKERS--OHIO--AKRON.

32.   *The political activities of artisans in Mexico City.*

ARTISANS--MEXICO--MEXICO CITY--POLITICAL ACTIVITY.

33.   *The pre-Lenten carnival in Baton Rouge, Louisiana.*

CARNIVAL--LOUISIANA--BATON ROUGE.
[See the scope notes under "Carnival" and "Carnivals."]

34.   *Dog laws of Portland, Maine.*

DOGS--LAW AND LEGISLATION--MAINE--PORTLAND.

35. *Bog men of England and Denmark.*

   BOG BODIES--ENGLAND.

   BOG BODIES--DENMARK.

36. *A new way to get the job done in the U.S.: contracting for services.*

   CONTRACTING OUT--UNITED STATES.

37. *Nineteenth century magazine illustration in Great Britain.*

   MAGAZINE ILLUSTRATION--19TH CENTURY--GREAT BRITAIN.

38. *A history of costume in 17th and 18th century France.*

   COSTUME--FRANCE--HISTORY--17TH CENTURY.

   COSTUME--FRANCE--HISTORY--18TH CENTURY.

39. *Mandatory retirement laws in Georgia.*

   RETIREMENT, MANDATORY--LAW AND LEGISLATION--GEORGIA.

40. *Depression glass of East Liverpool, Ohio.*

   DEPRESSION GLASS.
   [This subject heading cannot be subdivided geographically.]

41. *The problem of family abandonment in Indiana.*

   DESERTION AND NON-SUPPORT--INDIANA.

D. <u>Form and Topical Free-Floating Subdivision Headings</u>.

42. *The history of the Dewey Decimal Classification.*

   CLASSIFICATION, DEWEY DECIMAL--HISTORY.
   [See SCM:SH Instruction H 1095 for the use of the subdivision "History."]

264

43. *Soil density in Zurich Switzerland: a bibliography.*

> SOILS--SWITZERLAND--ZURICH--DENSITY--BIBLIOGRAPHY.
> *[See SCM:SH Instruction H 1095 for the use of the subdivision "Bibliography."]*

44. *The effects of drugs on the newborn: a compilation of essays.*

> INFANTS (NEWBORN)--EFFECT OF DRUGS ON.
> *[There is no subdivision that expresses "essays." See SCM:SH Instruction H 1210.]*

45. *Minority employment in the states of California and New York: a comparative statistical report.*

> MINORITIES--EMPLOYMENT--CALIFORNIA--STATISTICS.
>
> MINORITIES--EMPLOYMENT--NEW YORK (STATE)--STATISTICS.
> *[See SCM:SH Instructions H 1095 and H 2095 for the use of the subdivision "Statistics."]*

46. *U. S. copyright law for musical works: abstracts.*

> COPYRIGHT--MUSIC--UNITED STATES--ABSTRACTS.
> *[See SCM:SH Instructions H 1095 and H 1205 for the use of the subdivision "Abstracts."]*

47. *A history of fox hunting in Albemarle County, Virginia.*

> FOX-HUNTING--VIRGINIA--ALBERMARLE COUNTY--HISTORY.
> *[See SCM:SH Instruction H 1095 for the use of the subdivision "History."]*

48. *Fire towers and fire spotters of North and South Carolina: a directory.*

> FIRE LOOKOUT STATIONS--NORTH CAROLINA--DIRECTORIES.
>
> FIRE LOOKOUT STATIONS--SOUTH CAROLINA--DIRECTORIES.
>
> FIRE LOOKOUTS--NORTH CAROLINA--DIRECTORIES.
>
> FIRE LOOKOUTS--SOUTH CAROLINA--DIRECTORIES.
> *[See SCM:SH Instructions H 1095 and H 1558 for the use of the subdivision "Directories."]*

49. *Physics: a basic textbook.*

PHYSICS.
[*The subdivision "Textbooks" is not used for books that are textbooks on the subject. See SCM:SH Instruction H 2187.*]

50. *Macroeconomics for the layman.*

MACROECONOMICS--POPULAR WORKS.
[*See SCM:SH Instructions H 1095 and H 1943.5 for the use of the subdivision "Popular Works."*]

51. *Railroad accidents in late 19th century Pennsylvania.*

RAILROADS--PENNSYLVANIA--ACCIDENTS--HISTORY--19TH CENTURY.
[*See SCM:SH Instruction H 1095 for the use of the subdivision "History--19th century."*]

52. *Zeppelins: a photographic history.* [Over half of this book consists of pictures]

AIRSHIPS--HISTORY.
[*See SCM:SH Instruction H 1095 for the use of the subdivisions "History."*]

AIRSHIPS--PICTORIAL WORKS.
[*See SCM:SH Instructions H 1095 and H 1935 for the use of the subdivision "Pictorial works." This subdivision was not appended to the "Airships--History" because of the restriction to use only one free-floating subdivision.*]

53. *Yearbook of industrial psychiatry.*

INDUSTRIAL PSYCHIATRY--PERIODICALS
[*There is no subdivision that expresses "yearbook." (see SCM:SH Instruction H 2400). See Instructions H 1095 and H 1927 for the use of the subdivision "Periodicals."*]

54. *Campsites in Tennessee: a directory.*

CAMP SITES, FACILITIES, ETC.--TENNESSEE--DIRECTORIES.
[*See SCM:SH Instructions H 1095 and H 1558 for the use of the subdivision "Directories."*]

55. *Nursing home care and the Federal commitment*

NURSING HOME CARE--GOVERNMENT POLICY--UNITED STATES.
[*See SCM:SH Instruction H 1095 for the use of the subdivision*

"Government policy." The subject heading "Federal aid to nursing homes --United States" is somewhat narrower in scope than the topic implied by the title in that the subject heading confined Federal commitment to Federal aid only.]

56. *Japanese history, 1919 to 1945: a sourcebook.*

    JAPAN--HISTORY--1912-1945--SOURCES.
    [See SCM:SH Instructions H 1095, H 1647, and H 2080 for the use of the subdivision "Sources."]

57. *House repair for the homeowner.*

    DWELLINGS--MAINTENANCE AND REPAIR--AMATEURS' MANUALS.
    [See SCM:SH Instructions H 1095 and H 1943.5 for the use of the subdivision "Amateurs' manuals."]

E.   <u>Pattern and Other Free-Floating Subdivision Headings.</u>

58. *Thomas Alva Edison: a definitive biography.*

    EDISON, THOMAS A. (THOMAS ALVA), 1847-1931.
    [The heading for Edison was formulated from the rules for personal name headings in AACR2R. Unless otherwise indicated, the subdivision "Biography" is not added to the name heading for the biography of an individual (see SCM:SH Instruction H 1110).]

    INVENTORS--UNITED STATES--BIOGRAPHY.
    [See SCM:SH Instruction H 1330 for the provision of a subject heading for the class of persons of which an individual was a member.]

59. *The travelers' guide to Peru.*

    PERU--DESCRIPTION AND TRAVEL--GUIDE-BOOKS.
    [See SCM:SH Instruction H 1140 for the use of the subdivisions "Description and travel--Guide books' under the names of places.]

60. *Genealogy of the Carpenter family of Massachusetts.*

    CARPENTER FAMILY.
    [See SCM:SH Instruction H 1631 for an explanation of why the subdivision "Genealogy" is not used with a family name.]

    MASSACHUSETTS--GENEALOGY.
    [See SCM:SH Instructions H 1631 and H 1845 for an explanation of the use of '[local place]--Genealogy" as a second subject access point.]

61. *Control of the color fading of apples.*

APPLES--COLOR--FADING--CONTROL.
[See SCM:SH Instruction H 1180 for the use of the subdivisions "Color--Fading--Control."]

62. *Edgar Allan Poe as a character in mystery novels: a review.*

POE, EDGAR ALLAN, 1809-1849, IN FICTION, DRAMA, POETRY, ETC.
[The heading for Poe was formulated from the rules for personal name headings in AACR2R. See SCM:SH Instruction H 1110 for the use of the subdivision "In fiction, drama, poetry, etc." under the names of persons.]

63. *Camping and backpacking in the Great Lakes area.*

CAMPING--GREAT LAKES REGION.

BACKPACKING--GREAT LAKES REGION.
[See SCM:SH Instruction H 760 for the identification of geographic regions.]

64. *The foreign relations of Japan and France.*

JAPAN--FOREIGN RELATIONS--FRANCE.

FRANCE--FOREIGN RELATIONS--JAPAN.
[See SCM:SH Instruction H 1629 for the use of the subdivision "Foreign relations."]

65. *The Strait of Magellan along the Chilean coast.* [A general geography text]

MAGELLAN, STRAIT OF (CHILE AND ARGENTINA)--DESCRIPTION AND TRAVEL.
[See SCM:SH Instruction H 1530 for the use of the subdivision "Description and travel."]

66. *They fell for the Union: a listing of Pennsylvanian's who died for their country in the Civil War.*

UNITED STATES--HISTORY--CIVIL WAR, 1861-1865--REGISTER OF DEAD.

PENNSYLVANIA--HISTORY--CIVIL WAR, 1861-1865--REGISTER OF DEAD.
[See SCM:SH Instruction H 1200 for the use of pattern headings for wars and the subdivision "Register of dead." See also SCM:SH Instruction 1845 (Historical Materials, Including Local Historical Materials).]

67. *Lord Peter: English dilettante or true detective?* [A character created by Dorothy L. Sayers]

> SAYERS, DOROTHY L. (DOROTHY LEIGH), 1893-1957--CHARACTERS--
> LORD PETER WIMSEY.
> *[See SCM:SH Instruction H 1155.4 for the use of the subdivision
> "Characters" under the names of literary authors.]*
>
> WIMSEY, PETER, LORD (FICTITIOUS CHARACTER)
> *[See SCM:SH Instruction H 1610 for entry under the name of a fictitious
> character.]*

68. *Tunnel vision: retinitis pigmentosa research in the United States.*

> RETINITIS PIGMENTOSA--RESEARCH--UNITED STATES.
> *[See SCM:SH Instruction H 1150 for the use of the subdivision "Research."
> under the names of diseases.]*

69. *Diseases of lambs in Greene County, Pennsylvania: a statistical
evaluation.*

> LAMBS--DISEASES--PENNSYLVANIA--GREENE COUNTY--STATISTICS.
> *[See SCM:SH Instruction H 1148 for the use of the subdivision "Diseases"
> for domestic animals and Instructions H 1095 and H 2095 for the use of the
> subdivision "Statistics."]*

70. *Lost with the Titanic.* [A novel about the loss of the steamship Titanic in
1912]

> TITANIC (STEAMSHIP)--FICTION.
> *[The heading "Titanic (Steamship) was formulated from the rules for
> corporate name headings in AACR2R. See SCM:SH Instructions H 1105
> and H 1790 for the use of the subdivision "Fiction" under the names of
> corporate bodies.]*

71. *Henry Ford's contributions to the automobile industry.*

> FORD, HENRY, 1863-1947.
> *[The heading for Ford was formulated from the rules for personal name
> headings in AACR2R. See SCM:SH Instruction H 1110 for the use of the
> subdivision 'Contributions to [specific field or topic]" under the names of
> persons. For this title, the subdivision "Contributions to the automobile
> industry" was not used because it is the major field with which Ford was
> associated.]*
>
> AUTOMOBILE INDUSTRY AND TRADE--UNITED STATES--HISTORY.
> *[The subdivision "Biography" was not added because this work is not
> primarily biographical. and looks at Ford's contributions from an historical
> perspective. See SCM Instructions H 1095 and H 1645 for use use of the*

subdivision "History." The period subdivision "20th century was not added to the subdivision "History" because the history of this industry is essentially confined to the current century. If a significant part of the book dealt with the Ford Motor Company a third subject heading "Ford Motor Company--History" would also have been assigned.]

72. *The West Virginia University: pictorial views of the campus.*

WEST VIRGINIA UNIVERSITY--DESCRIPTION--VIEWS.
[The heading for the university was formulated from the rules for corporate name headings in AACR2R. See SCM:SH Instruction H 1151 for the use of the subdivisions "Description--Views" under the names of individual educational institutions.]

73. *Women in the fiction of Ernest Hemingway.*

HEMINGWAY, ERNEST, 1899-1961--CHARACTERS--WOMEN.
[See SCM:SH Instruction H 1155.4 for the use of the subdivision "Women" under the names of individual literary authors.]

WOMEN IN LITERATURE.

74. *Recruiting practices of the Central Intelligence Agency.*

UNITED STATES. CENTRAL INTELLIGENCE AGENCY--OFFICIALS AND EMPLOYEES--RECRUITING.
[The heading for the agency was formulated from the rules for corporate name headings in AACR2R. See SCM:SH Instruction H 1105 for the use of the subdivisions "Officials and employees--Recruiting" under the names of corporate bodies.]

F.

75. *How to catalog a rare book.*

CATALOGING OF RARE BOOKS.

76. *How to grow asparagus.*

ASPARAGUS.

77. *The conservation of museum collections.*

MUSEUM CONSERVATION METHODS.

78. *The folklore of holy wells and springs in Europe.*

 HOLY WELLS--EUROPE--FOLKLORE.
 [See SCM:SH Instruction H 1627 for the use of the subdivision "Folklore."]

 SPRINGS--EUROPE--FOLKLORE.

79. *How to train your homing pigeon.*

 HOMING PIGEONS--TRAINING.
 [See SCM:SH Instruction H 1148 for the use of the subdivision "Training."]

80. *The first book of astronomy.* [A book for children]

 ASTRONOMY--JUVENILE LITERATURE.

81. *The art of writing biographies.* [A book of techniques]

 BIOGRAPHY (AS A LITERARY FORM)
 [The free-floating subdivision "Technique" was not added to this heading because the heading "Biography--Technique" is a UF reference under "Biography (as a literary form)" thus indicating that "Technique" is implied in the meaning of that heading.

82. *A manual of archeology for the amateur archaeologist.*

 ARCHAEOLOGY--AMATEURS' MANUALS.
 [SCM: SH Instruction H 1943.5 for the use of the subdivision "Amateurs' manuals."]

83. *The chemical analysis of rocks.*

 ROCKS--ANALYSIS.

84. *Photography for children.*

 PHOTOGRAPHY--JUVENILE LITERATURE.
 [See SCM:SH Instruction H 1690 for the use of the subdivision "Juvenile literature."]

85. *Lawyers as characters in modern fiction.*

 LAWYERS IN LITERATURE.

86. *Coins and coin collectors.*

    COINS.

    COINS--COLLECTORS AND COLLECTING.

87. *A survey of veterinary hospitals.*

    VETERINARY HOSPITALS.

88. *A history of 18th century astrology.*

    ASTROLOGY--HISTORY--18TH CENTURY.
    [See SCM:SH Instruction H 1095 for the use of the subdivisions "History--18th century."]

89. *Vocational education for women.*

    WOMEN--VOCATIONAL EDUCATION.

90. *A dictionary of philosophy.* [In English]

    PHILOSOPHY--DICTIONARIES.
    [See SCM:SH Instruction H 1540 for the use of the subdivision "Dictionaries."]

91. *Children's furniture building for the home craftsman.*

    FURNITURE MAKING--AMATEURS' MANUALS.
    [See SCM:SH Instruction H 1943.5 for the use of the subdivision "Amateurs' manuals" and the difference between it and the subdivision "Popular works."]

    CHILDREN'S FURNITURE.
    [The subdivision "Amateurs' manuals" was not added to this heading because SCM:SH Instruction H 1943.5 calls for its use only under "technical subjects."

92. *Life on the stage: the biography of Helen Hayes.* [The American actress born in 1900]

    HAYES, HELEN, 1900-
    [The heading for Hayes was formulated from the rules for personal name headings in AACR2R. Unless otherwise indicated, the subdivision "Biography" is not added to the name heading for the biography of an individual (see SCM:SH Instruction H 1110).]

ACTORS--UNITED STATES--BIOGRAPHY.
[See the scope note under "Actors" and SCM:SH Instruction 1330 for the reason why the subject heading "Actresses" was not used. A third subject heading "Motion picture actors and actresses--United States--Biography" was not used because the title implies that this work concentrates on her theatrical career. If it had not, then this subject heading would also have been used.]

93. *The National League.* [A history of the professional baseball league]

NATIONAL LEAGUE OF PROFESSIONAL BASEBALL CLUBS--HISTORY.
[The heading for the National League was formulated from the rules for corporate name headings in AACR2R. See SCM:SH Instruction H 1105 for the use of the subdivision "History" under the names of corporate bodies.]

94. *Go Cubs! a history of the Chicago Cubs,* by Rogers. 1974. [The professional baseball team]

CHICAGO CUBS (BASEBALL TEAM)---HISTORY.
[The heading for the Chicago Cubs was formulated from the rules for corporate name headings in AACR2R. See SCM:SH Instruction H 1105 for the use of the subdivision "History" under the names of corporate bodies.]

95. *School architecture in California.*

SCHOOL BUILDINGS--CALIFORNIA.

96. *Witchcraft in Alabama.*

WITCHCRAFT--ALABAMA.

97. *Cheesebox on a raft: the Union ironclad Monitor.* [Centers on the activities of this ship during the Civil War]

MONITOR (IRONCLAD)
[The heading for the ship was formulated from the rules for corporate name headings in AACR2R.]

UNITED STATES--HISTORY--CIVIL WAR, 1861-1865--NAVAL OPERATIONS.
[If this work were limited to the Monitor's battle with the Merrimac, it would have been assigned the subject heading "Hampton Roads, Battle of, 1862" rather than tan this heading.]

98. *The Hogarth Press: the history of a great private press.*

    HOGARTH PRESS--HISTORY.
    [The heading for the press was formulated from the rules for corporate name headings in AACR2R. See SCM:SH Instruction H 1105 for the use of the subdivisions"History" under the names of corporate bodies.]

99. *Techniques of writing mystery and detective stories.*

    DETECTIVE AND MYSTERY STORIES--TECHNIQUE.

100. *A repair manual for the Buick automobile.*

    BUICK AUTOMOBILE--MAINTENANCE AND REPAIR.
    [See SCM:SH Instruction H 1095 for the use of the subdivision "Maintenance and repair." Note the difference between "Maintenance and repair" and "Repairing."]

101. *A bibliography of articles on motorcycles.*

    MOTORCYCLES--BIBLIOGRAPHY.
    [See SCM:SH Instruction 1095 for the use of the subdivision "Bibliography.]

102. *North American Indian embroidery.*

    INDIANS OF NORTH AMERICA--EMBROIDERY.

103. *Flowers in literature.*

    FLOWERS IN LITERATURE.

104. *How to win at the game Trivial Pursuit.*

    TRIVIAL PURSUIT (GAME)

105. *Modern paper manufacture in Japan.*

    PAPER INDUSTRY--JAPAN.

    PAPERMAKING--JAPAN.